FRAGMENTATION

FRAGMENTATION

New Production Patterns in the World Economy

Edited by

SVEN W. ARNDT

and

HENRYK KIERZKOWSKI

OXFORD

UNIVERSITY PRESS

OXFORD

UNIVERSITY PRESS

Great Clarendon Street, Oxford OX2 6DP

Oxford University Press is a department of the University of Oxford.
It furthers the University's objective of excellence in research, scholarship,
and education by publishing worldwide in

Oxford New York

Athens Auckland Bangkok Bogotá Buenos Aires Calcutta
Cape Town Chennai Dar es Salaam Delhi Florence Hong Kong Istanbul
Karachi Kuala Lumpur Madrid Melbourne Mexico City Mumbai
Nairobi Paris São Paulo Shanghai Singapore Taipei Tokyo Toronto Warsaw
with associated companies in Berlin Ibadan

Oxford is a registered trade mark of Oxford University Press
in the UK and in certain other countries

Published in the United States
by Oxford University Press Inc., New York

British Library Cataloguing in Publication Data

Data available

Library of Congress Cataloging in Publication Data
Fragmentation: new production patterns in the world economy/
edited by Sven W. Arndt and Henryk Kierzkowski.
p. cm.
Includes bibliographical references and index.
1. International division of labor. 2. Offshore assembly industry. 3. International
business enterprises. 4. Globalization. I. Arndt, Sven W. II. Kierzkowski, Henryk.
HF1412b.F698 2001 338.4'767—dc21 00-050502
ISBN 0-19-924331-X

1 3 5 7 9 10 8 6 4 2

Typeset by Newgen Imaging Systems (P) Ltd., Chennai, India
Printed in Great Britain
on acid-free paper by
T.J. International Ltd., Padstow, Cornwall

ACKNOWLEDGEMENTS

This book, and a conference in Burgenstock which preceded it, was made possible thanks to the generous financial support of the Swiss National Science Foundation, Swiss National Bank, Novartis and Nestlé. We are particularly grateful to Dr Ernst Buser of Novartis for his support and presentation at the conference. Support from the Lowe Institute of Political Economy is gratefully acknowledged.

CONTRIBUTORS

Sven W. Arndt
Director, Lowe Institute of Political Economy
and C. M. Stone Professor of Money, Credit and Trade
Claremont McKenna College

Leonard K. Cheng
Professor of Economics
Hong Kong University of Science and Technology

Alan V. Deardorff
John W. Sweetland Professor of International Economics
and Professor of Economics and Public Policy
University of Michigan, Ann Arbor

Holger Görg
Research Fellow
Centre for Research on Globalisation and Labour Markets
School of Economics
University of Nottingham

Giovanni Graziani
Professor of International Economics
Institute of Economics and Finance, Faculty of Law
University of Parma

Richard G. Harris
Telus Professor of Economics
Simon Fraser University

Ronald W. Jones
Xerox Professor of Economics
University of Rochester

Henryk Kierzkowski
Professor of Economics
Graduate Institute of International Studies
Geneva

Alberto Petrucci
Associate Professor of Economics
Università del Molise and LUISS (Rome)

Victoria Curzon Price
Professor of Economics
University of Geneva

Larry D. Qiu
Assistant Professor of Economics
Hong Kong University of Science and Technology

Beniamino Quintieri
Professor of Economics
Università de Roma 'Tor Vergata'
and Director of CEIS (Centre for International Studies
  on Economic Growth)

Frances Ruane
Associate Professor of Economics
Trinity College
Dublin

Guofu Tan
Associate Professor of Economics
University of British Columbia

Alexander J. Yeats
Former Principal Trade Economist, World Bank
Consultant, World Bank

CONTENTS

1

BK Title: ## Introduction

F11 F23
L23

SVEN W. ARNDT AND HENRYK KIERZKOWSKI

1. Fragmentation and International Trade

Over much of its development, trade theory has focused on explaining and assessing trade in end products. The international division of labor and the role of specialization are studied mainly in terms of final goods. Even the literature on intra-industry trade, which might naturally have been drawn to trade in parts and components, has tended to focus on the exchange of varieties of end products. There is, of course, a quite distinguished literature on trade in intermediate products, but its findings and insights exist more as an addendum to rather than an integral part of the main paradigm.

While trade in parts and components is hardly novel, its share in the total trade of nations has grown dramatically in recent years, as both imports and exports have risen in the United States and elsewhere. On the import side, computer makers import semiconductors, screens, and motherboards, while aircraft designed and engineered in the United States or in Europe are assembled with parts made in dozens of countries. On the export side, consumer appliances, automobiles, and a variety of other products are assembled in Mexico with parts made in the United States and shipped to the United States. Watches may be designed in Switzerland, but their components are often produced and assembled in hosts of other countries. Textiles and electronic products may be designed and marketed in Hong Kong, but they are largely produced in the Pearl River Delta.

In spite of these changes, economists still tend to think about comparative advantage in terms of end products and about international specialization in terms of complete industries and integrated products. Does the United States possess a comparative advantage in aircraft or in designing, engineering, and assembling them? Does the United States possess a comparative advantage in producing the more capital- and human capital-intensive parts of aircraft, but not the more labor-intensive parts and components? Does Mexico possess a comparative advantage in low-end automobiles or just in their assembly? Does Switzerland possess a comparative advantage in watches or just in designing and engineering them? Do questions like these address important issues or are they just splitting hairs?

Recent years have witnessed the emergence of intra-product trade as an increasingly important form of intra-industry trade. Needless to say, intra-product specialization can only take place where the various phases of a production process are physically separable, that is, where the manufacture of a product is amenable to *fragmentation*. Fragmentation is not a new phenomenon; nor is outsourcing. Both go back to the beginning of the Industrial Revolution or even predate it. In the modern era, however, both have acquired international dimension and complexity and probably represent one of the most important distinguishing features of contemporary globalization.

Production processes that permit fragmentation support a finer and more complex division of labor than those that do not. The various phases of production may now be spatially separated and undertaken at locations where costs are lowest. Spatial dispersion of production allows the factor intensity of each component, rather than the average factor intensity of the end product, to determine the location of its production. The international division of labor now matches factor intensities of components with factor abundance of locations.

Of course, the physical dispersion of production introduces certain costs, especially those of communication and coordination. For this reason, as well as a variety of restrictive trade policies and practices, spatial separation and outsourcing were traditionally limited to local or national markets. Recent advances in transportation and telecommunications technologies and reductions in trade and regulatory barriers have reduced the cost of cross-border production sharing. While distance has not become irrelevant, it has lost a great deal of its importance. As a result, international production networks involving producers operating in different countries or even on different continents have become not only feasible but also rational.

This volume examines this phenomenon and related issues from both the theoretical and empirical vantage points. In the remainder of this chapter, we set out some of the major findings and insights.

2. The Nature of Fragmentation

A general framework for analyzing fragmentation, whether domestic or international, was first presented by Jones and Kierzkowski (1990).

In Figure 1.1, the upper panel depicts a traditional production process: inputs are organized and combined to generate final outputs. All aspects of production are performed in one location. There may be many activities, so that coordination is necessary, but proximity helps keep the cost of coordination down. Fragmented production means that constituent activities may be organized into blocks which need not be performed in proximity to one another. The middle and lower panels of Figure 1.1 depict two examples of fragmented production, one rather simple and one more complex. When the constituent parts of production are spatially separated, coordination becomes more involved and complex.

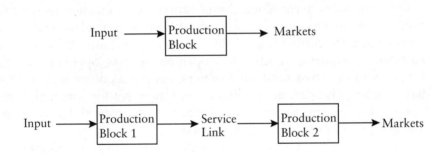

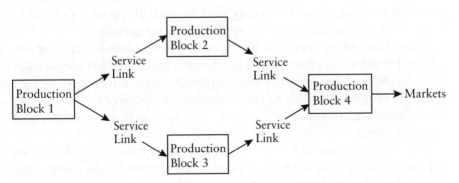

FIG. 1.1. Fragmentation and service links
Source: Jones and Kierzkowski (1990).

Coordination and related services are provided through service links. A service link is a composite of activities such as transportation, insurance, telecommunications, quality control, and management coordination to ensure that the production blocks interact in the proper manner. An important advantage of fragmentation is that it allows production blocks to be moved around so that components are produced in the best possible location. The speed and efficiency with which service links operate clearly have a bearing on the optimal degree of fragmentation.

In the past, fragmentation's primary impact was on the location of production blocks within nations. This was no doubt due in part to trade and regulatory barriers and to the fact that information about alternative production sites is more readily available domestically than internationally. But a crucial element limiting the dispersion of production was the cost and availability of service links. Domestic service links tended to be easier to establish and cheaper to operate.

In recent years, technological innovations, liberalization of international trade in services, convergence of legal and regulatory systems, and increased freedom of establishment have significantly reduced international coordination costs, thus opening up new opportunities for fragmentation across national frontiers. As cross-border service links have become cheaper, more reliable, and more readily obtainable, the options for locating production blocks have become global in scope. The tyranny of distance has been tamed.

While fragmentation may occur within a given firm, the mobility of production blocks implies that activities may be separated not only spatially but by ownership as well. An auto maker may produce ignition devices in a separate plant or obtain them from an independent subcontractor. Production blocks may thus be spatially apart, but close in ownership, or spatially close but separated by ownership.

Separability of ownership is an important determinant of the organizational structure of cross-border production sharing. Where separation of ownership is not feasible, multinational corporations and foreign direct investment are likely to play a dominant role. Where it is feasible, arm's-length relationships are possible and foreign direct investment is less important.

Component specialization may enable manufacturers to exploit characteristics of the production process that are specific to the component rather than the product. One of these may be component-specific scale economies. If a producer of a given component can supply makers of competing final products, he may achieve larger production runs and thus enjoy greater scale economies than would have been possible if production were fully integrated.

Finally, the ready availability of service links may encourage the development of technologies which are based on fragmented production, so that integrated technologies, that is, technologies which do not allow fragmentation, come to be replaced by fragmented technologies.

3. Fragmentation and Trade

Thus, while fragmentation has long been a feature of production in many industries, it was until recently primarily a domestic phenomenon. Subcontracting and outsourcing across borders were limited by the barriers enumerated above. Recent developments in the world trading system, together with important technological advances, have created new opportunities for extending production fragmentation across national frontiers. As a result, the share of components trade in the total trade of nations has risen significantly and many final products have become truly global, pulling together parts and components from many nations.

Offshore sourcing and offshore production have become commonplace in many industries, including the automotive, aircraft, computer, and apparel industries. National economies are becoming increasingly intertwined as production sharing spreads. These developments raise questions about implications and consequences. Who benefits and who loses when component production is moved offshore? Does production sharing with low-wage developing countries threaten jobs and depress wages in developed, high-wage countries?

For trade theorists, an important concern is whether and how the introduction of cross-border fragmentation alters the insights and conclusions of received trade theory. A number of chapters in this volume explore that issue. While some aspects of the question may be analyzed with the simplest of analytical structures, others require more complex modeling.

Traditional Trade Theory

At the broadest level, however, many of the insights of received trade theory continue to hold. Thus, the principle of specialization according to comparative advantage carries through to trade in components and parts. Similarly, matching factor intensities and factor endowments in the international allocation of production blocks continues to hold as a criterion for specialization. In these and other ways, the principles and propositions associated with received trade theory work well as the international division of labor is extended into the realm of parts and components. Most importantly, extending specialization to the level of components is generally welfare-enhancing.

Introduction of cross-border fragmentation does, however, complicate the analysis in several respects. It increases the number of products entering into trade, for example. The set of two final traded products in the simplest version of the standard trade model expands to six tradable items if each of the final products contains two tradable components. Who among two or more countries with divergent endowments and divergent cones of specialization will produce which of the several components and where will final products be assembled? The answer now depends not only on standard considerations of comparative advantage in the production blocks, but on the relative cost and efficiency of service links between any pair of countries. These service links often exhibit strong elements of increasing returns. Thus, it may be possible for the imperatives of communications networking to dictate specialization among countries which are identical in terms of factor endowments.

Output and Employment Effects

It can be shown that makers of labor-intensive consumer products in high-wage countries can increase output and employment and raise workers' wages by giving up home production of the most labor-intensive components of those products. In this way, offshore procurement can improve the competitiveness of an industry whose end products face competition from imports. Industry competitiveness rises, and with it employment, output, and wages. This outcome runs counter to the fears of critics of trade liberalization, but it makes sense when viewed through the lens of the theory of effective protection and it is consistent with what we know about the effects of technical progress.

The implications of cross-border fragmentation are not independent of the specifics of the arrangements. It matters, for example, whether the components involved are marketable commodities themselves, capable of being employed in the production of a variety of end products and thus tradable in world markets, or whether, instead, they are custom-made parts of specific products, with no alternative uses. Examples of the former include standardized semiconductors for use in automobiles, computers, consumer appliances, and the like. Examples of the latter include parts of a particular garment or of a particular airplane.

Scale Economies and Firm Size

The availability of production sharing offers new insights into the working of economies of scale. When production is fully integrated, the access to scale economies is limited by volume at the end-product level. With fragmentation, volume levels will rise wherever firms in one country supply not only their own industry, but foreign producers as well, thereby expanding the gains from scale. While this benefit may be found in the production of product-specific components, it is likely to be especially valuable with generic components. Apart from scale economies in production, the greater role of services in the context of fragmentation enhances the importance of scale effects inherent in service links.

Under fragmented production, moreover, it is no longer necessary for producers to master entire production chains and to organize them within single firms. The gains inherent in intra-product specialization and the potential savings in learning costs should encourage the creation of firms focusing on component production. Large and small firms can now use the global economy as their production partner. Multinationals, who played such an important role in promoting globalization, face a much more competitive environment in the form of small and medium-sized companies who operate successfully in the global production network. Size may be less of an advantage than it used to be.

Strategies for Economic Development

From the point of view of industrializing countries, the availability of component specialization broadens the choice of development strategies and generally reduces the hurdles to be overcome in the quest for industrialization. In the absence of component specialization, developing economies would have to master entire production processes in order to become viable competitors in world markets. Fragmentation and component specialization eliminate the need to gain competency in all aspects of production and allow emerging countries to enter into the network of global production sharing by focusing on mastery of just one facet of production or on no more than a limited subset of all the activities involved in making a final product. Given relative factor endowments, such countries may begin by developing competency in the more labor-intensive components of complex products and gradually move on to more capital- and human-capital-intensive activities. Production-sharing relationships with producers in developed countries facilitate knowledge transfer and thereby offer industrializing countries greater and cheaper access to advanced technologies.

Linking the Various Branches of Trade Theory

As already noted, the implications of cross-border production sharing may be profitably examined with the standard trade model. That approach alone, however, cannot capture the full scope of effects. Standard trade theory assumes that all industries are competitively organized, yet it is well known that multinational companies play an important role in offshore production activities of all types. The guiding principles, however, are readily transposed to the operation of multinationals. Offshore sourcing will be undertaken if it reduces costs relative to end-product prices, thereby expanding domestic value-added. Offshore sourcing or production will be organized to take advantage of cost conditions in various countries, which will be critically dependent on resource endowments. Such offshore production is more likely to be preceded by foreign direct investment. The less suitable are extant foreign production facilities, the more important are quality control considerations, and the more a multinational enterprise needs to protect industrial secrets.

If, as in the case of the standard trade model, the cost reductions brought about by offshore sourcing of labor-intensive activities enable the multinational to expand its market share in the domestic and/or foreign market for the end product, output levels will rise and, along with them, employment of capital and labor.

4. Tracking International Fragmentation Empirically

As noted earlier, published trade data do not make it easy to assess and evaluate the role of cross-border production. There is evidence, however, that the process described above is real and that it exerts some impact on international trade flows. Helleiner (1981) was one of the first to study the process of globalization from the perspective of transnational corporations and intra-firm trade. His findings support the thesis that a high and growing proportion of international commerce is carried out by transnational corporations in the form of intra-firm trade. Thus, about 30 percent of UK and Swedish exports in the mid-1970s took place on an intra-firm basis. Almost one-half of US imports in 1977 originated with a party related to the buyer by way of ownership (of 5 percent or more of the voting stock). Helleiner also documented the extraordinary growth of US imports under tariff items 807.00 and 806.30 attributed to reallocation of certain stages of production to countries such as Mexico, Taiwan, Singapore, Hong Kong, and Malaysia.

However, to focus only on multinationals as the agent of globalization is to underestimate the importance of the phenomenon. While some authors see outsourcing as the main manifestation of the globalization of production, Lawrence (1994), taking the imports of US multinationals as a measure of outsourcing, finds that there has been no spectacular growth in this trade category in recent years. Krugman (1986) considers foreign direct investment carried out by multinationals as the 'right' variable, but one in which there has been no dramatic change to explain the globalization of production. Neither multinationals nor foreign direct investment are necessary conditions for the cross-border dispersion of component production.

Feenstra (1998) looks at US imports in five categories: food and beverages; industrial supplies and materials; capital goods; consumer goods; and automotive vehicles and parts. While the combined share of food and beverages and industrial supplies and raw materials accounted for almost 80 percent of US imports in 1925, it represented only about 40 percent of total imports in 1995. This dramatic change came about primarily because of an expansion of imports in the capital goods category. While this trade aggregate is a mixed bag containing investment goods as well as intermediate inputs, Feenstra is right in arguing that:

These trends indicate that processed manufactured goods play an increasingly important role in U.S. trade. While some of these goods are sold directly to U.S. consumers, in many cases there will be additional value-added by American firms. Outsourcing takes on greatest significance when the products being imported are neither basic raw materials, nor finished consumer goods, but are at an intermediate stage of processing. In that case, it is very plausible that stages of the production process (or value chain) shift across borders as new trade opportunities emerge. The data ... indicate that products are being imported into the U.S. at increasingly advanced stages of production, which suggests that firms in the U.S. may have been substituting away from these processing activities at home.

Indeed, further empirical investigations made by Feenstra (1998) and Campa and Goldberg (1997) suggest that there has been a dramatic increase in imports of intermediate inputs across manufacturing industries in the United States and the United Kingdom in the last twenty years or so.

In the end, a full understanding of the nature and determinants of production sharing will require significant amounts of empirical work at both aggregate and disaggregated, that is, industry-, and perhaps even firm-specific levels. The latter part of this volume presents several first attempts at tracking the empirical nature of the phenomenon.

While anecdotal material abounds, systematic evidence is difficult to come by, in part because official statistics have until recently paid too little attention to trade in parts and components. As Yeats notes in his contribution to this volume, however, emerging evidence underscores the importance of this type of trade in some sectors of manufacturing. For its part, the anecdotal evidence suggests that motor vehicles, electronics, and apparel are industries in which cross-border production sharing plays an important role.

5. The Chapters in this Volume

Ronald Jones and *Henryk Kierzkowski* draw on earlier work (1990) for the essential definition of fragmentation as the decomposition of production into separable component blocks connected by service links. Traditionally, international service links were more difficult to establish and more costly to maintain, which explains why outsourcing has tended to be limited to national markets. In recent years, advances in telecommunications and other technologies have sharply reduced the costs of cross-border coordination and thus have encouraged the spread of outsourcing across national frontiers.

The chapter examines the implications of offshore sourcing with a Heckscher–Ohlin model, containing two factors, many goods, and fixed input coefficients. The model does, however, have an important Ricardian element in that it allows countries to have different technologies. When fragmentation is introduced into a world in which final goods are initially produced in integrated (that is, non-fragmented) processes, world prices of components as well as final products will change. Jones and Kierzkowski examine a range of possible outcomes, and conclude that although the welfare effect of fragmentation is generally positive, adverse terms-of-trade effects and hence declining welfare cannot be ruled out.

The chapter also examines the effects of scale economies, not in production, but in service links. Scale economies in service links make the level of output an important determinant of offshore sourcing and production. Growth in economic activity generally raises the demand for global networking.

The implications of international fragmentation for the distribution of income are also examined. They show that while fragmentation may reduce the real wages of unskilled workers, it may also increase them. The outcome depends on the interaction between factor endowments and factor intensities. An important distinction is made in this context between marginal and discrete changes in factor allocations.

Alan Deardorff approaches the issue with a Heckscher–Ohlin model of two factors, many goods, many countries, and two or more cones of specialization. Within cones, factor-price equalization rules; between cones it is absent. Thus, offshore sourcing is mainly an issue of trade relations between countries located in different cones.

After examining the conditions required to support offshore sourcing, Deardorff turns to its effect on factor prices and finds that it does not necessarily contribute to factor-price equalization across cones. The movement of relative factor prices in each cone depends on the relationship between factor proportions of fragments and average factor intensities in that cone. With respect to the role of trade barriers, Deardorff concludes that they may encourage as well as discourage cross-border fragmentation.

While the theoretical underpinnings of several chapters in this volume are thoroughly grounded in traditional trade theory and thus evaluate the effects of fragmentation from the point of view of countries, a full understanding of its implications cannot be achieved without examining the issue at industry and firm levels. *Richard Harris* does just that in his contribution.

He is interested in identifying the constraints that serve to limit the extent of international specialization in the presence of intermediate products. The analysis focuses on the fixed costs of operating global production networks and the costs of coordination technologies. A single industry, such as electronics, is modeled as consisting of component suppliers, some of whom supply only locally while others supply globally. Under certain conditions, including high global coordination costs and small markets, local suppliers will dominate the industry. Global networking facilities are assumed to be supplied by an international public monopoly, with access available to any firm at a common price.

In this model, trade is driven by specialization in component production and scale economies in component production and coordination. These conditions provide the basis for an explanation of the relative sizes of global and local firms in an industry. The volume of trade is shown to be related to plant-level scale economies, with both the volume of trade and the share of globally sourced components rising as plant fixed costs rise. As the size of the global economy expands, thus increasing the size of the market, the number of global components suppliers rises, while that of local suppliers fall.

Unlike the other contributions, this explanation of global sourcing does not depend on factor prices and factor intensities and thus may be important in understanding intra-product specialization among developed countries.

Returning to the Heckscher–Ohlin model, *Sven Arndt* examines the interaction between offshore sourcing and trade policy, focusing on the effect of trade protection at the end-product level and of preferential trade arrangements on factor prices, employment, and national welfare. While offshore sourcing is clearly welfare-enhancing under free trade, it exerts ambiguous welfare effects in the context of a *most favored nation (MFN)* tariff. When the trade regime is a free trade area, on the other hand, component specialization is welfare-enhancing. Rules of origin, a frequent component of free trade agreements, may inhibit member countries from fully exploiting the benefits of intra-product specialization.

Victoria Curzon Price considers three dimensions along which fragmentation may be pursued. They lie in product space, firm space, and geographic space, respectively. Since, in any given case, fragmentation may be pursued in more than one dimension, there exists a large number of potential combinations. The exercise underscores the complexity and multitude of possible arrangements. Curzon Price examines the main prototypes in terms of a variety of actual firms and industries. She also provides an overview of recent trends along the three dimensions of fragmentation.

Although the anecdotal evidence suggests that cross-border production sharing has become important, it has not been easy until recently to confirm that perception in more rigorous and systematic terms. In his chapter, *Alexander Yeats* examines trade data in the machinery and transport equipment group (SITC 7), where, after Revisions 2 and 3, approximately 50 individual three-, four-, and five-digit groups consisting solely of components are reported. He finds that in 1995 component trade made up 30 percent of total *Organization for Economic Co-operation and Development (OECD)* exports in SITC group 7 and that this ratio has been rising in recent years. He finds, on the import side, that trade in components is dominated by a very small number of product groups. Indeed, imports of parts of motor vehicles, office and adding machinery, telecommunications equipment, and switch gear account for 70 percent of all component imports under category SITC 7. Not surprisingly, the data reveal that the OECD tends to be a net exporter of parts in this group, suggesting that foreign assembly plays an important role in the industries involved. Developing countries are not only important recipients of components from advanced countries, but have seen their shipments of components rise as well in recent years. The United States and Germany are major importers of components.

Among probable explanations of these findings, Yeats considers tariff provisions governing offshore assembly, wage differentials, transport and other costs, and government policies. The theoretical chapters in this volume model a variety of causal linkages, but additional empirical research is needed to sort out the importance of various contributing factors.

Frances Ruane and *Holger Görg* examine the electronics industry in Ireland from the point of view of cross-border production and sourcing. The history of this industry in Ireland is explained in terms of the factor-endowment, factor-intensity arguments developed in the earlier chapters, but the authors note that a hospitable policy environment and the advantages of language and location within Europe also played a role.

Early in the industry's development, Irish plants assembled kits containing components that were sourced globally. Some of those components came from Asia, where labor costs were lower. In terms of key costs, Ireland found itself somewhere between Asia and the industrialized nations. If cross-border production sharing was going to work for Ireland, it would have to involve components and activities that made intensive use of its abundant supplies of medium-skilled, medium-priced labor. As the industry grew and expanded, it gave rise to the creation of industrial clusters and labor pools. This agglomeration in the area of Ireland's comparative advantage in the electronics industry enabled firms to exploit economies of scale and scope. This may be an important lesson for developing countries, by suggesting that industrialization does not require a country to master the production of entire products. Specialization at the component level may provide entry into a modern, globalized industry that would otherwise be denied or delayed.

In their review of the empirical evidence, the authors note that *inward-processing trade (IPT)*, involving imports into the country for processing and subsequent re-export, has grown very rapidly in both absolute and relative terms in Ireland. In 1997, for example, one-third of total imports consisted of IPT imports. In order to provide further insights into the nature and implications of intra-product specialization, the authors review the effects on employment and employment shares of medium-skilled and high-skilled workers and on factor remuneration.

Leonard Cheng, Larry Qiu, and *Guofu Tan* focus their inquiry on the role of *foreign direct investment (FDI)* in the international spread of fragmentation. The framework chosen is the relationship between Hong Kong and Guangdong province. The theoretical model consists of two factors (skilled and unskilled labor), a final good, and an intermediate good which is used in the production of the final good. Technologies and factor endowments are distributed in such a way between the two regions that both can produce the intermediate input, but only Hong Kong can produce the final product. The model is used to show that FDI encourages complete fragmentation, with Hong Kong producing the final good and China the input. This form of fragmentation reduces unemployment among unskilled workers in Hong Kong, while raising employment among skilled workers. Employment of unskilled workers in China, on the other hand, may rise or fall.

In the empirical application, the intermediate input of the model becomes manufactured (finished) products, while the final product of the model is represented by those manufactured goods plus the value-added of marketing, distribution, and other trade-related services. The focus is clearly on Hong Kong's re-exports of goods made in China.

The evidence shows a sharp rise in FDI flows from Hong Kong to China between 1988 and 1995, over which period the number of Hong Kong-invested enterprises in the province rose from 6,438 to 49,341. Most of the investment went into manufacturing, primarily in the electronics sector. Manufacturing output in Hong Kong fell from 22 percent of *gross domestic product (GDP)* in 1987 to 7.2 percent in 1995, while manufacturing employment declined from 34 percent of total employment to 11.4 percent.

Alberto Petrucci and *Beniamino Quintieri* examine the evolution of the Italian apparel industry. Unlike many industrial countries, Italy has been able to maintain relatively balanced trade in this sector. While apparel imports have grown in Italy, as elsewhere in the developed world, exports have also increased. The key to this experience has been specialization along the (vertical) quality dimension.

While Italian producers have lost competitiveness in lower quality, unskilled-labor-intensive, mass-producing branches of apparel, they have developed and exploited comparative advantage at the upper, high-quality, high-fashion, custom-made end of the quality spectrum. This is not a story about intra-product specialization within intra-industry trade, but one which gives an important example of intra-industry trade involving final goods between a high-wage, industrialized country and labor-rich, low-wage developing countries.

Giovanni Graziani focuses on the textiles and apparel industry and the role intra-product specialization has had in its recent development. Production in the industry is viewed in terms of a value-added chain, composed of four main stages or links, differentiated on the basis of factor intensities. Each stage or link, in turn, may be decomposed into a variety of operations, again differentiated according to factor intensity. It is on this basis that local and international outsourcing is examined. While such outsourcing is widespread and rising, the industry is characterized by a broad array of firms, ranging from large firms with highly integrated operations to small firms specialized on a single operation.

Graziani reviews recent developments in the industry in the *European Union (EU)*, the United States, and Asia. The focus is on the role of subcontracting in the structural changes that have been observed in the industry in recent years. For the EU, *outward processing traffic (OPT)* has been important, particularly in trade relations with certain Mediterranean and Central and Eastern European countries. The importance of this trade is directly related to the favorable tariff regime, relative labor costs, and proximity. For the industry in general, external scale economies and hence certain agglomeration patterns, matter more than internal economies of scale.

In the case of the United States, relations with Mexico and Caribbean Basin countries are important in this respect, and in Asia, the increasing importance to Hong Kong of component trade with China is examined. These discussions are followed by an evaluation of the costs and benefits of subcontracting to developing and developed countries.

Henryk Kierzkowski examines the role of various types of trade relations in the transitioning of the Central and Eastern European countries from planned to market economies. While the geographic reorientation of their trade is largely accomplished, opportunities remain for the structural transformation of trade in the direction of intra-industry trade, defined in the traditional manner, and, perhaps, beyond that toward intra-product trade.

Kierzkowski reviews developments in the reorientation of trade toward the West, in which the European Union and West Germany are pivotal targets. He turns next to the group's intra-industry trade, measured in the manner of Grubel-Lloyd, and finds significant levels of intra-industry trade with the EU—levels near those of Finland, Norway, and Portugal. Inasmuch as intra-industry trade involves product differentiation and inasmuch as the level of economic development is lower in the group than in the EU, it would be natural to expect the former to specialize in commodities at the lower end of the quality spectrum in each industry. Kierzkowski reports evidence from various studies that appears to support that expectation.

Kierzkowski next looks into the potential for international fragmentation or intra-product specialization between East and West Europe, focusing on outward-processing trade originating in the European Union. From the studies surveyed, he concludes that this type of trade has expanded significantly in recent years, particularly in textiles and clothing, with footwear as the next promising industry.

The empirical chapters in this volume are designed to illustrate the nature of the changes which are taking place in the pattern of production and trade around the globe. Both aggregate trade data and product- and country-specific case studies suggest the growing importance of production sharing and component trade. Better data and more empirical work are needed before we can fully understand and properly assess the implications of this phenomenon.

REFERENCES

Campa, Jose, and Goldberg, Linda (1997). 'The Evolving External Orientation of Manufacturing Industries: Evidence from Four Countries', *Economic Policy Review*, New York Federal Reserve Bank (July), 53–82.

Feenstra, Robert (1998). 'Integration of Trade and Disintegration of Production in the Global Economy', *Journal of Economic Perspectives*, 12/4 (fall), 31–50.

Helleiner, Gerald (1981). *Intra-firm Trade and the Developing Countries* (London: Macmillan Press).

Jones, R. W., and Kierzkowski, H. (1990). 'The Role of Services in Production and International Trade: A Theoretical Framework', in R. W. Jones and A. O. Krueger (eds.), *The Political Economy of International Trade* (Oxford: Blackwell).

Krugman, Paul, ed. (1986). *Strategic Trade Policy and the New International Economics* (Cambridge, Mass.: The MIT Press).

Lawrence, Robert (1994). 'Trade, Multinationals and Labor', *NBER Working Paper* (Cambridge, Mass.).

2

A Framework for Fragmentation

RONALD W. JONES AND HENRYK KIERZKOWSKI

1. Introduction

In current discussions of *globalization*, focus has been placed on the increased freedom of international trade in goods and services, as well as greater mobility of financial assets. However, recent patterns of globalization have exhibited a further phenomenon, namely, the role of advances in technology and lowered costs of services in fostering a *fragmentation* of vertically integrated production processes into separate segments that may enter international trade. The production of automobiles in most countries now makes use of components such as tires made by French or Italian producers, injection systems produced in Germany, computer chips manufactured in Malaysia, with software developed in the United States. Plunging international costs of telecommunication and developments of fax and Internet technology have allowed the production process to be widespread on a global basis with much less attention paid to national boundaries.

If the term fragmentation suggests destruction, it is creative destruction in the Schumpeterian tradition. Breaking down the integrated process into separate stages of production opens up new possibilities for exploiting gains from specialization. Although such fragmentation is likely to occur first on a local or national basis, significant cuts in costs of international coordination often allow producers to take advantage of differences in technologies and factor prices among countries in designing more global production networks.

The main focus of the theory of fragmentation of production is very akin to that of geography and trade. Indeed, international fragmentation of production *is* about geography. Our basic premise is that geographic parameters defining a firm are not fixed and reduced to a point in a dimensionless country. Technological advances reduce distance separating different regions, be they at home or abroad. With *the death of distance*, to borrow the title of Frances Cairncross's book, the geographic scope for modeling and organizing production processes expands. This expansion starts, we argue, at home but when it moves across national borders, a new type of international trade is created. Unlike the current literature on geography and trade, we predict that the death of distance will not only create trade in final goods but also trade in parts, components, and producers' goods.

A number of authors have investigated various aspects of fragmentation, often using their own framework and terminology. In a series of articles Sven Arndt (1996, 1997, 1998) has shown how intra-product specialization can be trade-enhancing and welfare-improving. Richard Harris (1993, 1995), on the other hand, concentrated on the role of telecommunications in establishing a new production paradigm. Alan Deardorff (1998) has investigated a two-country model in order to focus upon the determination of international prices in a setting in which production processes get fragmented. Gordon Hanson (1996) has illustrated the fragmentation phenomenon in the case of Mexico and its closer association with production in the United States.[1] Our discussion in the present chapter builds upon our two earlier analyses of international fragmentation (1990, 2000), focusing upon the importance of service links in connecting fragmented production blocks.

The next section of this paper probes the fundamentals of the fragmentation process and how prices may adjust in global markets. The key role of services and the importance of increasing returns are highlighted in Section 3. Section 4 explores in more detail possible causes of the increased degree of fragmentation now observed in world markets. A phenomenon of utmost interest in current policy debates is the effect of globalization on the distribution of income within a country, especially in the United States. Section 5 investigates the connection between fragmentation and wage rates for less skilled workers. The final section of the paper suggests various further consequences of the fragmentation phenomenon, especially as regards the changing nature of markets in the global economy.

2. Fundamentals of Fragmentation

The term, 'fragmentation', refers to a splitting up of a previously integrated production process into two or more components, or 'fragments'. As we detail in the next section, such fragmentation is made possible by utilizing activities from the 'service' sector. Here we focus more intensively on a simple characterization of the process, with the help

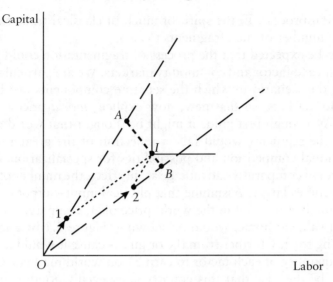

FIG. 2.1. Fragments of an integrated technology

of Figure 2.1. For an economy in an initial equilibrium, with commodity prices given by world markets and factor prices determined by the country's technology, endowments, and world commodity prices, suppose that internationally traded commodity I is produced with rigid input coefficients of two factors, say capital and labor. Point I indicates the factor input bundle required to produce $1 worth of this integrated good at the going prices. Assume that production requires a combination of two segments. Points 1 and 2 illustrate the fixed input requirements for these segments, and their vector summation must be reflected in point I. In the initial situation the production process and conditions of trade do not allow an actual split of I into these two parts. There is no market price for each component, but the costs of these segments can be obtained by the presumed fixed input/output coefficients and the equilibrium values of the wage rate and return to capital. Thus points A and B, lying on the line whose slope is given by the initial factor price ratio $(-w/r)$, shows amounts of capital and labor for each segment that would add up exactly to $1. The appropriate weights for A and B in I would then be reflected in their share of costs in the integrated activity.

With fragmentation it becomes possible to trade directly in the separate segments. To simplify, we assume away here the explicit costs involved in breaking down a vertical link as well as any costs involved in assembling components 1 and 2. If such assembly costs were to be considered, there would in effect be a tripartite fragmentation of the production process. In the spirit of much of classical trade theory, we limit the number of such fragments to two.

It is to be expected that the process of fragmentation could involve a disturbance to factor and commodity markets. We are particularly interested in the scenario in which the separate components can be traded on world markets, so that new, now explicit, *world* prices are determined. As a rough first guide it might be thought that world prices for each of the segments would fall, a reflection of the greater degree of international competition and possibilities for specialization according to Ricardian comparative advantage as, in effect, the number of tradable items becomes larger. Assuming that physical input–output coefficients remain unaltered, a fall in the world price of *A*, compared to its initial imputed value at home, would be shown in Figure 2.1 by a movement of *A* along the ray further from the origin, because it would now take a greater quantity of each factor to earn $1 on world markets. Of course it might be the case that this country is especially good at producing fragment *A* relative to other countries so that, when international fragmentation occurs, the price of *A* is driven up beyond the imputed price (or cost) of *A* in this country's pre-trade state. Whatever the comparison of autarky and trade prices for the separate sections, we assume that the greater degree of Ricardian specialization reflecting comparative advantage in these separate fragments leads to a world price for the final commodity that falls short of its price before fragmentation. Thus in Figure 2.2, a ray from the origin through point *I* would hit the chord connecting the amounts of labor and capital required to produce $1 worth of the two fragments at the newly established world prices at point *I'*, lying northeast of *I*. The ratio *II'/0I* would reveal the consequent relative fall in the world price of obtaining a unit of the final integrated commodity.

The Hicksian composite unit-value isoquant for this country, such as depicted in Figure 2.2, serves to illustrate the possible patterns of production and factor prices before and after fragmentation. Given world prices in the initial state for commodities 1, 2 and *I*, and assuming fixed input coefficients throughout, suppose the unit-value isoquants for these three commodities are as shown in Figure 2.2, with the connecting chords outlining the original Hicksian composite unit-value isoquant. Thus if the country's endowments are not extreme, it will originally be producing commodity *I* and commodity 1, or *I* and 2. (We do not consider the possibility that the country could produce only commodity 1 or commodity 2, with resulting losses in employment for capital or for labor.) Also illustrated are points *A'* and *B'*, which take into account the

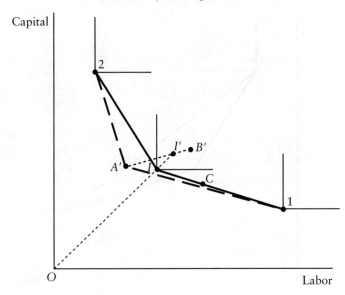

FIG. 2.2. The Hicksian composite unit-value isoquant

new world prices for post-fragmentation individual segments which can now enter trade. As drawn, for this country it is no longer possible to produce fragment *B'*. There must be some one or more countries, however, whose technology in producing *B* is sufficiently superior so that for such a country point *B'* lies on *its* Hicksian unit-value composite isoquant.

In thinking about the possible overall welfare improvement for this country as a consequence of international fragmentation, note that the new Hicksian composite isoquant is superior to the old. This would be a probable consequence of fragmentation if the world price of a composite bundle appropriate to assembling *I* had not changed. Such a result follows because of the convexity of the original composite isoquant and the fact that with *I* a positive convex combination of the two fragments, at least one of them must lie closer to the origin (than the original composite) by a finite amount.[2] Is this enough to guarantee that the country as a whole benefits from fragmentation? Yes, if prices of other traded goods are not disturbed (as assumed in Fig. 2.2). However, in general, with a realignment of all traded goods prices as a consequence of fragmentation, it might be the case that a country's terms of trade could sufficiently worsen so that it is made worse off.

Not considered in Figure 2.2 is the possibility that price falls for both fragments *A* and *B* could suffice to make it impossible for this country to

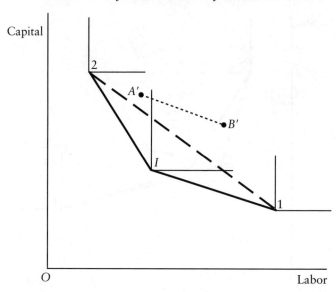

Fig. 2.3. A loss of both fragments

produce either fragment even if initially its production pattern was heavily concentrated in commodity *I* (that is, the country's endowment ray would pass close to point *I*). Such a possibility is illustrated in Figure 2.3. In Jones and Kierzkowski (2000) the analogy is made of such a scenario with that of an Olympic gold winner in a mixed event, such as the decathlon, who might return with no medals if the integrated event were to be broken down into separate components. What is revealed is that being an effective competitor in an integrated event may result from productivity in each of the separate fragments being neither very high nor very low, but that potential rivals exist which are superior in particular fragments, only to be dragged down by low productivities in the remaining ones. In school the valedictorian may have a uniform A− average in all subjects, even though there are one or more others in the class who have received A+'s in each of the subjects but have earned only C's in others. A finer degree of specialization is possible with fragmentation, and this serves to reward those countries that are particularly good at producing some fragment, but whose superiority is not of such a caliber in others. Fragmentation allows a greater scope for application of Ricardian comparative advantage.

Must the country which is illustrated in Figure 2.3 be made worse off by fragmentation? The Hicksian unit-value isoquant, which after fragmentation is clearly inferior, does not tell the whole story. The country's consumers may be heavily biased in their tastes for commodity I, and price falls in the components after fragmentation may more than offset the welfare effects of moving to the more limited Hicksian composite isoquant.

International fragmentation results in a realignment of production patterns among countries. Emphasized above is the possibility that the technological performance of inputs in various countries differs (as would be reflected in different Hicksian isoquants), leading to a Ricardian emphasis on technology and comparative advantage. But Heckscher–Ohlin elements are also involved. Although Figures 2.2 and 2.3 are somewhat limited in showing only three commodities producible (prior to fragmentation), they suffice to suggest that relatively capital-abundant countries will produce commodities 2 and I and relatively labor-abundant countries commodities 1 and I. Ricardian comparisons are useful in differentiating among the shapes of the Hicksian composite isoquants among countries, and Heckscher–Ohlin distinctions about endowment proportions indicate which portions of the Hicksian composite are relevant for a country's production. Later we shall indicate a role for the specific-factors model in the analysis of fragmentation.

We have so far established that a combination of Ricardian and Heckscher–Ohlin models can be very illuminating in explaining the phenomenon of production fragmentation and its effects on wages and other factor prices. But it is quite pertinent to ask whether another theoretical framework may not be better suited to explain the emergence of international production frameworks. In particular, imperfect competition could possibly provide a more realistic description and explanation of international fragmentation.

It is quite possible to build a model of fragmentation based on imperfect competition. Indeed, the chapter by Richard Harris in this volume does so in a very elegant manner. However, it is hard to say whether international fragmentation of production is driven by imperfect competition *per se*. We leave this question open, hoping for an answer to come out of future empirical research and case studies. Does Nike's reallocation of sports-shoes production to Malaysia require an imperfect competition model or the old Ricardian framework stressing that productivity and wage differences across nations are powerful enough to explain what is going on? Similarly, US–Mexico outsourcing in the textile industry may also be based mainly on wage/productivity differentials and a perfect competition model seems a reasonable choice in this case. Of course, computer and pharmaceutical industries could hardly be assumed to be competitive. Without in-depth case studies the question cannot be answered categorically.

In our judgment, however, although increasing returns to scale and imperfect competition may or may not be relevant in modeling *production blocks*, they appear, at least to us, to be crucial in *service links*. We even take it to an extreme by assuming the existence of only fixed costs in production of services connecting various stages of production. The emergence of the Internet comes close to justifying our assumption. Modeling of other services such as insurance, banking, transportation, and coordination should rely on a monopolistic competition framework.

3. The Role of Services in Fragmentation

In the Uruguay Round of talks leading up to the creation of the World Trade Organization much attention was paid to the possibility of bringing services under the rubric of international agreements to liberalize trade. In Jones and Kierzkowski (1990) we suggested how integrated production processes could be characterized by a series of production blocks which are connected by various service links. The notion whereby a larger scale of output can result in a finer division of labor, promulgated two centuries ago by Adam Smith, is essential in our discussion of the role of services such as transportation, communication, and coordination in linking increasingly fragmented production blocks and reducing average costs.

We do not deny the importance of service activities within a simple production block since inputs have to be organized, supervised, and coordinated before production can take place. The role of services is further emphasized when more than one production block is involved, because these blocks must be linked to generate efficient output. It is this kind of service link which we wish to emphasize. We propose to accept two stylized facts about the costs of these service links. First, purely domestic service links are less costly than those required to connect production blocks located in more than one country. This could readily be the case for all individual services, but here we only assume such a cost disparity characterizes aggregate service links. Secondly, production of services displays strong increasing returns to scale. Indeed, we would argue that such economies of scale are more likely to be found in service activities than within production blocks.

This pair of stylized facts is taken to extremes in our subsequent diagrammatic treatment whereby production blocks exhibit constant

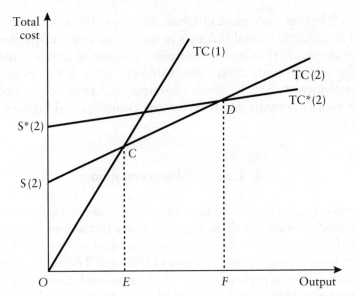

FIG. 2.4. Fragmentation with growth of output

returns to scale (as in Figs. 2.1–2.3) and service links involve only constant fixed costs and zero variable costs. In Figure 2.4 ray TC(1) represents total costs within a simple production block. Also portrayed are two possible cost configurations: TC(2) integrates two domestic production blocks, with vertical intercept measuring the constant service costs of such integration, whereas TC*(2) reflects costs for a production process combining one domestic production block with one foreign production block. The country assignment is dictated by considerations of Ricardian comparative advantage, and/or Heckscher–Ohlin type of matching factor-intensity rankings with relative cheapness of factors. Our assumptions are reflected in the higher service costs, OS*(2), associated with fragmentation in the international arena and the linearity of the cost functions. Also illustrated in Figure 2.4 is that intersection point D lies to the right of intersection point C. This is consistent with the following scenario to describe the production process as industry output expands from low levels. At first a single block is the most efficient way in which to organize production. When scale of output OE is reached, further expansion of output entails a switch to (domestically) fragmented production with costs given by the TC(2) schedule. However, after output level OF is attained, it pays to bring a foreign production block into the process; although this involves higher costs of the service links, the lower marginal costs of production reflected in

$TC^*(2)$ make this route more efficient. An alternative route would entail switching to international linkages at an earlier stage, dispensing with larger-scale purely domestic operations—this would require point D to lie to the left of point C. Not illustrated in Figure 2.4 is an extension of the argument to greater levels of output and switches to more production blocks perhaps involving several countries and higher costs of service links.

4. Causes of Fragmentation

In the preceding account of fragmentation we assumed that some change takes place 'off-stage' to allow fragments of a production process to be marketed separately whereas previously they had to be integrated with only the final product traded on world markets. Technical progress in the service sectors is perhaps the most obvious candidate. Tales abound of the fantastic reduction in the cost of international telephone calls, of reductions in transport costs and the availability of Internet connections, of much greater ease and lower costs of making banking transactions, all of which make coordination of production blocks in various locations around the globe feasible.[3] As well, increased knowledge of other cultures and laws is important. In arranging arm's-length transactions between countries it helps to know what legal procedures to follow in case the conditions of a contract are not met. Assurances of reliability in timing of shipments is essential if fragmentation at the global level is to be achieved.

We have argued that economies of scale in service activities can be quite pronounced. Significant set-up or fixed costs coupled with low marginal costs typify many of the service links required to support fragmentation. As a consequence, sheer growth in economic activity serves to induce higher levels of networking on a global basis. Furthermore, in many countries there has been a tendency to loosen the degree of governmental regulation of service activities domestically. In the United States, for example, airline deregulation and greater competition in telecommunications have altered the costs of business organization.

At the international level the efforts to liberalize barriers to service trade can be expected to encourage the tendency toward greater fragmentation of economic activity, and this for several reasons. If a country can for the first time obtain such services from the international market without governmental obstruction, costs of service links are obviously reduced. But more is involved. Liberalization encourages both an increase in scale of activity and an increase in the degree of market competition in the service industries. As the experience in telecommunications in the United States and Europe is revealing, greater competition induces reductions in cost.

5. Fragmentation and Income Distribution

International fragmentation of economic activity is a phenomenon associated with globalization, and in both the United States and Europe fears have been expressed in voluble tones as to the unsettling effect on the distribution of income of such trends in world production and trade. In particular, the criticism is often voiced that for such advanced countries globalization poses a threat to unskilled labor, either in the form of lower real wages or (especially in Europe) of higher levels of unemployment.

Figure 2.2 can usefully be harnessed to display some of the possibilities for income distribution associated with fragmentation. Think of the two categories of inputs as an amalgam of physical and human capital on the vertical axis and unskilled labor on the horizontal. Start by considering the situation of a country which is relatively unskilled-labor-abundant in the specific sense of having an endowment ray in Figure 2.2 passing south-east of point I (and allowing production of commodities I and 1). As already discussed, fragmentation for a country such as this involves the loss to global competition of the labor-intensive fragment, B'. It is just such a loss which prompts observers to fear that fragmentation induces a fall in the level of real wages for the unskilled, as is apparent from the lower slope of $A'1$ (compared with $I1$), coupled with the magnification effect standard in Heckscher–Ohlin theory. The reasoning, as expounded in Jones and Kierzkowski (2000), is that for such a country fragmentation is like technical progress in the capital-intensive sector of the economy, since at initial factor prices point A' represents an improvement over point I.

However reasonable it sounds to suggest that should a country lose the labor-intensive fragment of production to foreign competition, real wages will suffer, this need not be the outcome. Consider the case of a country whose endowment ray cuts the chord connecting 2 with A' in Figure 2.2. In such a country fragmentation has resulted in an *increase* in the real wage for unskilled workers. Indeed, it is easily seen that the level of employment of unskilled workers in the surviving capital-intensive fragment, A', is even higher than originally found in the integrated activity I. Note that compared with the previous case considered, it

is precisely a relatively capital-abundant country that has less to fear
from losses of labor-intensive fragments to world markets.

Referring once again to Figure 2.2, the fate of a country whose endowment ray lies within a cone defined by rays OA', and OI is difficult to
reconcile with standard Heckscher–Ohlin logic. Such a country initially
produces commodities 2 and I, and fragmentation that results in the loss
of segment B' but retention of fragment A' is akin to technical progress
in the country's labor-intensive activity. Nonetheless, its real wage falls.
The problem is that standard Heckscher–Ohlin logic applies to small
changes in technology, whereas the process of fragmentation is definitely not a marginal phenomenon. Figure 2.5 (based on the analysis
in Findlay and Jones, 1998) helps to clarify the issue. The solid locus
illustrates the connection between endowments and relative factor prices
in the initial pre-fragmentation state. The economy we are considering
has endowment proportions shown by point k, with a wage/rent ratio
shown by point D, producing commodities 2 and I. The dashed locus in
Figure 2.5 reveals that fragmentation of the type shown in Figure 2.2 is
like technical progress that has a labor-saving bias. (The vertical dashed
section labeled A' in Fig. 2.5 lies to the right of the original stretch
labeled I, since activity A' in Fig. 2.2 is capital-intensive relative to I).
For marginal changes it is standard in trade theory to argue that bias
does not matter. But clearly in Figure 2.5 this is no longer the case for

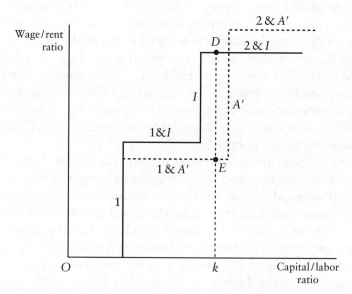

FIG. 2.5. Technical progress and wage behavior

finite changes, of the type expected with fragmentation. The shift is from point D in Figure 2.5 to point E.

The example illustrated above, wherein the loss of a labor-intensive segment results in a drop in unskilled wages only for relatively labor-abundant countries, does not generalize to all cases. (Several others are discussed in Jones and Kierzkowski, 2000.) For example, in Figure 2.3 a relatively capital abundant country, producing commodities 2 and I, would suffer a loss in the real wage of unskilled workers with fragmentation, but workers in more labor-abundant countries would gain. The purpose of the argument here is not to dispute the wisdom of the observation that losses of labor-intensive activities to other countries in trade spells trouble for unskilled labor, but to suggest that this is not always the case. The issue of the effects of international fragmentation on the distribution of income is more subtle than popular discourse suggests.

As a final exercise we utilize Figures 2.6 and 2.7 to discuss the possible effects of fragmentation when two countries share the same technology.[4] In both diagrams the relatively labor-abundant country initially produces commodities 1 and I, with its wage/rental ratio shown by the slope of the chord connecting isoquant corners I and 1, while the relatively capital-abundant country produces 2 and I at a higher wage/rental ratio. In addition, in Figure 2.6 each country produces a number of other commodities, with world prices reflective of that country's factor-price

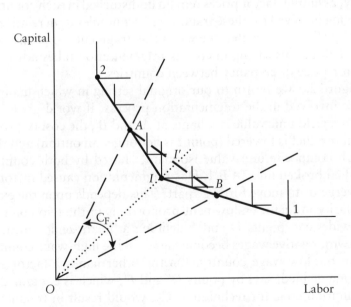

FIG. 2.6. Fragmentation and unchanged factor prices

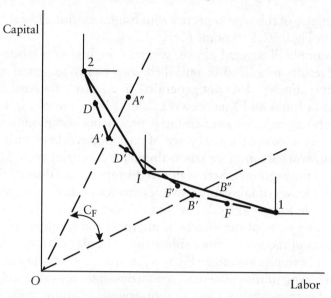

FIG. 2.7. Convergence and divergence of factor prices

ratio as well as the commonly-shared technology. After fragmentation each country produces one segment of the vertical process for producing I: A' in the capital-abundant country and B' in the labor-abundant country, assuming factor prices remain undisturbed in each country. The cost saving involved for these fragmented economies is, in relative terms, shown by II'/OI. Note that the wider the 'fragmentation cone', C_F, the greater will be this saving in cost as fragmentation takes advantage of the factor-price discrepancy between countries.

In Figure 2.7 we return to our original setting in which many countries are involved in the fragmentation process. If world prices for the fragments yield unit-value isoquants at A' and B', the cost of producing the final product is lowered (point I is no longer an option) and the new Hicksian composite unit-value isoquant, shared by both countries, is the dashed broken line $2A'B'1$. Has fragmentation caused factor prices to converge or to move further apart? This depends upon the extent of dissimilarity in factor endowment proportions in the two countries. If this is wide (e.g. points D and F defining a 'factor-endowment cone', not drawn), relative wages become higher in the high-wage country and lower in the low-wage country. On the other hand, a factor endowment cone defined, say, by points D' and F', which is contained in the fragmentation cone for techniques, C_F, would result in fragmentation causing each country to produce both segments and their factor prices to be driven to equality. In the event that competition in world markets pushes prices of fragments even lower (say to A'' and B''), a wide endowment cone (defined by rays OD and OF) would bring factor prices closer together but not all the way to equality. The economist's favorite phrase, 'almost anything can happen' seems appropriate for the income-distribution fall-out of fragmentation. This implies, however, that the loss of a labor-intensive segment due to the process of fragmentation need *not* necessarily harm the interests of labor.

Wage-rate behavior is sometimes analyzed in a context of the specific-factors model (e.g. as in Jones and Engerman, 1996). For example, if unskilled labor is mobile among sectors (with physical capital and skilled labor the specific factors), technological change in any sector will tend to spill over to register benefits to unskilled labor unless progress has a significant labor-saving bias. The point we wish to stress here is that the Hicksian unit-value isoquant apparatus utilized in Figures 2.2 and 2.3 need not be restricted to the standard all-factors-mobile Heckscher–Ohlin scenario. Instead, suppose that productive activity takes place in many sectors of the economy, and in each there is a specific type of physical or human capital employed, fixed in amount. However, suppose that within each such sector there are a number of industries which employ the type of specific capital identified with that sector. Then the analysis of fragmentation in some such industry can build upon the type of Hicksian unit-value isoquant displayed in Figures 2.2 or 2.3. The major alteration is that the quantity of unskilled labor employed by that sector becomes endogenous.[5]

6. Consequences of Fragmentation: Concluding Remarks

The role of services has been highlighted in our discussion but not whether services themselves become internationally tradable and subject to fragmentation. Thus production blocks could be fragmented internationally by making use of fairly integrated non-traded national service links, such as banking or accounting services. However, much of the current change in technology has allowed fragmentation in *international* service links. Providers of service activities in transportation and communication have made frequent use of locations in the Caribbean, say, to provide answers to queries about hotels, airline possibilities, and telephone numbers from sources worldwide. A flourishing software sector has emerged in Bangalore to design new packages and trouble-shoot difficulties and problems posed to them by firms in the United States,

Western Europe, and elsewhere. Indeed, given the existence of different time zones, there is an advantage in being able to pose the query at the end of the day in Pacific Coast Time and have an answer ready at the start of work the next morning!

One major consequence of the process of fragmentation into more simple production blocks is that new firms can spring up to take over some such blocks and to supply a *number* of other (competing) firms with its output. Thus further economies of scale are generated and demand for the block can exhibit greater stability than would be the case if separate firms all performed identical processes.

Since the mid-1980's, and particularly in the 1990's, large and well-known American electronics companies such as Apple, IBM, NCR, Philips, ATT, Hewlett Packard, and DEC have been abandoning their internal manufacturing operations in droves and turning to contract manufacturers such as SCI to build their products. At the same time, many younger, faster growing electronics firms, many of them based in Silicon Valley, CA, have always used contract manufacturers; few new firms have built internal manufacturing capacity even as they have grown (e.g. Sun Microsystems, Silicon Graphics, and Cisco Systems). (Sturgeon, 1997)

Think of how wasteful it would be if each separate firm were to install its own e-mail apparatus or fax system in order to connect its own production blocks.

International fragmentation of vertical production processes into separate production blocks often results in these blocks being sufficiently simple that they find potential uses in other activities seemingly remote from the original final product. Thus computer chips are used not only in computers, but also in cars, micro-vans, cameras, and so on. In addition it is now easier and more convenient for consumers to obtain what can only be described as custom-made final products without the cost of hands-on treatment at a traditional retail outlet. For example, Levi-Strauss allows customers to order 'at the click of a mouse' (Cairncross, 1997) jeans tailored to individual measurements. Dell Computers allows customers to skip the retail outlet and order via the Internet a computer with a great number of individually specified parameters and to expect this customized product to be delivered in a matter of days (Davis and Meyer, 1998). Dell passes on the order to a number of separate (mainly foreign) subcontractors. Such fragmentation would have appeared totally strange to the IBM of the 1960s, intent on providing completely integrated products in-house.

Examples of fragmentation need not be limited to the computer industry. Nike, for example, has found that its comparative advantage lies in design and marketing, leaving unto others all the manufacturing. The famous camera, Leica, has its lenses produced in Germany, and its body and electrical parts produced in Spain, Canada, and the Far East.

In our earlier discussion of fragmentation (Jones and Kierzkowski, 1990) we pondered the role of multinationals. We stated that international fragmentation was taking place both within multinational organizations and by means of arm's-length arrangements in the market. Here we suggest an update with a bias. As the price of international service links declines, and as knowledge of potential international suppliers and legal systems becomes more widespread, we now suggest that the necessity for containing various production blocks under the umbrella of a multinational organization is systematically being reduced. But we leave unto others the task of testing the proposition that there is an increasing role to be played by separate firms (perhaps smaller than in the past), connected only by the rules of the international market-place.

NOTES

1. Further contributions to the literature are found in Cairncross (1997), Borrus and Zysman (1997), Borrus (1997), Zysman *et al.* (1996), Davis and Meyer (1998), and Feenstra (1998).
2. Indeed, even if commodity I originally lies *within* the Hicksian composite unit-value isoquant (so that I cannot be produced by this country), after fragmentation a segment such as A' could lie *on* the new isoquant. An exception could be shown in Fig. 2.2 if final commodity I was produced (along with the first commodity) as well as another commodity, C, and it was commodity C that was fragmented instead of commodity I. It might be the case that the fragments at the new world prices would lie *along* the $I1$ linear segment.
3. Australia has in the past decades produced a series of notable films. It has also been host to the production end of some films coordinated from Hollywood. Such fragmentation has recently been further encouraged since internet transmissions have obviated the need to fly rushes from Australia to California.
4. This is the focus of the related paper by Alan Deardorff (1998), to whom we are indebted for stimulating conversations on this topic.
5. For an analysis of this type see Jones and Marjit (1992).

REFERENCES

Arndt, Sven (1996). 'International Sourcing and Factor Allocation in Preference Areas', unpublished manuscript.
—— (1997). 'Globalization and the Open Economy', *North-American Journal of Economics and Finance*, 8/1.

Arndt, Sven (1998). 'Globalization and the Gains from Trade', in K. J. Koch and K. Jaeger (eds.), *Trade, Growth, and Economic Policy in Open Economies* (New York: Springer-Verlag).

Borrus, Michael (1997). 'Left for Dead: Asian Production Networks and the Revival of U.S. Electronics', BRIE Working Paper 100 (Berkeley).

—— and Zysman, John (1997). 'You Don't Have to be a Giant: How the Changing Terms of Competition in Global Markets are Creating New Possibilities for Danish Companies', BRIE Working Paper 96A (Berkeley).

Cairncross, Frances (1997). *The Death of Distance* (Boston: Harvard Business School Press).

Davis, Stan, and Meyer, Christopher (1998). *Blur* (Reading, Mass.: Addison-Wesley).

Deardorff, Alan (1998). 'Fragmentation in Simple Trade Models', unpublished.

Feenstra, Robert (1998). 'Integration of Trade and Disintegration of Production in the Global Economy', *Journal of Economic Perspectives*, 12/4 (fall), 31–50.

Findlay, Ronald, and Jones, R. W. (2000). 'Factor Bias and Technical Progress', *Economics Letters*, 68: 303–8.

Hanson, Gordon (1996). 'Localization Economies, Vertical Organization, and Trade', *American Economic Review*, Dec.

Harris, Richard G. (1993). 'Globalization, Trade and Income', *Canadian Journal of Economics*, Nov.

—— (1995). 'Trade and Communications Costs', *Canadian Journal of Economics*, Nov.

Jones, Ronald W., and Engerman, Stanley (1996). 'Trade, Technology and Wages: A Tale of Two Countries,' *American Economic Review*, 86: 35–40.

—— and Kierzkowski, Henryk (1990). 'The Role of Services in Production and International Trade: A Theoretical Framework', in Ronald Jones and Anne Krueger (eds.), *The Political Economy of International Trade* (Oxford: Basil Blackwell).

—— —— (2000). 'Globalization and the Consequences of International Fragmention', forthcoming in Rudiger Dornbusch, Guillermo Calvo, and Maurice Obstfeld (eds.), *Money, Factor Mobility and Trade: A Festschrift in Honor of Robert A. Mundell* (Cambridge, Mass.: MIT Press).

—— and Marjit, Sugata (1992). 'International Trade and Endogenous Production Structures', Ch. 9 in W. Neuefeind and R. Riezman, *Economic Theory and International Trade: Essays in Memoriam J. Trout Rader* (New York: Springer-Verlag).

Sturgeon, Timothy J. (1997). 'Turnkey Production Networks: A New American Model of Industrial Organization?', BRIE Working Paper 92A (Berkeley).

Zysman, John, Doherty, Eileen, Schwartz, Andrew (1996). 'Tales from the "Global" Economy: Cross National Production Networks and the Re-organization of the European Economy', BRIE Working Paper 83 (Berkeley).

3

Fragmentation across Cones

ALAN V. DEARDORFF

F11 F23
L23

1. Introduction

The subject is still fragmentation, as it was in an earlier paper motivated by the previous conference in this series.[1] This time I want to explore further how fragmentation may matter for the prices of factors. This question is most interesting in the context of a Heckscher–Ohlin trade model in which factor prices are *not* equalized by trade, especially if this is due to the countries having sufficiently different factor endowments to make *factor price equalization (FPE)* impossible.[2] In such a world, with a large number of both goods and countries (but only two factors, to keep things manageable), goods and countries fall into two or more cones of specialization.[3] Within these cones, countries share identical factor prices, but between cones they do not. Fragmentation either will not occur, or is not particularly interesting, within these cones. Therefore I will look primarily at fragmentation across cones.

In Section 2 I begin by examining the circumstances under which a new fragmentation technology will be used. There are no surprises here, and the purpose is mainly just to clarify the context of the analysis. A fragmentation technology will be used, under free trade, only if the cost savings from producing fragments in countries with different factor prices are large enough to offset any need for additional resources. In the two-factor model, a relatively simple geometric construction can determine whether or not this is the case. The section also briefly considers the role of tariffs, which can both prevent and stimulate fragmentation depending on whether and where tariffs are imposed on intermediate and final goods.

Sections 3 and 4 provide results that may be more unexpected. Both ask how fragmentation will affect factor prices. In Deardorff (1998) I noted that fragmentation in some sense increases the likelihood of FPE, and indeed it is quite possible that fragmentation will in fact bring factor prices across countries closer together, and even equalize them.

However, in a world of many goods, the introduction of a single fragmentation technology is unlikely to accomplish that. The question then
becomes whether fragmentation necessarily brings factor prices closer
together across countries, and the answer is no. Instead, the direction of
change of relative factor prices in each cone depends systematically on
how the factor proportions of fragments compare to the average factor
intensities within the cones where the fragments are produced.

The analysis in Section 3 is entirely graphical, and it is also to some
extent impressionistic, since the graphs do not really enable one to nail
down exactly what factor prices will be after conditions change. In Section 4, therefore, I examine the same issue more explicitly, but in the
context of a special case of the model in which all preferences and technologies are Cobb–Douglas. In this context it is feasible to express factor
prices under free trade in terms of the intensities of use of the factors
in producing industries. From that it is possible to show more explicitly
that relative factor prices can be pushed further apart by fragmentation.

2. When does Fragmentation Happen?

Consider two countries, or groups of countries, with different factor
prices under free trade. Unit isocost lines for both countries are shown
in Figure 3.1 as lines ACD for the labor-abundant country, which I will
call *South*, and BCE for the capital abundant country, *North*.

As discussed in Deardorff (1979), with free trade we can identify
which country will produce each (final) good by finding prices that place
the good's unit-value isoquant (the isoquant for producing one dollar's
worth of that good) just tangent to the outermost, or envelope, of the
two isocost lines. As a result, all of the goods that capital-abundant
North produces will be more capital intensive than all of the goods that
South produces, with the possible but not necessary exception of a good
whose unit-value isoquant is tangent to both isocost lines on either side
of their intersection at point C.[4] Since if there are many goods most
are therefore not produced in both countries, I will consider only goods
that are produced in only one. One such is good X, whose unit-value
isoquant is shown in the figure.

Now suppose that fragmentation of the technology for producing X
becomes possible. That is, there now exist two different factor combinations (or sets of them) that together permit production of the same
amount of good X given by the isoquant. When will these fragments be
used instead of the original technology? I will assume in this section that

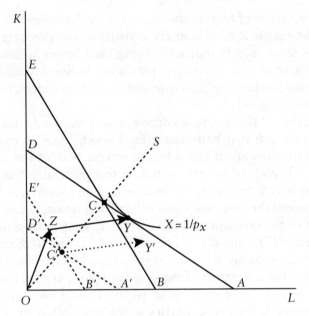

FIG. 3.1. Cost saving from costless fragmentation

good X and its fragments constitute a sufficiently small part of the total economies that changing to the fragmented technology will not cause a noticeable change in the factor prices in either country. Such changes will instead be the topic of Section 3.

If the fragments of technology together were to use a smaller amount of the factors than the original one, then of course they would necessarily be used somewhere, perhaps both of them in the same country as before. As discussed in Deardorff (1998), that possibility is really a combination of both technological improvement and fragmentation, and I will not consider it here. Instead, I will assume always in this chapter that fragmentation uses at least as many resources as the unfragmented technology. Therefore, fragmentation is at best only costless, and in general it will be costly in terms of resources used, if it requires larger amounts of factors. I will consider both cases in this section.

Costless Fragmentation

Consider, then, costless fragmentation. When and where will it be used? Suppose in Figure 3.1 that the same amount of good X produced by the isoquant $X = 1/p_x$ can now also be produced using one fragment that requires the vector of factors shown as OZ and another fragment that requires the vector ZY.[5] These are constructed in this case to add to exactly the same factors that were being used before in *South*, where good X was produced. Therefore producers in *South* could switch to the fragmented technology and it would do them no harm, but it would also do them no good.

But note that of the fragments drawn, one, OZ, would not have been produced in *South* if it had been a final good, since its capital–labor ratio is above the cut-off given by the intersection of the two isocost lines at C.[6] Therefore we expect that if this particular fragmentation opportunity arises, fragment OZ will be used in *North*, not *South*.

That is indeed the case, and costs will fall as a result, as can be verified by the rest of the construction in Figure 3.1. First draw a new pair of isocost lines, $A'C'D'$ and $B'C'E'$, parallel to ACD and BCE respectively, but both contracted inward toward the origin by the same proportion, and such that the outermost of the shrunken pair passes through the tip of the arrow, OZ. Since the original isocost lines showed the combinations of factors in the two countries worth one dollar, these new ones show the combinations worth some other amount, in this case the cost of producing the fragment OZ in *North*.[7] Since $A'C'D'$ is an isocost line, all other points on it cost the same in *North*, including point C', which therefore represents the cost of producing fragment OZ in both *North* and *South*. If we now add the other fragment, ZY, to this, we get a bundle of factors that costs the same, in *South*, as the combined fragmented technology when part of it is used in *North*. That is, draw vector $C'Y'$ equal in length and direction to ZY, starting at point C'. The tip of this arrow at Y' shows a bundle of factors that costs the same in *South* as the total fragmented technology, so long as the more capital-intensive fragment is produced in *North*, where the relative price of capital is lower.

Therefore, the fact that point Y' lies inside isocost line ACD tells us that use of the fragmented technology, even though it is just costless in the sense of using exactly the same total factors as the original technology, actually reduces cost if the fragments are produced in different countries. It also shows us the size of the cost savings, which is measured by the distance of Y' inside ACD.

Costly Fragmentation

Now consider costly fragmentation: a fragmentation technology that uses more combined factors than could have produced the good before.

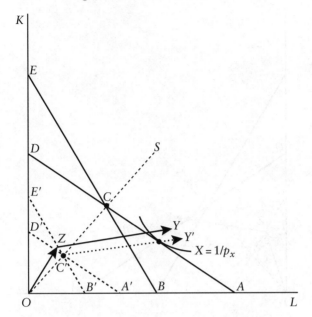

FIG. 3.2. Cost increase from costly fragmentation

Such a case is shown in Figure 3.2, where the fragmented technology is again shown by vectors OZ and ZY. This time, however, the two together extend beyond the X isoquant, requiring more total factors. The same construction as in Figure 3.1 now yields a point Y' that is also beyond the isocost line ACD. Thus, even though in this case one of the fragments could be more cheaply produced in the other country, doing so would not save enough to make up for the greater total factor usage of the fragmented technology.

Therefore, if fragmentation is costly, it may not be used at all, even though one of the fragments could be done more cheaply in the other country. What matters is the size of the cost saving from exploiting different factor prices (the savings seen in Fig. 3.1) compared to the cost of the extra resources required.

Figure 3.3 shows a case of costly fragmentation that *is* cost-saving if done in different countries. The construction is the same as in Figures 3.1 and 3.2; it just turns out differently. Of course I have made it do so by changing two things about the shapes and positions of the curves compared to Figure 3.2. I have made the capital intensity of the fragment OZ greater, so that moving it to *North* could save more cost, and I have reduced the length of the vector ZY, reducing the real cost of the new technology in terms of real resources.

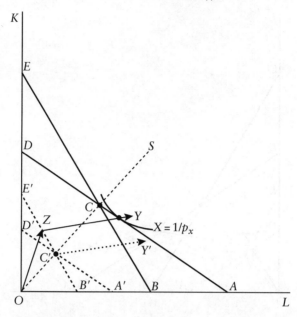

FIG. 3.3. Cost saving from costly fragmentation

These several figures give us a complete picture of when fragmentation will be used, starting from free trade, in a world of two factors, many goods, and two cones. There are several directions one could go from this for a more complete understanding of the issue. I will consider just two: multiple cones, because they are straightforward; and trade impediments, because they are important. I suspect that the extension to more than two factors is also straightforward for those who visualize easily in three dimensions, but I will not attempt it here.

Before doing the case of multiple cones, however, I would ask the reader to do a bit of drawing for themselves in Figures 3.2 and 3.3. In both cases, move the arrow ZY around in the figure, keeping its base on the kinked line $E'C'A'$ and drawing the locus traced out by its tip, Y. The result is an exact image of $E'C'A'$ itself, transposed up and to the right by the vector ZY. The new curve has its kink at point Y', and it extends to the right and left of Y' in lines that are parallel to ACD and BCE respectively. The difference between the cases of Figures 3.2 and 3.3 is simply that this new curve lies wholly outside ACE in Figure 3.2, while part of it passes inside ACE in Figure 3.3, where fragmentation reduces cost.

This technique can easily be applied to situations with more cones. Suppose, as shown in Figure 3.4, that there are four cones instead of two.

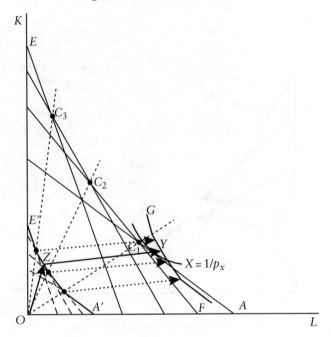

FIG. 3.4. Cost saving fragmentation with four cones of specialization

The outer envelope of the four isocost lines is $AC_1C_2C_3E$. Good X is produced in the most labor-abundant cone, and again, a fragmentation technology becomes available that uses factor vectors OZ and ZY. This time, fragment OZ could be done at least cost in the second most capital-abundant cone, two cones away from the original X. This can be seen, as before, by shrinking the envelope $AC_1C_2C_3E$ in toward the origin until it just touches vector OZ, which it does in the C_2C_3 cone. The shrunken envelope is labeled $A'E'$, and I now make an exact copy of it, transposing it northeast by the vector ZY. This forms the curve FG, which also has three kinks corresponding to C_1, C_2, and C_3. From the fact that FG passes inside the envelope $AC_1C_2C_3E$, we can conclude that this fragmentation technology will reduce costs, and therefore that it will be used.

With more than two cones, it is also easily possible that neither fragment of a new technology will be employed in the country that originally produced the good. Such an example is shown in Figure 3.5. Here there are three cones, and I consider the introduction of fragmentation in production of a good, X, that is produced in the middle cone. The fragments, however, differ sufficiently in capital intensity that one of

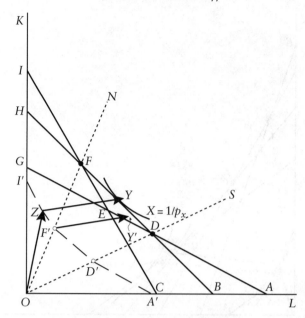

FIG. 3.5. Fragmentation off both shores

them, OZ, is most efficiently produced in the most capital-abundant cone, while the other, ZY, belongs in the most labor-abundant cone. In the case shown, although the combined fragments use more capital and labor than the original technology for producing X, our earlier construction indicates that the fragmented technology is cheaper if performed in these other cones. That is, point Y' is inside the middle cone's isocost line, $BDFH$. Therefore, when fragmentation becomes possible, if factor prices remain unchanged the entire X industry will shut down in the middle cone and production of the two fragments will arise in the other cones. Of course, if the X industry is large enough, this will induce changes in factor prices, and it may well be that these changes will permit a portion of the X industry in the middle cone to survive. But the potential for complete elimination of an industry is certainly present.

Trade Barriers

Now consider briefly what happens if there are barriers to trade, such as transport costs and/or tariffs. These permit the price of a good to be higher inside one country than in another, so long as the country with the higher price does not export the good. In the diagrams here, that means that the price of the good in any country that exports it must place its unit-value isoquant tangent to the envelope of isocost lines, as before. But price in a country that imports the good, or in one that does not trade it at all because of a trade barrier, will place the unit-value isoquant in closer to the origin than that. If the country produces the good itself, then domestic price must be high enough to place its isoquant just tangent to its own isocost line.

What does this do to our story? Not much. Although trade impediments, if sufficiently pervasive, will surely change factor prices, this will make them even more likely to be unequal across countries than if trade were frictionless and free. In any case, we can take those factor prices as given for drawing diagrams like Figures 3.1 to 3.4.

However, several effects of trade barriers can easily be understood without recourse to the figures. First, if there is no barrier to trade in X, but there is a barrier to trade in any intermediate input, call it Z, that accompanies fragmentation, then that barrier may render fragmentation unprofitable even when it would otherwise lower costs, as in Figure 3.3. There, for example, suppose that fragment OZ produces an intermediate input that must then be combined with the resources in vector ZY to produce good X. While the true cost of the intermediate input produced in the capital-abundant country is the same as factor bundle C', the cost to users of it in the labor-abundant country will be higher than this if there is an import tariff on it. It would not take a very large tariff to raise the cost above that of producing X with the old technology, in which case the tariff would prevent fragmentation from occurring.

Secondly, if there is a barrier to trade in X itself, but no barrier to trade in the intermediate good Z, then even fragmentation that would not have lowered cost with free trade might still be used. In Figure 3.2, for example, we saw that the fragmented technology would not be used under free trade. But suppose that the capital-abundant country places a tariff on imports of final good X, and suppose also in this case that it is fragment ZY that produces the intermediate input and fragment OZ that completes the processing to produce good X. The tariff on X will raise its price inside the capital-abundant country, and if large enough it can easily raise it above the cost of first importing the intermediate input and then producing X domestically using the fragmented technology.

These two examples indicate that fragmentation can be both encouraged and discouraged by trade barriers.

3. How does Fragmentation affect Factor Prices?

In Deardorff (1998) I pointed out that fragmentation has the potential to bring about factor price equalization. This will happen in a situation of free trade if the factor endowments of countries are sufficiently different to prevent FPE initially, and if costless fragmentation enlarges the sets of feasible factor uses enough to accommodate those differences across countries.[8]

But there is no guarantee that this will happen. On the contrary, if there are many goods and if fragmentation becomes possible in only some of them, then the potential for fragmentation to make any difference at all to the economy will be reduced. Indeed, this was my justification in Section 2 for considering the possibility that factor prices might not change at all.

Here I look at a middle position. Suppose that fragmentation is quantitatively important enough to matter for factor prices, but not important enough to equalize them across countries. Then in what direction will factor prices move? The answer might seem obvious, from the fact that a large amount of fragmentation at appropriate factor intensities would equalize factor prices. Then surely, one might think, a smaller amount of fragmentation will bring them closer together. That need not be the case, however.

Let the initial situation, prior to fragmentation, be that shown in Figure 3.6. Factor prices in *North* and *South* with free trade are given, as before, by the unit-isocost lines BCE and ACD respectively. Each country (or region) is producing a large number of goods, the unit-value isoquants of which are shown and labeled simply X_1, X_2, and so on. In general there could be a good produced in both countries, but I will assume that there is not. Instead, *South* produces all of the world's demand for goods X_1 to X_S and *North* produces all of the world's demand for the remaining goods, X_{S+1} to X_N.

Now suppose that fragmentation becomes possible for any one of these goods, say good X_f produced in *South*. As before, the factor requirements of the fragments are shown as the vectors OZ and ZY. Since OZ is in the northern cone, and since I have drawn this fragmentation as costless, we know from Section 2 that the fragmented technology will be used. Consider now the pressures that use of this technology in the two countries will put upon factor prices. These pressures are suggested by the three heavy arrows in the figure, but they require some explanation.

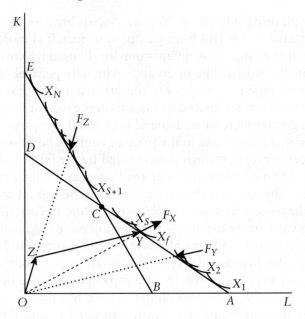

FIG. 3.6. Fragmentation pressures on factor prices

As *North* begins to produce fragment OZ, this creates additional demands for both factors in amounts given by vector OZ. These demands are added to the factor demands that the country already has for producing other goods. This will tend to bid up the prices of both factors, pushing the unit-isocost line inward toward the origin, so I indicate that with an arrow that points inward in the reverse direction of the OZ vector. How this will affect relative factor prices in *North* is something that I will consider in a moment.

First, though, consider *South*. There, since the good whose technology is being fragmented is initially produced there, two things happen. First, production of good X_f ceases, reducing demands for both factors by the amounts that were employed there. Since this by itself would reduce factor prices and push the isocost line outward, I draw the arrow F_X pointing away from the origin in the direction of the capital–labor ratio in industry X_f. Secondly, new production of the fragment ZY requires factors in the ratio given by its slope, so I draw a line parallel to ZY from the origin and indicate another arrow of pressure on factor prices, F_Y, pointing inward where it crosses *South's* isocost line.

It seems intuitively clear that these arrows are suggestive of how the isocost lines will shift, and perhaps rotate, as a result of fragmentation.

The arrow pointing inward on *North's* isocost line, for example, suggests that factor prices will both go up, and since it is more or less in the middle of the range of isoquants previously used in *North*, this will tend to shift the isocost line in an approximately parallel fashion, not particularly changing its slope. On the other hand, if that arrow had been, say, much further up and to the left on the isocost line, representing a much greater increase in demand for capital compared to labor, it would suggest a greater rise in the price of capital and thus a flattening of the isocost curve, as though it were tilted by the push of the arrow.

Similarly, in *South* the outward arrow F_X suggests falling factor prices that, because the arrow is drawn high among the capital intensities of *South's* industries, will make *South's* isocost line steeper. At the same time, the inward arrow for the more labor-intensive fragment, F_Y, tends to raise factor prices, and may also reinforce that rotation. For the case shown, then, the three arrows together seem to suggest not much change in relative factor prices in *North*, accompanied by a rise in the wage–rental ratio in *South*. To avoid clutter, I have not drawn the resulting new isocost lines in Figure 3.6, but the reader can add them if interested. In *North* the new isocost line would be shifted inward from BCE slightly, without much change in slope. In *South* ACD would be rotated somewhat clockwise, pivoting somewhere low on the segment AC, since there is a net reduction at initial prices in demands for factors in *South*. Together, in this particular case, the changes seem to take us in the direction of FPE.

But if you accept this argument, then such a move toward factor price equality is not at all assured. It depends crucially on where the heavy arrows happen to be, and thus on the factor intensities both of the fragments and of the original technology. There are many possibilities, including that relative factor prices move in the same direction in both countries and that they both move either together or further apart.

Figure 3.7 shows a case in which relative factor prices move further apart. In the case shown, it is the most labor-intensive good, X_1, for which a fragmentation technology becomes available, with a capital-intensive fragment, OZ, that can be performed in *North* at lower cost, although it is then the most labor-intensive process being used there. The more labor-intensive fragment, ZY, is of course even more labor-intensive than X_1, although not by much. Once again, arrows F_Z, F_Y, and F_X show the pressures on unit-isocost lines, via factor markets and factor prices, due to the fragmentation. Fragment OZ, being the most labor-intensive process in *North*, increases the wage there more than the rental and makes the isocost line steeper (not shown). Fragment ZY

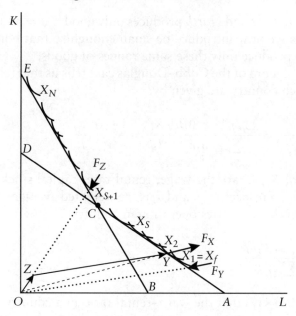

FIG. 3.7. Fragmentation that drives factor prices apart

would do the same in *South* if it were not for the offsetting downward pressure on wages due to the cessation of production of X_1. The latter necessarily involves more resources than the fragment ZY, and therefore can easily dominate it, causing the wage–rental ratio to fall. Therefore this is a case in which fragmentation can cause the relative wage to fall in *South* and rise in *North*, the two ratios thus moving further apart.

4. Factor Price Determination

These conclusions about effects on factor prices may seem somewhat less than certain, since I have not provided a full model of how they are determined, and indeed they are only examples of what might happen. But that they are valid examples can be shown rather simply in the following more explicit version of the model.

Suppose that all preferences are identical and Cobb–Douglas, with β_j the share of each consumer's expenditure on good j. Suppose that all production functions are also Cobb–Douglas in factors capital and labor, with α_j the capital share and $1 - \alpha_j$ the labor share in industry j. Finally, suppose that in the initial equilibrium *South* produces only goods $J_S = 1, \ldots, s$ and *North* produces only goods $J_N = s+1, \ldots, n$. Let any changes we now introduce be small enough so that both countries continue to produce only these same ranges of goods.

Then the algebra of the Cobb–Douglas case tells us that relative factor prices in each country are given by:

$$\omega_i^0 = \frac{w_i^0}{r_i^0} = \frac{\sum_{j \in J_i} (1 - \alpha_j)\beta_j}{\sum_{j \in J_i} \alpha_j \beta_j} \frac{K_i}{L_i} = \frac{1 - \bar{\alpha}^i}{\bar{\alpha}^i} \frac{K_i}{L_i} \qquad (3.1)$$

where w_i, r_i, K_i, L_i are the wage, rental rate, capital stock, and labor force of region i respectively, and $\bar{\alpha}_i$ is the weighted average of the capital shares, α_i, in the industries operating in country i:

$$\bar{\alpha}_i = \frac{\sum_{j \in J_i} \alpha_j \beta_j}{\sum_{j \in J_i} \beta_j}$$

Equation (3.1) says that the wage–rental ratio in a country depends on its factor endowments and on the relative weighted averages of the labor shares compared to the capital shares in its own production. Given the goods that a country or region produces, the relative returns to factors depend inversely on their endowments. But given their endowments, the relative returns also depend positively on the average factor intensities of their own industries. This is the feature of the model that I will use here. The higher the average labor intensity of the goods that a country produces, for example, the higher the country's relative wage.

Now let an industry, $j' \in J_S$, become costlessly fragmented. This means that it is split into two parts, j_1' and j_2', that together produce good j'. Let these fragments also be Cobb–Douglas as follows: fragment j_1' produces an intermediate input, z, using the production function

$$z = K_{z1}^{\alpha_{z1}} L_{z1}^{1-\alpha_{z1}}$$

and fragment j_2' produces final good j' with production function

$$x_{j'} = \left(K_{z2}^{\alpha_{z2}} L_{z2}^{1-\alpha_{z2}} \right)^{1-\gamma} z^\gamma$$

Thus, of the share of expenditure $\beta_{j'}$, that goes to good j', a fraction γ is paid to capital and labor employed in fragment j_1' producing the intermediate good z, while the fraction $1 - \gamma$ is paid to capital and labor in the second fragment, j_2', producing the final good.

Suppose for concreteness that $\alpha_{z1} > \alpha_{j'} > \alpha_{z2}$. Also, consistent with this, let fragment j'_1 be produced in *North*, and fragment j'_2 in *South*, as in the figures. *North's* new wage–rental ratio can be found from eqn (3.1), adding the appropriate terms into both numerator and denominator for the fragment j'_1:

$$\omega_N^1 = \frac{(1 - \alpha_{z1})\gamma\beta_{j'} + \sum_{j \in J_N}(1 - \alpha_j)\beta_j}{\alpha_{z1}\gamma\beta_{j'} + \sum_{j \in J_N}\alpha_j\beta_j}\frac{K_N}{L_N}$$

$$= \omega_N^0 + (\bar{\alpha}^N - \alpha_{z1})\Omega_N \tag{3.2}$$

where

$$\Omega_N = \frac{\gamma\beta_{j'}}{\left(\alpha_{z1}\gamma\beta_{j'} + \sum_{j \in J_N}\alpha_j\beta_j\right)\bar{\alpha}^N}\frac{K_N}{L_N} > 0$$

The expression for ω_N^1 in eqn (3.2) is evidently larger than ω_N^0 if α_{z1} is smaller than $\bar{\alpha}^N$, the weighted average of the α_j's in J_N, as was the case in Figure 3.7.

Similarly, the new wage–rental ratio in *South* is found from eqn (3.1) by adding a term in top and bottom for new fragment j'_2, and also subtracting the term for the no-longer-produced good j' itself, since it should no longer be included in the summations:

$$\omega_S^1 = \frac{(1 - \alpha_{z2})(1 - \gamma)\beta_{j'} - (1 - \alpha_{j'})\beta_{j'} + \sum_{j \in J_S}(1 - \alpha_j)\beta_j}{\alpha_{z2}(1 - \gamma)\beta_{j'} - \alpha_{j'}\beta_{j'} + \sum_{j \in J_S}\alpha_j\beta_j}\frac{K_S}{L_S}$$

$$= \frac{-[(1 - \alpha_{j'})\gamma - \delta]\beta_{j'} + \sum_{j \in J_S}(1 - \alpha_j)\beta_j}{-[\alpha_{j'}\gamma + \delta]\beta_{j'} + \sum_{j \in J_S}\alpha_j\beta_j}\frac{K_S}{L_S}$$

where

$$\delta = (\alpha_{j'} - \alpha_{z2})(1 - \gamma) > 0$$

This can be manipulated to yield

$$\omega_S^1 = \omega_S^0 - \left[(\bar{\alpha}^S - \alpha_{j'}) - \frac{\delta}{\gamma}\right]\Omega_S \tag{3.3}$$

where

$$\Omega_S = \frac{\gamma\beta_{j'}}{\left((1 - \gamma)\alpha_{z2}\beta_{j'} + \sum_{j \in J_S - j'}\alpha_j\beta_j\right)\bar{\alpha}^S}\frac{K_S}{L_S} > 0$$

Thus ω_S^1 is less than ω_S^0 if α_{z2} and $\alpha_{j'}$ are sufficiently close together, so that δ is small in eqn (3.3), and if the original good, j', was less capital intensive than the average industry in *South*. Again, this was the case in Figure 3.5.

5. Conclusion

Fragmentation, as defined here, is a diverse phenomenon. When a production process is split into parts, this can be done in a wide variety of ways, and it matters greatly to the economies involved what form the fragmentation takes. In this chapter I have looked at just two issues— whether and where fragmented technologies will be used, and the effects of fragmentation on factor prices. In both cases, the answers depend on the nature of the fragmentation. Most important for the results, in both cases, are the factor intensities of the fragments. Also important for the viability of a fragmented technology is its total use of resources.

For the use of fragmented technologies, the analysis shows that even a costly fragmentation technology, one which uses more resources than the original, may be viable. This is true, however, only if countries lie in different diversification cones and (at least) one of the fragments lies in a different cone than the original, unfragmented technology. In that case, the viability of the fragmented technology depends on a tradeoff between its extra cost in terms of resources and the cost saving that can be achieved by performing fragments in countries where factor prices favor them.

Regarding the effects of fragmentation on factor prices, it is of course possible that fragmentation will equalize them across countries. When this does not happen, however, it need not be the case that factor prices are drawn closer together by fragmentation. Instead, the effects on relative factor prices in the countries where the fragmentation takes place depend fairly systematically on the factor intensities of the fragments, as well as that of the original technology. What matters, however, is how these factor intensities compare to the average intensities of processes in use in each country before fragmentation, not their intensities compared to all goods produced globally.[9]

NOTES

My greatest thanks to Arvind Panagariya, with whom I discussed the issues addressed in this chapter and who helped me to see the results and the topic more clearly.

My thanks also to Sven Arndt, Ron Jones, and Henryk Kierzkowski who got me started on this topic, and to Chong Xiang and Chul Chung who have helped me to clarify these ideas.

1. See Deardorff (1998).
2. See Deardorff (1994) for clarification of just how factor endowments must differ in order for FPE to be impossible.
3. See Deardorff (1979).
4. For there to be more than one such good there would have to be factor-intensity reversals, which I assume here do not exist.
5. For simplicity I will take the fragments to be Leontief fixed-coefficient technologies. If substitution is possible, that can only make the use of the fragments more attractive. However, it somewhat complicates the analysis of where a fragment will be produced, since the relevant vectors in each country are those that minimize costs at the country's factor prices.
6. That is, for the output of the fragment OZ to be produced in *South*, its price would have to place a unit-value isoquant corresponding to OZ tangent to ACD. But at that price, anyone producing it in *North* would earn a positive profit. Hence, the equilibrium (zero-profit) price for such a fragment is lower, and it would not be produced in *South* without protection.
7. If shrinking the isocost lines to OZ had hit OZ in segment $A'C'$, then this would be the cost of producing the fragment in *South*.
8. If fragmentation is costly, then since it will not be used if factor prices are equal, it cannot cause complete FPE.
9. Davis (1996) has made a similar point for the effects of trade liberalization in a multi-cone model.

REFERENCES

Davis, Donald R. (1996). 'Trade Liberalization and Income Distribution', NBER Working Paper No. 5693.

Deardorff, Alan V. (1979). 'Weak Links in the Chain of Comparative Advantage', *Journal of International Economics*, 9 (May).

—— (1994). 'The Possibility of Factor Price Equalization, Revisited', *Journal of International Economics*, 36.

—— (1998). 'Fragmentation in Simple Trade Models', Research Seminar in International Economics Working Paper No. 422, University of Michigan, 7 Jan.

4

A Communication-Based Model of Global Production Fragmentation

RICHARD G. HARRIS

1. Introduction

An important characterization of the globalization of trade, and in particular of trade in manufactures, is the increased fragmentation of production as defined by Jones and Kierzkowski (1990). The basic idea they advanced is that it is important to open the 'black box' of the production function and focus attention on differences among the basic component processes of a production system. For example, an electronics plant may have historically produced a number of different components and then assembled them into a final product at a single geographic location. Over time these separate processes which were once agglomerated within a single plant have been segmented, with their location being geographically dispersed both within national economies and across international economies. From the point of view of the country losing an activity, this is also referred to as 'outsourcing' by the resident home country firm.

The possible reasons for 'fragmentation' and its consequences are a primary concern of the chapters in this volume. There are a number of explanations for the observed increased specialization of plants and the consequent fragmentation of global production structures. One is differences in factor intensities across the different processes within the firm as emphasized in the chapters by Deardorff and Jones and Kierzkowski in this volume. That perspective suggests that fragmentation results as a response to factor price or endowments differences across countries in line with comparative advantage analysis. Another set of explanations is based on the reduction in global trade barriers which allows greater vertical specialization in response to Ricardian productivity differentials. A third set of possible explanations is motivated by the potential gains to specialization of the Smithian sort, emphasized in models of trade in intermediate inputs such as that developed by Ethier (1979). It is the latter set of explanations which is most closely related to the model developed in this chapter.

An obvious question in models with variable degrees of specialization in intermediates is what factors constrain the degree of specialization. One part of the answer are fixed costs at the level of individual plants which Ethier emphasized. However, I will argue this is not enough to give rise to a satisfactory theory of fragmentation. Potentially more interesting are the fixed costs of running global 'production networks'. A production network is defined as a set of links and infrastructure linking a large number of related production units. These may be closely related firms, as for example within a fully vertically integrated *multinational enterprise (MNE)*, or less closely related on ownership grounds, but related on a customer–supplier basis as is often the case, for example in just-in-time inventory systems. The recent business case literature on production networks provides a rich ethnography on cases that would fall under what we have labeled 'fragmentation'.

Production systems involving design, production, delivery, and installation consist of thousands of complex components all of which require coordination technologies. Coordination technologies as discussed by Becker and Murphy (1992) are a central limiting factor on the size of the firm. The view taken here is that the firm is too narrow a unit of analysis for the problem of global fragmentation. A more natural unit of analysis is the production network. In the case of production networks, a major limitation on coordination across the network are communication and transport technologies. Changes in these technologies, it will be argued, are a major force in driving fragmentation. Of the two technologies (transport and communications), most of the most dramatic innovations of the last two decades have been in communication with the development of internet-based public communications networks. It is important to emphasize that network industries operate on infrastructure which has the characteristic of an *international quasi-public good*. It is the change in the extent and magnitude of international increasing returns which derive from this infrastructure which will be the driving factor of the model of fragmentation developed in this chapter.

The literature subsequent to the initial Jones and Kierzkowski contribution has gone in a number of directions. There are some models of fragmentation based on factor-intensities differences between processes—originally emphasized by Jones and Kierzkowski (1990), including papers by Arndt (1998) and Deardorff (Ch. 3, this vol.), and Jones and Kierzkowski (Ch. 2, this vol.). Related are the models

of vertical specialization such as that of Ishii and Yi (1998). Partially
related to the model of this chapter are the models of trade and geography following Krugman (1992) which deal with the interaction of
transport costs and firm-level economies of scale.

The trade and geography literature has focused largely on the opposite
question of international agglomeration which is related, but somewhat
tangential, to the fragmentation issue. In addition there is a crucial difference between trade with the transport costs which this literature has
emphasized, and trade subject to coordination/communication barriers
emphasized here. The trade and geography models use Samuelson's ice-
berg model of transport costs; costs of transport over space are per unit
product, usually thought of as the cost of shipping a product of given
weight or volume per unit distance. Communication costs are different
in that the cost of communication is almost entirely, if not solely, a
fixed cost; once a communications 'network' is installed, marginal costs
of sending messages are very low. In this chapter this is approximated
by the assumption that the only communication costs are fixed costs.
Communication costs of trade, however, are dependent on the overall
complexity of the message sent. Highly specialized production networks require larger volumes of messages—or in slightly different terms,
require networks capable of transferring more complex information.

Communications costs also differ from transport costs in the nature
of the supply of communication/coordination services. Communication
services are often provided by supply networks which are characterized by elements of both natural monopoly and public goods at an
international level. Natural monopoly is present because of the strong
fixed-cost nature in the provision of linkages between any two locations. Exclusion is possible, however, so that networks are public goods
in only one dimension—a degree of non-rivalry in consumption of network services. It is certainly the case that some transport services such
as air and road transport are subject to similar considerations. Generally, however, the act of 'transport' corresponds to the act of physically
transferring an object from one location to another. It has been traditional in the trade literature to emphasize the marginal cost of that
transfer rather than the fixed cost. Communication facilitates the transfer of a commodity highly complementary to economic exchange and
specialization—information—rather than the physical commodity itself.
Changes in the communications network, therefore, rather than simply
reducing the cost of a transfer of a commodity over space (the message
unit), at the same time provide for the shrinkage in time of a coordination activity between any two agents as emphasized by Jim Melvin

(1990) and others. Transactions time is in most models of international trade largely ignored. Yet one defining characteristic of many transactions in 'coordination services', as opposed to transactions in goods, is the time dimension—they must be provided very quickly, and repeatedly—durability is completely absent in many instances. Changes in communications technology are therefore responsible for the coordination of closely related production systems over vast distances where this was not previously possible.

A third set of reasons for thinking that communications barriers to trade are different than transport costs is that the communications are subject to an important consumption externality emphasized in the industrial organization literature on network externalities. My value of being connected to the phone system is dependent upon the fact that many other people are likewise connected. The central concept of a network as an ongoing link between large numbers of users is much more complex than the notion of a transport link connecting one supplying region with another—a point-to-point, one-time connection. The presence of joint consumption externalities in a network gives rise to a number of issues different than encountered in the trade and transport cost literature. One emphasis in this chapter is, given that communication is complementary to international exchange, that any change which impacts on the extent of the consumption externality will have implications for the volume of international transactions.

2. A Model of Production Networks and Trade in Intermediate Components

In this section a model is developed in which there are economy-wide network costs which must be incurred to trade in intermediate inputs or as we shall often refer to them—components. It is best to think of this as a model of a single manufacturing industry such as electronics, but with an 'industry' defined in both the vertical and horizontal dimensions, such that all key suppliers are included within the domain of the network. A key simplifying assumption of the model is that a single 'economy' is of a geographic extent sufficiently small that provided an industry is locally sourced there are no coordination costs. One way to think about this is that production with a single local economy[1] takes place on a given and unchanged network. Specialization, defined as increasing the number of plants dedicated to specific components, comes at a cost as fixed costs are plant-specific. The size of the market then clearly limits the degree of specialization. What makes international sourcing of components different than local sourcing is that firms supplying components internationally, that is, are engaged in export, must incur a cost associated with being on the global industry network. The network is thought of as a global quasi-public network such as the Internet. The network costs are taken as parametric by a single firm, but are endogenous at the level of the global economy.

The model is also best thought of as one of trade and production links between economies with similar levels of development—it is not a North–South model of trade in manufactures. Thus we imagine the world economy to consist of M symmetric economies in terms of geography, resources, technology, and tastes. In a symmetric equilibrium in each economy there are potentially two kinds of production platforms supplying components: those who produce only for the local economy and those who produce locally for the global economy—the scale of the latter is much larger than the former. Going global in this model means not only exporting, but also implies a substantial increase in firm size. In that respect it provides an explanation not only of fragmentation, but also a prediction on the size structure of global as opposed to local suppliers.

2.1. *Model Structure*

The Network Communications Market

It is assumed there exists a global coordination network linking the suppliers of the industry in all M markets. The network is public in that any firm can have access at some common price. It is international in scope. It provides all the necessary services to operate as supplier within this industry. The market structure of the network supply side can be thought of as an international public monopoly, or closely related national public monopolies, that sells its service at average cost. Various assumptions can be made on the network technology.[2] The simplest is that costs of a network are dependent on the size of the market served and the number of firms (users) of the network. Thus if total costs of a network of covering M markets and u users is denoted by $K(M, u)$, the cost per user is simply

$$N(M, u) = K(M, u)/u \tag{4.1}$$

The number of network users will be identified with the total number of globally sourced components. This assumption emphasizes the public-good fixed-cost nature of a communications network, and also the congestion effect of additional users on the network. If there were only fixed costs to supplying the public network, and there were no congestion costs, then N would be decreasing in u—more users can share the common costs of constructing the network. However, if the network is subject to congestion, more users raise the cost of providing a network of given communications quality—thus at some point N will be increasing in u. K, and thus N, is always increasing in the number of markets served. The marginal cost of extending the geographic extent of the network size will also be increasing at some point, although the presumption is that over some range there will be social increasing returns in the cost. Clearly physical geography matters for some forms of communication, but satellite linking has reduced dramatically the costs differences based on the nature of land links. It is important to recognise that in the case of communications technology, market size is measured in two dimensions. There is size measured by the density of users for a given geographic area. Market size can also be represented by geographic size, given the number of users. In each dimension we can think of there being either increasing or decreasing returns to scale. Note also there is an important symmetry assumed in this model in that the cost linking any pair of markets is presumed to be the same. This may adequately describe satellite links, but clearly would not describe coordination links associated with transport technology.

A key assumption of the model is that the pricing policy of the public communications supplier is such that it always charges the true average cost. This is a dramatic simplification and ignores a host of issues linked to network competition emphasized in the industrial organization literature on network industries.[3] The assumption that the communications supplier prices at average cost can be viewed as a first approximation to more general pricing rules. In reality the organizational structure of industries providing coordination services differs vastly across countries, running from regulated or government-owned monopoly to small-numbers competitive oligopoly.

Tastes, Resources, and Production

In each market there is a single representative consumer who supplies (inelastically) an amount of labor L, and consumes a single homogeneous final consumption good in quantity U. L is the same in terms of quality and quantity across all M economies. In the middle-products tradition of Jones and Sanyal (1982) the final good is assumed to be non-traded. The final good is supplied by a competitive sector which shall be referred to as the final assembly, or simply assembly stage, of the manufacturing sector. Further, to keep matters as simple as possible, and without much loss of generality, it will be assumed that assembly occurs with no value-added from the primary factor labor. If there are k components used in assembling the final good, each supplied to the local assembly operation in quantity z_i, $i = 1, \ldots, v$, then the output of the final good is given by an Ethier-type production function

$$U = \left(\sum_{i=1}^{v} z_i^{\rho} \right)^{1/\rho} \tag{4.2}$$

The elasticity of substitution between components, $\sigma = 1/(1-\rho)$, is presumed to be greater than one, and thus there are increasing returns to specialization as the number of components k increases. The interpretation of the z_i is best not thought of as separate 'varieties' of horizontally differentiated inputs. In the spirit of the Ethier model the z can best be thought of as indexing the level of inputs provided by distinct suppliers. As v changes, what changes is the level of input specialization. Thus, for example, if two components which were previously put together and provided by one supplier are now provided separately by two separate suppliers each operating a separate plant, this would correspond to an increase in v. Representative market welfare in this set-up is given by consumption of the final assembled good in each market, U.

Component producers incur fixed and variable costs to produce a component. Fixed costs are plant costs plus network costs if a component supplier is globally linked. Thus if a component supplier supplies x units of its component but supplies only locally, its cost will be

$$TC^L(x) = awx + fw \tag{4.3}$$

where w is the wage rate. All factor inputs are labor, so ax is the variable labor inputs and f is plant-specific fixed labor inputs.

Global component suppliers use factors located in a single market but deliver components in all markets (at least in equilibrium). A global supplier uses the global public communications network in order to coordinate both with users and other component suppliers—each global supplier can be thought of as a participant in a global production network.[4] Recall for simplicity that it is assumed local suppliers are not subject to coordination costs. If a firm operates globally, its network cost is Nw so that its total cost at output scale x will be

$$TC^G(x) = awx + fx + Nw \tag{4.4}$$

By virtue of market symmetry, factor prices will be the same in all markets, thus w is identical across all economies, and can be taken as the numeraire; henceforth we set $w = 1$ in all economies.

International trade is driven by specialization in component production and scale economies (fixed costs) in both the production of components and the fixed costs of coordinating a global production network. To simplify matters, attention will be focused on the fixed costs of providing the global network versus the traditional-plant fixed costs of production. Given the production function for final assembly, the elasticity of demand for each component is given by $\varepsilon = 1/(\rho - 1)$.[5] The component-supplying sector is assumed to be monopolistically competitive—that is, they set prices but take other prices as given and set a mark-up consistent with the individual demand curves. Free entry in the long-run view ensures that revenues cover both variable and fixed costs. Thus the price of each component i will be given by

$$p_i = \frac{1}{\rho}aw, \tag{4.5}$$

and in equilibrium will be the same for all components across all markets. Define $\lambda = 1/\rho > 1$ as the mark-up factor.

Let d stand for the number of global component-supplying firms per local market. Thus the number of components available through international trade is $n^* = dM$. The number of local components is denoted by k. The total number of components available to final goods producers in each economy is therefore $n = n^* + k$. International trade facilitates increased specialization by letting a component produced in one economy be available for final assembly in all economies. Components that are sourced locally on the other hand must be produced in each separate market.

Global suppliers must incur both fixed plant costs as well as the network costs associated with coordination defined as $N(n^*, M) = K(n^*, M)/n^*$. $K(\cdot)$ is the total cost of providing the entire (global) network; it depends upon the number of markets, M and the number of components traded within the network, n^*. Each 'network user' is identified with a distinct global component supplier. N is increasing in M since a larger network with larger nodes must have larger costs. The network may be subject to congestion effects so that K is also ultimately increasing in n^*, as congestion starts to set in on the network. From the point of view of per user network costs, N first decreases in n^* due to the spreading of fixed costs over a larger number of users and the possible existence of network externalities. There are two factors which tend to generate rising per user network costs. The first are congestion costs which can occur as users are added to a given network. Secondly, there are the physical costs of installing and linking additional users. For the latter reasons the average cost per user will ultimately flatten out and then increase as the number of users rises. In a symmetric equilibrium it is assumed the cost of network provision is spread evenly across all markets so that labor inputs required by the network are spread across all markets; thus the demand for labor per local market due to network provision is K/M. Output scale of a representative global component producer is defined as y^* and a local component supplier by y.

Equilibrium Conditions

Equilibrium requires zero profits for all suppliers, with the labor market and goods market clearing. Adding-up conditions for the usual reasons will ensure trade balance is satisfied. The key endogenous variables are the output scale of each type of component supplier and the number of global and local component suppliers.

The zero profit condition for each local supplier is given by

$$py = ay + f \tag{4.6a}$$

Using the mark-up rule for prices, equilibrium output scale is given as

$$y = \frac{f}{(\lambda - 1)a} \tag{4.6b}$$

For global suppliers the zero profit condition is

$$p^*y^* = ay^* + f + N(n^*, M) \tag{4.7a}$$

and output scale is

$$y^* = \frac{f + N}{(\lambda - 1)a} \tag{4.7b}$$

As all components sell at the same price, given a common marginal cost of production, it is immediately evident that for both types of organizations to coexist, in equilibrium the scale of the global firm must be larger than that of the local firm; that is, $y^* > y$. Labor market clearing in each local market requires that labor demand equal labor supply L. Hence

$$L = kay + day^* + kf + dN(n^*, M) + df \qquad (4.8)$$

In each market total income is wL which must equal the total revenue of all component producers, which given $w = 1$, is L. With n components, revenue per component in each market is L/n. Equilibrium in the goods and components market thus requires that

$$px = L/n = L/(k + n^*) \qquad (4.9)$$

where x is local demand per component. In equilibrium $y = x$ and $y^* = Mx$. Thus global firms are exactly M times the size of the local firms. The existence of two types of firms offering similar products but using different technologies raises the issue of whether an equilibrium exists that can sustain both types of technology. We will proceed on the basis that this can occur and then will establish conditions under which such equilibrium occur. It is useful to note that revenue per component, using the zero profit and mark-up rule for local firms, is given by

$$px = \frac{\lambda}{\lambda - 1}f$$

Substituting for the price-mark-up condition and rearranging the zero profit conditions we also get that

$$(\lambda - 1)ay = f$$
$$(\lambda - 1)ay^* = f + N(n^*, M) \qquad (4.10)$$

Taking the ratio of these two equations implies that $y^*/y = (f + N)/f$. Using the demand conditions gives the restriction that in this type of equilibrium the number of globally sourced components, n^*, must satisfy

$$f = \frac{f + N(n^*, M)}{M} \qquad (4.11)$$

Equation (4.11) is a technological arbitrage condition—it says that for the two technologies (global and local sourcing) to coexist each must have equal average costs of production at equilibrium outputs. In this set-up this is equivalent to saying that M local firms have a fixed cost structure equal to one global firm. Equation (4.11) can be rewritten as

$$f(M-1) = \frac{K(n^*, M)}{n^*} \tag{4.12}$$

For given M and f eqn (4.12) determines n^*, the total number of components which are traded internationally. The number of locally sourced inputs, k, is then determined by eqn (4.9).

2.2. *Sustaining both Local and Global Suppliers in an Equilibrium*

An *international equilibrium* is defined as one in which both local and global firms coexist, and its properties depend upon the structure of the global network cost function, $K(\cdot)$. If $N(n^*, M)$ is U-shaped in n^* there exists the potential for multiple solutions to eqn (4.12). This is illustrated in Figure 4.1 below.

There are two potential equilibrium levels of globally sourced components in Figure 4.1; n' and n''. The first corresponds to a region of increasing returns in the number of users due to the fixed cost-sharing effect. In the other equilibrium $N(\cdot)$ is increasing in n^* so that the incremental costs of adding new users plus congestion more than offsets the cost-sharing effect of a larger number of users. The situation depicted in Figure 4.1 might be thought of as typical of modern networks and one has to appeal to some economic criteria to choose among these potential

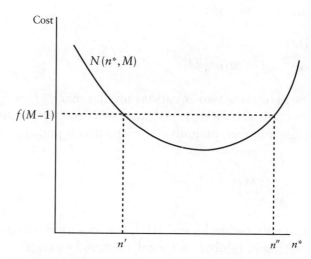

FIG. 4.1. Sustainability of both local and global component production

equilibria. Recall that network services are supplied by an international public monopoly pricing at average cost. We shall assume that in any situation of temporary disequilibrium, cost savings or increases are immediately passed on to network users via a change in the price of network use. Under this assumption there is a strong case based on a stability argument that only n'' can be sustained as a viable equilibrium. The equilibrium at $n^* = n'$ is unstable because a small increase in n^* would reduce the cost of network services to all global firms, and would thus lead to an increase in their profits and additional entry increasing n^* further. This adjustment process would only end when $n^* = n''$ and any additional entry would lower the profits of global component suppliers. For these reasons we shall use this stability argument to focus on the normal case in which $n^* = n''$ and $N(\cdot)$ is increasing in n^*.

From a social point of view, it is clear welfare would be improved if users of the network were charged marginal cost; in this case the marginal cost of their entry to the network. At an equilibrium such as n'' the marginal cost of congestion to additional users is in excess of the price being charged, which is average cost. 'Congestion' in this model is equivalent to there being too many global component producers and hence too much trade. On the other hand at n' equilibrium the economies of scale in the communications network are not being fully exploited; this leads to too many local firms and not enough global firms.[6]

2.3. Trade Volume and Fragmentation Indexes

Imports of components in a single market are given by netting out the home sales of the resident global suppliers from sales of all global firms in the home market. Hence imports in value terms are

$$p(n^* - d)x = \frac{\lambda}{\lambda - 1} f(n^* - d) \tag{4.13}$$

where the zero profit condition on local sales has been used ($px = ax + f$). The total world trade volume, VOL, is given by adding up imports across all markets which gives

$$\text{VOL} = M \frac{\lambda}{\lambda - 1} f \left(n^* - \frac{n^*}{M} \right)$$

$$= (M - 1) \frac{\lambda}{\lambda - 1} n^* f \tag{4.14}$$

Recall that in an international equilibrium

$$f(M-1) = \frac{K(n^*, M)}{n^*}, \tag{4.15}$$

so

$$\text{VOL} = \frac{\lambda}{\lambda - 1} K(n^*, M) \tag{4.16}$$

Thus the volume of international trade is directly proportional to total network costs.

A natural index, or metric, of fragmentation is the ratio of locally sourced production to global production defined as

$$\text{FRAG} = \frac{(n^*/M)y^*}{ky} = \frac{n^*}{k}$$

2.4. *Comparative Statics: Costs and Market Expansion*

A change in production fixed costs, *ceteris paribus*, raises the importance of economies of scale to both local and global suppliers. An increase in f from eqn (4.11) implies that K/n^* must rise. That is network costs per global firm must rise in equilibrium if production costs to local firms rise and both types of firms are to coexist given the technological arbitrage condition. The effect on n^* of a change in f depends upon the properties of the N function. Under the stability condition assumed, an increase in f leads to an increase in n^*, which implies an increase in n^*f, the total production fixed costs associated with global production. From eqn (4.14) increases in plant fixed costs alone increase the volume of trade as n^*f increases. From eqn (4.9) as x rises with an increase in f and n^* increases, k, the number of local sourced components, will fall.

What about changes in a, the marginal cost of component production? Since eqn (4.9) implies revenue per component is independent of a, the total number of components in each market is independent of a. Reductions in a lower prices and increase the output volumes of both local and global suppliers. The number of global and local suppliers is independent of any changes in marginal costs of production. Note also that reduction in a leads to no changes in the volume of trade from eqn (4.14).

Summarizing we have

Proposition 1: An increase in plant fixed costs leads to (a) an increase in the volume of trade, (b) an increase in the number of globally sourced components, and (c) *a decrease in the number of locally sourced components.* (d) *The volume of trade and number of global and local component suppliers are independent of the marginal costs of production.*

The significance of this proposition is that the volume of international trade can be 'explained' by the extent of traditional-plant-level scale economies. Larger fixed costs associated with plant specialization alone push additional firms into 'going global' via expansion of global production networks and reduction in production for local sourcing only.

An increase in M, the number of markets, or the 'size' of the global economy such as occurred when the Cold War ended, would imply that the scale of the average global supplier must rise relative to that of the local supplier from eqn (4.10). The net effect on n^* would depend upon the exact properties of the network cost function at the initial equilibrium and the value of production fixed costs relative to the marginal cost of extending the network to another market. The equilibrium response of n^* to a change in M is given by differentiating eqn (4.12) so that

$$\frac{\mathrm{d}n^*}{\mathrm{d}M} = \frac{f - N_M}{N_{n^*}} \tag{4.17}$$

The sign of eqn (4.17) depends on the size of plant fixed costs relative to the marginal cost per user of extending the network to another market. With current technology it would be reasonable to assume that marginal network size cost (per user) is low relative to plant-level fixed cost so that f exceeds N_M. Under these circumstances and the assumed stability condition, n^* increases as market size increases. Thus an increase in the size of the global economy will lead to an increase in the number of global components, and from eqn (4.9) a reduction in the number of locally sourced components. From eqn (4.10) the output scale of the global firm unambiguously increases as the size of the world economy increases.

2.5. *Economic Growth: Factor Endowments versus Market Expansion*

An increase in income per market generated by factor supply growth, or an increase in L, holding the number of markets constant, might generally be thought to lead to an increase in international trade. Equations (4.9) and (4.10) imply that holding technology constant, an increase in factor endowments in each economy, *ceteris paribus*, will lead to an increase in the total number of components. From eqn (4.11), however, the split of this increased number of components between local and global suppliers falls entirely on an increase in the number of local sourced components with no change in the number of global components. Thus increases in factor supplies, holding the number of markets and productivity constant, leads to a decrease in the ratio of trade to income—economic growth caused by increases in factor endowments reduces the relative importance of trade. This of course is quite contrary to the known empirical fact of a positive relationship between trade and income growth.[7] The other type of income growth however occurs due to an expansion in the number of markets, M. An increase in the size of the global economy will increase the volume of trade provided that the number of global components increases with market size as discussed above. In any case, provided total network costs rise, from eqn (4.16) trade volumes will rise, and will rise in proportion to total world income, ML.[8] Trade is the mechanism by which the fixed costs of running the global communications network are covered.

Proposition 2: (a) *Factor endowment growth leads to no increase in the number of globally sourced components, an increase in the number of locally sourced components and a reduction in the ratio of trade to income.* (b) *Market expansion growth, provided global network costs rise, leads to an increase in the ratio of trade to income.*

3. Globalization as Technological Change in Global Networks

In this section the case for viewing globalization as a response to a reduction in communications costs is within the context of the model developed. There is ample evidence that the ICT revolution has dramatically reduced these costs, particularly over the last two decades, although the telephone and telegraph led to a similar step change in international networking costs earlier in this century.

We focus attention on the case of an *international* equilibrium so that both global and local firms coexist. For sufficiently large network costs there is also an equilibrium with only a locally sourced supplier (and thus no trade) but we exclude this case from consideration. Interest focuses on the number of firms and on the volume of trade as technological change occurs and there are possibly large shifts in the structure of the equilibrium.

An innovation such as the Internet can be viewed as a downward shift in the network cost function $N(\cdot)$ such that costs at all n^* are lower. From eqn (4.14) it is clear that the volume of trade will increase as n^*, the number of global suppliers, increases in response to the decline in network costs per user; furthermore as the total number of components produced is unchanged, the number of local components must decline in response to this change in the extent of globalization.

The welfare consequences of this innovation are not so obvious, however. Utility of the representative consumer in each market is given by

$$U = n^{1/\rho}z$$

where $n = k + n^*$ and z is local input per component to final goods production. Substituting for z we find that given $0 < \rho < 1$, U is increasing in n, the total number of components. In particular as $z = L/(\lambda a n)$

$$U = n^{\lambda - 1}\frac{L}{\lambda a} \tag{4.18}$$

Reductions in network costs shift the composition of sourcing between local and global suppliers such as to leave n unchanged. Thus welfare is unaffected by cost reductions on the global network.

Proposition 3: Technological change which decreases the cost of global production networks will lead to (a) *an increase in the volume of trade relative to income;* (b) *an increase in the number of global sourced components and decrease in locally sourced components. However, this type of technological change has* no effect *on welfare.*

In this model technological improvements in global communications networks have no effect on real income even though they increase the volume of trade and the extent of globalization. The reason is that technological arbitrage between the local and global sourcing of production forces sufficient reduction in local component sourcing to offset all benefits that trade allows through increased international specialization. In effect, domestic specialization losses exactly offset global specialization gains.

4. Fragmentation as Scale-Based Technological Change

An alternative technology-based explanation of the global fragmentation of production is the scale-biased nature of technological change: in particular, that technological change has reduced marginal costs relative to fixed costs. In this model, this is equivalent to a reduction in the ratio of a to f. One could also make the case that, at the same time, technological change has increased absolutely the level of plant fixed costs, f. We shall refer to such technological change as absolutely pro-scale biased in that both a has declined and f has increased. For small changes in both f and a, we can restrict our attention to international equilibrium. Within that type of equilibrium the consequences of such changes that follow from what has already been established are:

1. n^* (absolute degree of outsourcing) must increase;
2.   the total level of specialization must decrease and thus k (local component sourcing) decreases;
3.   output price decreases (relative to wages);
4.   output per firm increases;
5.   trade volume increases.

Some of these trends are consistent with some of the broad facts on globalization with the exception of point 2. The one ambiguity is on welfare. The impact on welfare hinges on the relative effects of the degree of specialization relative to the price impact (or equivalently the impact on x—component sales per market). Without exact numbers on the relative changes in f and a it is not possible to get an unambiguous prediction on welfare. Substituting and solving we have that

$$\mathrm{d}\log U = (1 - \rho)\mathrm{d}\log f - \mathrm{d}\log a \tag{4.19}$$

Consequently, provided the percentage fall in marginal costs relative to the percentage increase in fixed costs exceeds the inverse of the elasticity of substitution, $1/\sigma$, welfare will increase with this type of biased technological change. The benefits from price reductions exceed the losses due to decreased specialization. It could be the case then that some of the consequences of fragmentation are due in part to this type of scale-biased technological change.

5. From the International to the Global Economy

Thus far attention has been focused on the *international equilibrium* in which both local and global supplier coexist. It is reasonable to expect that eventually a fully global equilibrium will evolve in which all local forms of component sourcing are squeezed out. It turns out that this is the case and we shall consider in detail the determinants of each type of equilibrium and how they might evolve.

A global equilibrium is a configuration in which all component suppliers are on the global network. In this case there are no local component suppliers and the arbitrage condition on technologies is replaced by a type of integrated equilibrium condition. However, in addition there is an economic restriction on parameters such that in a global equilibrium no local supplier could enter and make positive profits. This leads to the following possible outcomes that can be summarized in terms of the factor endowments and fixed costs that the economy incurs with different degrees of fragmentation. Given the mark-up pricing rule, zero profits, and market clearing, there is always a fixed fraction of income in each economy available to cover fixed costs. Let $c = L(\lambda - 1)/\lambda$ denote the total income available to cover fixed costs.

A *global equilibrium* exists if there exists a level of global specialization in components, $n^* = n_G^* > 0$ such that the following pair of equations hold.

$$\frac{\lambda}{\lambda - 1}L < fn_G^*$$

$$\frac{\lambda}{\lambda - 1}L = \frac{n_G^*}{M}(f + N(n_G^*, M)) \tag{4.20}$$

The first equation in eqn (4.20) is the requirement that any local entrant loses money at the equilibrium scale of sales in each market.[9] The second condition is the labor market clearing condition. In a global equilibrium $k = 0$.

The conditions for the existence of an *international equilibrium* can be expressed as the existence of an $n^* = n_I^* > 0$ such that the following pair of equations hold.

$$f(M - 1) = N(n_I^*, M)$$

$$\frac{\lambda}{\lambda - 1}L > \frac{n_I^*}{M}(f + N(n_I^*, M)) \tag{4.21}$$

The first condition is the familiar technological arbitrage condition. The second is a resource availability condition. Given n_I^* global firms, there are sufficient resources available for local component suppliers to exist. It will be useful to note that the first condition in eqn (4.21) (using zero profits and the mark-up pricing rule) is equivalent to the condition that

$$fn_I^* = \frac{n^*}{M}(f + N(n_I^*, M))$$

It is possible there exist solutions to both equation systems (4.20) and (4.21). In such cases there is a multiple equilibrium.

To illustrate the various equilibrium and comparative statics it is useful to introduce a new diagram. Let the function $g(n^*)$, defined on n^*, the number of global firms, be defined as follows:

$$g(n^*) = \frac{n^*}{M}(f + N(n^*, M)) \tag{4.22}$$

This is the total fixed costs of n^* global component suppliers divided by the number of markets, or you can think of this as per market fixed costs for global suppliers. The $g(n^*)$ function can be either decreasing or increasing in its arguments, but generally will be increasing over the range over which N is increasing in n^*; furthermore $\lim_{n^* \to 0} g(n^*) > 0$ if there are elements of fixed costs in the $K(\cdot)$ function. In addition, the condition that average cost be rising at the international equilibrium level of component specialization is equivalent to the condition that $g'(n^*) > f$ so that in the case of an international equilibrium g cuts the line fn^* from below. In Figures 4.2 through 4.4, n^* is on the horizontal axis and on the vertical axis we have values of $g(n^*)$, fn^*, and horizontal lines at the value $c = L(\lambda - 1)/\lambda$.

An international equilibrium is illustrated in Figure 4.2 at the value $n^* = n_I$. Note that c (fixed cost resources) lies above the intersection

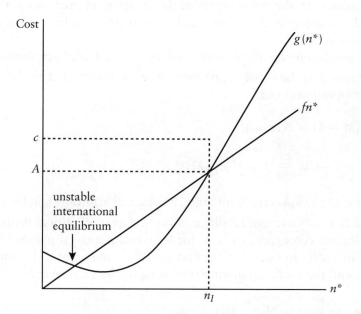

FIG. 4.2. International equilibrium

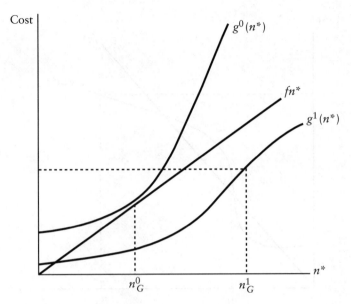

FIG. 4.3. Global equilibrium

of the g function with the line fn^*. The resources given by the distance Ac on the vertical axis are available to cover the fixed costs of local component suppliers. As network costs fall, as already established, the g function shifts down and the number of global components increases. Note that were g to lie entirely above the fn^* line, the only feasible equilibrium would be autarkic (no trade in components). As g shifts down, eventually the (stable) international equilibrium emerges.

The global equilibrium configuration is depicted in Figure 4.3 with costs g^1 and $n^* = n_G^1$ indicating the number of global firms. Network costs have fallen sufficiently that the relevant constraint is that $c = g(n^*)$ and $g(n^*)$ lie below the fixed cost line fn^*. The evolution of equilibria is now clear from these two figures as technological changes proceed with continuous reductions in network costs. For a critical cost level indicated by the cost function g^0 there is a sudden shift to global production with n_G^0 firms 'going global'—think of the emergence of MNE's in the earlier part of this century. However, in the course of gravitating toward that equilibrium, economic growth in factor supplies increases c and at the same time technological change in communications networks lowers N. The combined effect of these is to simultaneously increase the size of the local and global economies.

Full globalization can only emerge if the pace at which network costs fall rapidly exceeds that of factor endowment growth (the rate at which

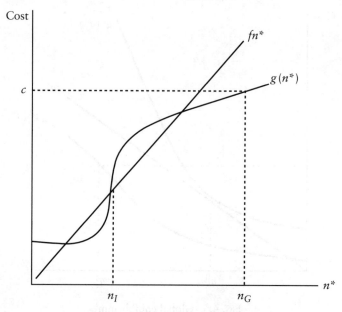

FIG. 4.4. Multiple equilibrium

c grows) such that the intersection $g(n^*) = c$ falls below the fn^* line. In these circumstances the rapid shift to global production networks has reduced the $c - g(n^*)$ 'gap' which was previously available to support local component production in international equilibria.

Multiple Equilibrium

In Figure 4.4 a multiple equilibrium case is depicted—in this instance there is a global equilibrium in which all n_G firms are global firms. However, there is also a stable international equilibrium with n_I global firms. Public policy could have a significant impact in this instance by determining the type of entry which was most likely to occur as global network costs fall. If protectionism were to preclude global firms from entering all markets then as the $c - g(n^*)$ gap opens up in response to the increased efficiency of communications, entry of local components suppliers would occur rather than the entry of global firms. The figure also indicates the potentially discrete nature of the change in equilibria as communications costs fall. As $g(n^*)$ continues to shift down, eventually the stable international equilibrium will disappear leaving only the global equilibrium. When both equilibria exist there is a clear welfare ranking of these two types of equilibria as shown in the following proposition.

Proposition 4: *In the case of multiple global–international equilibrium, a global equilibrium always has more global components than does an international equilibrium, and is welfare-superior to the international equilibrium.*

Proof of the first part of the proposition is by contradiction. If $n_I^* > n_G^*$ then the last inequality of eqn (4.21) and the last equality of eqn (4.20) cannot be simultaneously true. Recall that utility of the representative consumer in each market is given by eqn (4.18) where $n = k + n^*$. Let x and y denote the values of n^* in the global and international equilibrium respectively. Then eqn (4.20) implies that $fx > g(x)$. Using both eqn (4.20) and eqn (4.21) and labor market clearing, we have that $g(x) = fk + g(y)$, where k is the number of products produced locally in each market in the international equilibrium. Using eqn (4.20) and substituting, we have that $g(y) = fy$. Putting these inequalities together implies that $fx > f(k+y)$. Since $k+y$ equals the total number of products in the international equilibrium, these must be less than the total number of products in the global equilibrium.

The implication of Proposition 4 mitigates to some extent the negative welfare results of technical change in communications networks that were noted in the case of international equilibrium in Section 3. With enough technological change in communications, global equilibria emerge at the same time that international equilibria also exist. If the economy could switch from the international to the global equilibria, there would be a discrete increase in world welfare and in the fragmentation of production. Furthermore, subsequent decreases in communications costs would be welfare enhancing. While this model is purely static, it also suggests that there could be some abrupt shifts in the structure of the economy with little apparent shift in technology if these shifts represent a shift from an international to global equilibrium configuration.

6. Conclusion

A model of global production systems was developed which emphasized the role of the fixed cost associated with international trade networks— in particular communications networks—which are subject to increasing returns. These fixed network costs to the firm and the market size associated with 'going global' are important determinants of the extent of global outsourcing or fragmentation. The model provides an alternative explanation of the fragmentation of production systems to those explanations based on factor–price differences and factor–intensity differences across related activities of manufacturing firms. The model suggests that the process of fragmentation can be attributed in part to the search for gains from specialization among developed countries. The key argument advanced here is that the limits to that specialization are found in the existence of global and industry-wide coordination costs. The rapid improvements and extensions in communications networks such as the Internet may substantially lower these coordination costs among related suppliers and customer firms in manufacturing industries. Given the global scale economies implicit in these international public networks, the process of fragmentation may have a considerable way to go.

NOTES

1. Throughout the chapter I shall use the terminology 'local economy' to refer to a single geographically concentrated economy. Economic trade and integration refer to the linking of multiple 'local economies'.
2. In order to make the model tractable, the assumptions on the communications network and market structure are clearly dramatic simplifications of that used in the industrial organization literature on telecommunications for example. A good example of this type of modeling is Oren and Smith (1981).
3. See Katz and Shapiro (1985, 1986) for some of the original modeling of network industries in which competition occurs.
4. A more complicated but important extension of the model would be to have competing production networks.
5. Which is also equal to the negative of the common elasticity of factor substitution among intermediate inputs.
6. This does not deal with the question of whether the degree of specialization is too high or low relative to some world optimum.
7. The long-run evidence on trade and income growth is reviewed in Harris (1993) and more recently by Ishii and Yi (1997).
8. This can be seen by dividing VOL in equation (4.14) by ML. Provided n^* rises with an increase in M, the ratio of trade to income increases. If n^* decreases with M, however, there is no presumption in favor of increased trade to income ratios as the number of markets increases.
9. Dividing both sides of the first part of this inequality by n^* give revenues to a new entrant on the left-hand side and costs on the right hand.

REFERENCES

Arndt, S. W. (1998) 'Globalization and the Gains from Trade', in K. J. Koch and K. Jaeger (eds.), *Trade, Growth and Economic Policy in Open Economies* (New York: Springer-Verlag).

Becker, G., and Murphy, K. (1992). 'The Division of Labor, Co-ordination Costs, and Knowledge', *Quarterly Journal of Economics*, 107.

Ethier, W. (1979). 'Internationally Decreasing Costs and World Trade', *Journal of International Economics*, 9.

Harris, R. G. (1993). 'Presidential Address: Globalization, Trade and Income', *Canadian Journal of Economics*, 26.

——(1995). 'Trade and Communication Costs', *Canadian Journal of Economics*, Nov.

Ishii, J., and Yi, Kei-Mu (1997). 'The Growth of World Trade', *Federal Reserve Bank of New York, Research Paper* No. 9718.

Jones, R. W. and Kierzkowski, H. (1990). 'The Role of Services in Production and International Trade: A Theoretical Framework', ch. 3 in R. W. Jones and A. O. Krueger (eds.), *The Political Economy of International Trade* (Oxford: Blackwell).

—— —— (2000). 'Globalization and the Consequences of International Fragmentation', forthcoming in Rudiger Dornbusch, Guillermo Calvo, and Maurice Obstfeld, (eds.), *Money, Factor Mobility and Trade: A Festschrift in Honor of Robert A. Mundell*, (Cambridge, Mass.: MIT Press).

Katz, M. L., and Shapiro, C. (1985). 'Network Externalities, Competition and Compatibility', *American Economic Review*, 75/3 (June).

—— —— (1986). 'Technology Adoption in the Presence of Network Externalities', *Journal of Political Economy*, 94/4 (Aug.).

Krugman, P. (1992). *Geography and International Trade* (Cambridge, Mass.: MIT Press).

Melvin, J. R. (1990). 'Time and Space in Economic Analysis', *Canadian Journal of Economics*, 23.

Oren, S. S. and Smith, S. (1981). 'Critical Mass and Tariff Structure in Electronic Communications Markets', *Bell Journal of Economics*, 12 (Aut.).

Sanyal, K. and Jones, R. W. (1982). 'The Theory of Trade in Middle Products', *American Economic Review*, Mar.

5

Offshore Sourcing and Production Sharing in Preference Areas

SVEN W. ARNDT

F11 F13
F23 L23

1. Introduction

The traditional approach to trade analysis has shown a strong preoccupation with trade in end-products. There is, of course, a comprehensive and elegant literature on trade in intermediate products,[1] but it leads a rather separate and cloistered existence. This emphasis finds its underpinnings in the assumption that production is a spatially concentrated and functionally integrated process. We are used to thinking about products as 'made' in a country. Trade in components and cross-border dispersion of production, both characteristics of intra-product specialization, have no place in this approach.

In the real world, by comparison, offshore component production and assembly have been among the more noticeable features of recent advances in globalization. Trade in components is growing rapidly and the shares of foreign value-added in exports and of domestic value-added in imports are expanding everywhere.

Multinational enterprises (MNEs) play an important role in the cross-border dispersion of production, especially where technology transfer and coordination are important. This suggests that the phenomenon may be studied from the firm, as well as the country, perspective. Markusen (1984) examines the implications of multi-plant operations by MNEs when economies are present in the concentration of 'headquarters' activities such as R&D, marketing, finance, and so on, while production is geographically dispersed.

This chapter examines the implications of offshore sourcing under alternative trade policy regimes. As shown in Section 2, offshore sourcing is unequivocally welfare-enhancing under free trade, but may raise or lower welfare when trade restrictions are present. Section 3 looks at offshore sourcing in low-wage developing countries and examines the implications of rules of origin in that context. Section 4 concludes the discussion.

2. Component Specialization and Trade Policy

At given world prices, the cost savings achieved through offshore sourcing improve competitiveness and create profit opportunities which raise output and employment.[2] When world prices are variable, such cost savings allow firms to lower end-product prices and thereby increase sales and raise market share.

We start with the traditional model involving trade in two final products, X and Y, produced with two factors of production, capital, K, and labor, L. Figure 5.1 presents the basic analytical structure, where unit-value isoquants X_0 and Y_0 reflect the traditional pattern of spatially concentrated and functionally integrated production technologies. The initial factor–price ratio, w/r, is consistent with given world commodity prices.

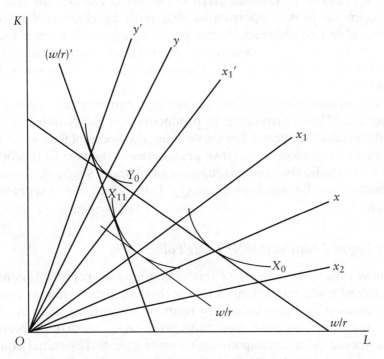

FIG. 5.1. Integrated versus fragmented production

We introduce the possibility of offshore sourcing by assuming that good X, the country's labor-intensive, import-competing product consists of two activities, x_1 and x_2, the first more and the second less capital-intensive than the product overall.[3] Suppose that technological breakthroughs make it possible to physically separate the location of the two activities and that the labor-intensive component may be obtained from a trading partner at significant cost savings.

Assume that the factor cost of assembling product X is included in the cost of activity x_1.[4] This implies that the X-industry's production function is now fully described by its x_1-isoquants. The factor content of a unit of X is the quantity of capital and labor employed in activity x_1, plus the amounts of labor and capital needed to produce the quantity of x_1 that will pay for imports of x_2. Thus, if imports of x_2 were available at zero cost, then the x_1-isoquant associated with the original X-isoquant, X_0, would fully describe the resource cost of producing X_0 units of X. Otherwise, the resource cost of imports of x_2, measured in terms of exports of x_1, must be taken into account. Then, the x_1-isoquant representing the full resource cost of X_0 units of X will lie farther away from the origin along ray Ox_1. We suppose that X_{11} is that isoquant.

With prices of final goods given in the world market, the cost savings open up profit opportunities that must be eliminated in order to re-establish equilibrium. Factor prices adjust until the new factor–price ratio, $(w/r)'$, is tangent to the original Y-isoquant and the new X-industry isoquant, X_{11}. Capital–labor ratios increase in both industries.[5]

To determine the effect on output and employment, we turn to Figure 5.2. The improvement in productivity in the X-industry shifts out the production possibility curve along the horizontal axis.[6] If P_d is assumed to represent the relative price between the two final products under free trade, then the introduction of offshore sourcing moves the production equilibrium from Q_1 to Q_2. This shift clearly raises national welfare.

Most Favored Nation (MFN) Trade Policy

We now turn to examine the effect of component specialization in the presence of trade restrictions. Suppose that our focus country, country A, imposes a non-discriminatory tariff on imports of good X. Suppose that P_w is now the free trade price ratio, so that P_d becomes the domestic price corresponding to tariff rate t. The initial equilibrium before the introduction of offshore sourcing is given by points Q_1

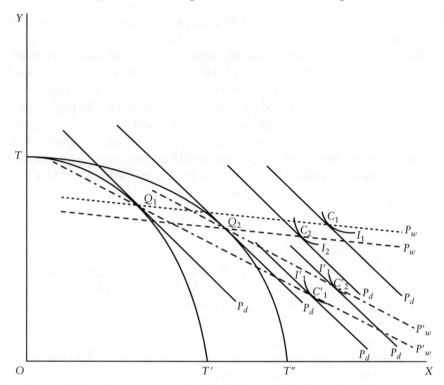

FIG. 5.2. Offshore sourcing and trade policy

and C_1. When component specialization is introduced in the import sector, the production possibility curve moves out along the X-axis to TT''. The small-country assumption ensures that in the world market for end-products, the relative price ratio remains undisturbed at P_w. The outward rotation of the production possibility curve causes its tangency with the domestic price line to move in a south easterly direction to point Q_2, where X-output is larger than before and Y-output smaller. Consumption moves to point C_2 on indifference curve I_2. This change represents a clear reduction in national welfare.[7]

This is, however, not the only possible outcome. Consider a steeper world price ratio for the end-products like P'_w. For convenience, we choose quantities such that a smaller tariff, t', applied to the world price ratio P'_w again yields a domestic price ratio equal to P_d. This allows the production points for the two cases to be identical and thus directly comparable at points Q_1 and Q_2. The difference in outcomes lies in the consumption equilibria and the change in welfare. In the second case, consumption is at point C'_1 before component specialization and at point C_2' after its introduction. The change represents an unambiguous improvement in welfare.

We conclude, therefore, that introduction of component specialization into an MFN tariff situation may raise or lower welfare. Welfare is more likely to fall as the distortion due to the tariff rises relative to the efficiency gains generated by component specialization. In the cases examined, the efficiency gains are identical by construction, but the tariff is larger in the first, welfare-reducing situation. The key result, here, is that implementation of component specialization into a protectionist environment may reduce welfare, whereas its introduction under free trade raises welfare unambiguously.[8]

Preferential Trade Policy

Much like traditional trade theory, the customs union literature has also focused on trade in end-products. As the *North American Free Trade Agreement* (NAFTA) (and its predecessor, the maquiladora program) has shown, however, PTAs may facilitate trade in components. This section analyzes the implications.

MFN-based protection is the starting-point in Figure 5.3, where the object is to assess the welfare effects of a *preferential trade arrangement* (PTA), which frees trade in both end-products and components. It is, of course, well known that PTAs may raise as well as reduce welfare, depending on whether trade-creating elements dominate or fall short of trade-diverting influences.

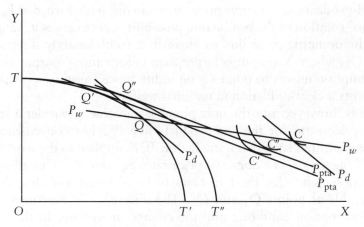

FIG. 5.3. Offshore sourcing and preferential trade policy

Production is initially at Q and consumption at C. Formation of the trade area is assumed to change the price of X from P_d to P_{pta}. The price change shifts domestic production from Q to Q' and imports to the trade partner. The change in the output bundle moves productive resources away from X toward Y. In the figure, the outcome represented is welfare-reducing, with consumption now at C' and thus on a lower indifference curve than C. We know from the theory of customs unions, however, that welfare improvements are also possible.

If formation of the free trade area is accompanied by intra-product specialization in the X-sector, then the production possibility curve expands along the X-axis.[9] The tangency point between P_{pta} and the new production possibility curve moves down to Q''. We once again encounter the familiar result of rising X-output and falling Y-output. Consumption moves to C'' and hence to a higher indifference curve. Component specialization thus mitigates the negative welfare effects of this free trade agreement. More importantly, whereas component specialization may reduce welfare when it is introduced into an environment of MFN protection, it unambiguously augments welfare in the context of a preferential trade arrangement.

Terms-of-trade effects come into play when country A is a large member of the PTA, for then the increase in X-output in the region (and decrease in Y-output) will tend to depress the relative price of X, causing the PTA price ratio to rotate in a counter-clockwise manner and leading to a further increase in national welfare.

Factor Prices and Factor Proportions

This section examines the implications for factor prices and factor allocation by referring back to Figure 5.1. Suppose that the initial commodity price ratio, for which isoquants X_0 and Y_0 are defined, is the MFN price ratio P_d of Figure 5.3. Then, introduction of the PTA and the resultant change in the price ratio to P_{pta} shifts the family of X-isoquants out from the origin in Figure 5.1, while moving the family of Y-isoquants in toward the origin in order to reflect, respectively, reductions in the price of end-product X and increases in the price of end-product Y. These shifts are not shown in the figure to avoid congestion, but it is clear that outward relocation of X-isoquants reduces the wage–rental ratio and inward relocation of Y-isoquants reinforces that adjustment.

This, of course, is the well-known Stolper–Samuelson result that a decline in the relative price of a commodity reduces the relative price of the factor used intensively in its production. What is important for

present purposes, however, is that this change in factor prices is orthog-
onal to the effect on factor prices of component specialization in the
X-industry. The net effect thus depends on the relative strengths of
the two tendencies. If the effect of preferential trade liberalization on
commodity prices is large relative to the cost savings of component specialization, then the wage–rental ratio will fall. From the point of view of
workers, therefore, component specialization should be a welcome feature of any trade agreement that introduces tougher price competition
at the level of end-products.

This result is pertinent to the fears of NAFTA critics. If introduction
of the free trade area brings only a decline in the price of the import-
competing end-product, X, then wages in the industry will come under
pressure and employment and output will decline. To the extent, however, that the free trade area also encourages intra-product specialization
in the X-industry, wages will fall less or even rise and industry output
and employment will fall less or even rise.[10] If the effect of intra-product
specialization dominates the terms-of-trade effect, workers will be better
off and jobs will be more plentiful in the import-competing end-product
industry than before.

If the main effect of a PTA with a low-wage country is to introduce component specialization in the import-competing sector, perhaps
because the end-product price is governed by trade relations with
non-members and thus unaffected by the arrangement, then it will
be welfare-enhancing. This consideration may be part of a country's
strategic objective in joining a preference area, namely, to capture
the cost-saving benefits of cross-border component production for the
competitive struggle with non-members in end-product markets.

3. Repercussions in the Partner Country

During implementation of the PTA, partner country B removes tariffs
on imports of Y from country A and as a result the price of Y falls in
B. In Figure 5.4, the price change is reflected in a shift of the unit-value
isoquant from Y_0 to Y_0'. This raises the wage–rental ratio from w/r to
$(w/r)'$, with tangencies to the new Y-sector isoquant and the original
X-isoquant at points a and b, respectively.

In addition to the change in the terms of trade, the PTA clears the
way for component specialization in the X-sector. For country B, component specialization means that it abandons production of component
x_1 in favor of imports from country A. Consequently, the X-industry's

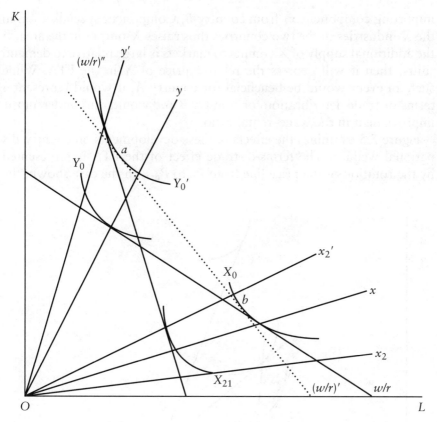

FIG. 5.4. Offshore production and the partner country

production technology is now represented by the x_2-isoquants (which are assumed to include the resource cost of assembling the end-product). We assume that the relevant new isoquant is X_{21} (which would be tangent to the original factor–price ratio (w/r) on a lower expansion path than ox). Expansion paths for component x_1 have not been drawn in order to avoid cluttering. The new equilibrium factor–price ratio must reflect both the terms-of-trade change and the cost savings of component specialization, that is, it must be tangent to Y_0' and X_{21}. That ratio is $(w/r)''$, which causes capital–labor ratios to rise to Oy' and Ox_2', respectively. Component specialization in the country's export industry clearly reinforces the terms-of-trade effect on the factor–price ratio.[11]

There may, however, be a further effect which works in the opposite direction. It will be recalled from the earlier discussion that X-output rises in country A, when that country specializes in component x_1, while importing component x_2 from country B. Component specialization in the X-industries of the two countries thus raises X-output in the area. If the additional supply of X coming to markets is large relative to demand shifts, then it will depress the relative price of X in the PTA. While such an event would be beneficial for country A, it would represent a terms-of-trade deterioration for country B and would thus undercut the improvement in the wage–rental ratio.

Figure 5.5 examines the effects of these developments on country B's national welfare. The terms-of-trade effect of the PTA is represented by the rotation of the price line from P_b to P_{pta}. In the case shown, the

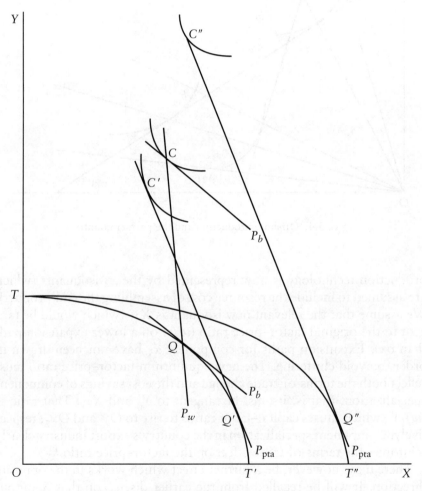

FIG. 5.5. Welfare effects in the partner country

PTA has been drawn to be trade-diverting for country B, with consumption moving to C' prior to implementation of component specialization. That specialization shifts the production possibility curve out along the X-axis. Production shifts to Q'', while consumption moves to point C''.

Thus, while standard inter-product specialization among the members of a preference area may raise or lower national welfare, the effect of intra-product specialization is unambiguously welfare-enhancing. In the case shown, intra-industry specialization of the component type transforms a welfare-reducing PTA into a welfare-creating one. In general, PTAs which stimulate intra-product specialization among members will be more beneficial than those which do not.

Rules of Origin

When the option of component trade is introduced into an MFN system, components will be obtained from the lowest cost source. The bias inherent in preferential trade arrangements, however, has the effect of diverting component trade to the partner country for the same reasons that trade in end-products is diverted. In free trade areas, with their uncoordinated tariff policies, such diversion may be further encouraged by rules of origin. Any tendency for rules of origin to shift sourcing of components from low-cost outsiders to higher-cost partners erodes the cost savings inherent in component specialization. This is an inefficiency which prevents the production possibility curve from shifting out as far as otherwise and thereby reduces the welfare gains. Rules of origin thus keep countries from fully exploiting the benefits of intra-product specialization.

4. Concluding Observations

While outsourcing of parts and components has long been a feature of production in many branches of manufacturing, offshore sourcing and, more importantly, offshore production of parts and components appears to have become more prominent and more widely practiced in recent years. This upsurge has doubtless been facilitated by innovations in communications and transportation and by trade liberalization at both multilateral and regional levels.

Under conditions of free trade, extension of the international division of labor to the level of parts and component activities is welfare-creating. If component production is subject to variations in factor intensities, it will affect comparative advantage across countries. Hence, intra-product specialization will be welfare-enhancing. If component production is subject to economies of scale, then geographic concentration of a component's production will bring further welfare gains.

While this basic principle applies regardless of whether trade is free or not, the welfare effects of intra-product specialization are not independent of the trade regime. In the presence of MFN tariffs, for example, introduction of intra-product specialization in the import-competing sector may raise or lower national welfare. When intra-product specialization is introduced in the context of a preferential trade arrangement, on the other hand, national welfare is increased unambiguously. Thus, any tendency for a preference area to generate trade in components increases the likelihood that it will be welfare-improving.

Finally, to the extent that rules of origin and local content requirements force firms to shift sourcing of components from low-cost non-members to higher-cost members, they are welfare-reducing.

NOTES

I am indebted to Alan Deardorff, Ronald Jones, and Henryk Kierzkowski and to conference participants for valuable comments and suggestions.

1. For examples of that literature, see Ethier (1984), Hazari *et al.* (1981), and Sanyal and Jones (1982).
2. See Arndt (1997, 1998*a*, 1998*b*), Deardorff (1998), and Jones and Kierzkowski (1997).
3. The capital–labor ratio along expansion path *ox* is thus the weighted average of the capital–labor ratios of the two component activities.
4. This assumption makes assembly and production of component x_1 non-separable. If assembly is modeled as a separate activity, then it may also be cheaper offshore.
5. For additional details, see Arndt (1997, 1998*a*, 1998*b*).
6. For details, see Arndt (1997, 1998*a*, 1998*b*). See Johnson (1971) for a classic study of trade and technical progress. See also Hazari *et al.* (1981) for an example from the earlier literature on trade in intermediate products. For an application to the economics of multi-plant operations by MNEs, see Markusen (1984).
7. See Johnson (1967) for a related discussion concerning protection and technical progress.
8. For a small country, the shift to offshore sourcing does not affect the terms of trade. A large country, on the other hand, may affect global supply conditions when *X*-output rises and *Y*-output falls and thereby turn the terms of trade in its favor. In that case, the world price line would rotate in a counter-clockwise direction with obvious welfare-enhancing consequences.

9. It is immaterial in the first instance whether offshore sourcing involves the partner country or the outsider. If the latter is the low-cost producer of the component and there are no discriminatory trade barriers on components, then component imports will originate there. Preferential treatment of component imports from the PTA partner, as under rules of origin, is considered below.

10. In the 2 × 2 world with completely integrated labor markets and perfectly mobile labor, the effect on factor prices spreads throughout the economy. In the real world, the spillover will be more limited; it may spread to neighboring industries or regions, but need not affect the entire economy.

11. The intellectual foundations of the present analytical approach are to be found in the literature on trade and technical progress. That literature finds that output and employment will rise in a sector which enjoys technical progress *except* when that progress is 'saving' in the sector's non-intensive factor, in which case the outcome is ambiguous. Thus, for example, output may rise or fall in the capital-intensive sector if technical progress is labor-saving. It is shown in Arndt (2000) that there is no ambiguity.

REFERENCES

Arndt, S. W. (1997). 'Globalization and the Open Economy', *North American Journal of Economics and Finance*, 8/1.

—— (1998*a*). 'Globalization and the Gains from Trade', in K. J. Koch and K. J. Jaeger (eds.), *Trade, Growth, and Economic Policy in Open Economies* (New York: Springer-Verlag).

—— (1998*b*). 'Super-Specialization and the Gains from Trade', *Contemporary Economic Policy*, 16 (Oct.).

—— (2000). 'Technical Progress and Trade Revisited', mimeo. Claremont, Calif.: Lowe Institute of Political Economy.

Deardorff, A. (1998). 'Fragmentation in Simple Trade Models', mimeo, Dec.

Ethier, W. J. (1984). 'Higher Dimensional Issues in Trade Theory', in R. W. Jones and P. B. Kenen (eds.), *Handbook of International Economics*, i (New York: North-Holland).

Hazari, B. R., Sgro, P. M., and Suh, D. C. (1981). *Non-traded and Intermediate Goods and the Pure Theory of International Trade* (London: Croom Helm).

Johnson, H. G. (1967). 'The Possibility of Income Losses from Increased Efficiency or Factor Accumulation in the Presence of Tariffs', *Economic Journal* (Mar.).

—— (1971). *Two-Sector Model of General Equilibrium* (Chicago: Aldine Atherton).

Jones, R. W., and Kierzkowski, H. (2000), 'Globalization and the Consequences of International Fragmentation', forthcoming in Rudiger Dornbusch, Guillermo Calvo, and Maurice Obstfeld (eds.), *Money, Factor Mobility and Trade: A Festschrift in Honor of Robert A. Mundell* (Cambridge, Mass.: MIT Press).

Markusen, J. R. (1984). 'Multinationals, Multi-plant Economies, and the Gains from Trade', *Journal of International Economics*, 16: 205–26.

Sanyal, K., and Jones, R. W. (1982). 'The Theory of Trade in Middle Products', *American Economic Review*, 72 (Mar.).

6

Some Causes and Consequences of Fragmentation

VICTORIA CURZON PRICE

1. Introduction

'Fragmentation' refers to the growing complexity of the modern chain of production, which divides and redivides previously integrated systems into ever more specialized and distinguishable units.

The components of many objects have not only originated in many different places, but the components themselves have an equally chequered geographic history. The actual molecules making up a pen or a computer will have crossed many frontiers, probably back and forth across the same frontiers several times, changing owners all the time, before reaching their final destination, at which point the physical molecules will have been rearranged into something useful. Arguably, the value-added in the process is 'just services'. In other words, the service-content of the goods we buy is very great indeed. Identifying the diverse national 'origins' of a modern product is nowadays quite impossible.

What drives this process of fragmentation? What are some of its consequences? This chapter starts with an attempt to define fragmentation as a combination of a geographic dimension and a set of managerial strategies (running from vertical integration to complete outsourcing). The most 'fragmented' firm is the international 'virtual' corporation, which has decoupled management from production on a global basis. In the second part, the claim is made that this form of fragmentation is increasing and that the Coasian reasons for firms' existence are shrinking. The chapter concludes with the hypothesis that globalization, far from generating only ever larger, fewer, monopolistic firms, also favors the development of more numerous, highly specialized firms and the maintenance of competition.

2. A Definition of Fragmentation

To reduce the problem of definition to manageable proportions, one is tempted to concentrate on just that part of the chain of production which takes place within a single firm, under its ownership and control, but in different countries (the traditional multinational firm). But in so doing, we run the danger of missing some interesting and relatively new and growing aspects of fragmentation. For instance, while the ownership dimension captures nicely the international aspects of fragmentation which occur within a particular corporation, as it seeks for instance to relocate labor-intensive 'bits' of the chain abroad without losing control over its part of the chain, it misses the growing trend toward international outsourcing of part of the production process, such as, for instance, when Gucci arranges for its smart leather goods to be produced by independent firms in South East Asia, instead of sewing them up in its own workshops in China or arranging for an independent contractor to do so in Milan. The outsourcing dimension of international fragmentation lies somewhere in between total ownership on the one hand, and complete arm's-length transactions on the other. Two important elements make outsourcing different from traditional arm's-length transactions: the long-term nature of the relationship and the amount of information, in the form of detailed instructions and specifications on the part of the customer, which accompany the outsourcing.

In what follows, we shall try to combine these two dimensions in order to indentify the locus of the novelty of the fragmentation concept.

2.1. *The Spatial Dimension*

Part of the chain of production is undertaken in another country, with transactions taking place *either* at arm's length, on open markets, between different economic agents at an identifiable price, *or* within the same firm. This is the dimension usually explored by international trade theory, which does not worry much about the question of ownership of the chain of production, but is very interested in the international aspects of production and consumption. We shall call this the 'A-dimension' (see Figure 6.1), which runs on a scale going from autarky to extreme geographic fragmentation of production, but for simplicity we divide line A into only two segments, A1 (locally produced goods) and A2 (goods with high global content).

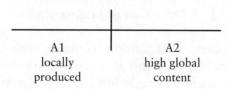

	A1	A2
	locally	high global
	produced	content

FIG. 6.1. The spatial dimension

The actual destination of the product does not concern us—it might be consumed locally or exported. We are only interested in the production side.

2.2. *The Integration/Specialization Dimension*

Exactly over what part of the chain of production does a firm extend its activities? In the 1950s and 1960s the corporate fashion was for the creation of conglomerates, uniting under a single managerial roof a host of different businesses, not necessarily connected in any way with each other. This was the heyday of 'management as a science': the same scientific approach could be used to manage anything. US General Electric was known, in its day, for manufacturing thousands of products, and managing hundreds of separate business units. It almost came to grief before slimming down its portfolio to manageable proportions. But even fairly 'focused' firms can be found producing an odd assortment of goods. Why should Peugeot, an automobile manufacturer, also produce pepper grinders? Why should BP go in for fish farming? Perhaps there were synergies to begin with, but this is rarely enough for the long run. Even the refocused conglomerate is disappearing fast. Nowadays, management is obliged to 'downsize' and 're-engineer'. As firms sell off bits of themselves, or fall victims to corporate raiders, new, smaller, more specialized firms appear from the debris. This is a major source of *specialization fragmentation.*

Another aspect of specialization, or managerial fragmentation, occurs within the already refocused, specialized, lean-and-mean firm, when part of the integrated production process of management function suddenly becomes available on the open market. At this point, the 'product' or managerial function/service can continue to be produced internally, or bought in from outside ('contracting-out'). Once this occurs, as we shall see, the writing is on the wall: sooner or later the well-managed firm will divest itself of this activity, unless it decides to concentrate

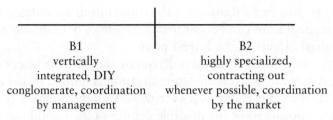

B1	B2
vertically integrated, DIY conglomerate, coordination by management	highly specialized, contracting out whenever possible, coordination by the market

FIG. 6.2. The integration/specialization dimension

on it to the exclusion of all others. The badly managed firm will be taken over or go bankrupt and the inefficient link in the chain will become an independent business sector. The end-result is the same: increasing fragmentation of the chain of production and pattern of management and more numerous, and more specialized, producers. One can clearly see that each distinct specialized unit is really 'just' supplying a service, transforming and combining molecules, but not 'producing' them. This, it seems to me, is the new dimension of managerial fragmentation. It delves deeply into the chain of production and even into the managerial structure of the firm, since various service functions like billing, accountancy, or recruitment can be increasingly outsourced.

We shall call this the B-dimension, which runs all the way from the vertically integrated, unspecialized, conglomerate 'do-it-all-yourself' type of firm, to the highly specialized enterprise which never manufactures itself what is cheaper to buy in from outside. Increasingly, in developed countries, this firm manufactures nothing at all directly, but contracts out all but its innermost core competence. It is a pure service entity. The B-dimension concerns corporate strategy rather than products.

The totally homogenized product is only found in economic textbooks. There are, for instance, hundreds of different qualities of steel, so 'steel' does not really exist *per se* as a marketable product. However, when markets were smaller and technology less refined, steel was steel. Changing technology and larger markets have thus created opportunities for firms to specialize in different types of steel. As Smith, Stigler, and many others have long ago remarked, specialization brings extra efficiencies in its own right, all the way from the humble learning-curve effect to economies of scale, so we have no difficulty in explaining the trend. Nike farms out its production of shoes to subcontractors, which allows it to concentrate its energies on the design of the next generation of footwear. Firms need not employ an expensive team of full-time accountants, but can contract out this function to an outside supplier. Thus even small firms can benefit from economies of scale and get access to the highest quality at the lowest price.

This ever finer fragmentation is driven by the familiar forces of larger markets. Adam Smith's dictum 'specialization is limited by the extent of the market' is as true today as it ever was. An interesting by-product of the process appears to be the possible demise of the mammoth firm and its replacement by much smaller firms efficiently producing specialized production services.

These different forms of fragmentation can be combined to give two-by-two distinct product/firm types of fragmentation—or the absence thereof. Sometimes the boxes contain very different animals, since these two dimensions are of course by far not the only possible distinguishing characteristics. They can be used to identify the sources of change and what appears to be new about the phenomenon.

3. Fragmentation—A Non-exhaustive Taxonomy

3.1. *Local Firms/Products*

Referring to 'The Fragmentation Box' (Fig. 6.3), the baseline A1, B1 firm/product is relatively standardized, inspired by a do-it-all-yourself mentality with negligible global content. It is the exact opposite of 'fragmentation' along whichever dimension one wishes to view it. The general store in a small town comes to mind as a fast-disappearing example, killed off by the motor car and competition from the modern shopping mall. The great monopolized public utilities also belong here. As we know, they are an endangered species. Since privatization and deregulation has hit them, they have been split up, downsized, and re-engineered as never before. Even the great *Electricité de France* may lose its monopoly of electricity supply in France—and in the meantime it has gone abroad to *advise* other electricity monopolies (e.g. in the Ukraine) on how to run their business. It has entered the international energy consultancy business (the A2, B1 segment). Some privatized telecommunications firms are arguably also in the multinationally fragmented A2, B1 segment, while state-run postal services are stuck in the starting blocks. On the other hand, some of Europe's monolithic state education systems may be moving to the A1, B2 box: there is certainly no danger that they might 'go multinational', but they are beginning to

	B-dimension: is the firm or the market the chosen instrument of coordination?	
	The vertically integrated, do-it-yourself firm. Management does the job of coordination B1	The specialized firm, contracting out if possible. Markets do the job of coordination B2
A-dimension: goods with a high proportion of local content A1	A1, B1 *General store in small town, monopolized public utilities, vertically integrated retailers*	A1, B2 *Dentists, artisans, building firms, hospitals seeking efficiency gains from outsourcing, members of a specialized agglomeration complex*
A-dimension: Goods with a high proportion of international content A2	A2, B1 *Traditional MNCs, keeping control over the production chain to preserve proprietary technology and know-how*	A2, B2 *International subcontracting parts of the production process, leading to intra-product trade and 'supply chain management' transactions, costs kept low by agglomeration effects*

FIG. 6.3. The Fragmentation Box

contract out the management of difficult, non-performing schools to private management institutions.

3.2. *Local, Specialized Firms*

The A1, B2 firm/product, is local, but is very specialized (like a dentist producing fillings). Here we find the typical non-traded professions and specialized artisans, where a great deal of fragmentation takes place along the specialization dimension, but not along the others. One might also place hospitals in the A1, B2 box, since they are simultaneously highly specialized, local, supply individually tailored services, but increasingly contract out, for instance, catering, laundry, cleaning, maintenance, and laboratory analyses. Some hospitals no longer employ nurses directly, but contract out this seemingly core activity to a nursing-services agency. At one moment, the hospital might just become a Coasian locus for a multitude of contracts (see below) but at this point it would have slipped into the 'new' fragmentation category described below. The construction industry would tend to be in this box, since it is often very local, but each independent firm is highly specialized.

3.2.1. Local, 'Fragmented' Firms forming Part of an
Agglomeration Complex

Industrial agglomerations of particular economic activites, composed of many specialized firms, like Silicon Valley, have long intrigued economists. They are part of the fragmentation story too, for an alternative to an agglomeration of independent firms would be to combine them all under a single, vertically integrated mammoth enterprise. But this would be inefficient for the reasons already outlined. Various 'pull' factors, which create positive externalities and thus reduce costs, have been identified by many authors:[1] positive externalities based on mass production of specialized inputs, specialized labor, specialized services, shared consumers, shared infrastructure (especially universities), flow of information, the efficiency of markets as coordinating agents, the corresponding inefficiency of management beyond a certain degree of complexity, and so on.

In the A1, B2 segment we thus find the small, local, skilled subcontractor offering essentially *services* to other companies. Its comparative advantage is an ability to take orders and manufacture or supply services to a high degree of specification. The firm may 'produce' or offer its services in only one location, but it will probably be the international link in a global chain of production. The small firm in Northern Italy producing part of a highly design-specific spectacle frame on contract for Armani, Rayban, Vuarnet, or Porsche (though why should an automobile firm sell sun-glasses?) comes to mind, especially if one knows that it is part of an 'agglomeration' complex, where the gold-plating is done by another independent family firm and about 200 firms collaborate to produce in a fragmented and flexible way a highly differentiated and changeable fashion product.[2]

It is important to note that the particular firm which gets the contract to perform the process does so in competition with other equally competent firms. This kind of arrangement can only be efficient if the market for sun-glasses is very large indeed. This is an example of what we mean by *intra-product* fragmentation. But this type of fragmentation flourishes *precisely* because it occurs in an identifiable geographic location, where informal information flows between the units and strong positive externalities bind the nest of firms together. The hospital which contracts out nursing services will only get good results if there are many hospitals and many service providers, offering similar (but often subtly differentiated) products. The truly spectacular benefits will only come when specialization and economies of scale, in turn, hit the nursing services supply industry as well, spreading pecuniary externalities[3] throughout the agglomeration and creating a Silicon Valley for health care.

We note in passing (*a*) that local firms/products are capable of being part of the new fragmentation process and (*b*) that there are forces pushing local firms/products out of the baseline no-fragmentation box into some form of fragmentation—either spatial or specialized.

3.3. *Multinational Firms Producing Goods Internationally*

In the A2, B1 box we find the large *multinational corporation* (MNC), producing a standardized set of goods in several locations in a vertically integrated way. This represents 'traditional spatial fragmentation'. Much has been written about it, and many examples can be found, ranging from Coca-Cola to Exxon. Scale economies and firm-specific technology are important characteristics.[4] Such firms wish to keep control of the production chain, even if it could be split up, in order to preserve their proprietary technology and know-how, or because there are other sources of rents (such as mineral rights) which might be endangered if it contracted out too many 'core' activities. Their many activities are fragmented across the globe, but they keep them under one ownership roof. The costs of managing such a complex unit have to be offset by economies of scale and/or technological advantage. These firms are optimizing production possibilities around the world. They tend to participate, in Dunning's terminology, in 'efficiency-seeking' foreign direct investment.[5] A pharmaceutical company, for instance, which concentrates its R&D function in Europe, North America, and Japan (to benefit from the best of the different scientific outputs of various higher-education systems), produces its active ingredients in two locations (just to be on the safe side if there's a fire), and ships them to many locations for galenic preparation, close to the consumer (and possibly also close to the medical regulators) is still low on the B scale, but far ahead on the A scale. It hesitates to share proprietary technology with subcontractors, which means that it still does plenty 'in-house'.

3.4. *The 'Virtual', 'Hollow', or 'Network' Corporation*

The A2, B2 box is occupied by firms/products where *international* subcontracting has become important. For example, instead of producing radios in a wholly owned subsidiary in Malaysia, Philips decides to sell the factory, and subcontract its radio production to an arm's-length independent supplier (or suppliers). It may supply bits that go into the radio, or just the design. Instead of getting the gold-plating done in Northern Italy, Porsche decides to try out an Indian firm.

The goods themselves need not be very sophisticated or difficult to make (footballs? furniture? T-shirts?), the firms that 'create' them may not be multinationals at all in the conventional sense of the term (i.e. they need not themselves produce in more than one location, and indeed may not produce at all), but they contract out the actual physical production to a wide range of producers, who may themselves contract out to yet other firms, some of which happen to be in another country. These firms/products may be household names worldwide with a small home base (Gucci, Benetton). It is the type of firm for which outward processing regimes have been developed (reimport of worked-up clothing cut out by laser in a developed, high-labor cost country, stitched into clothes in a low-labor cost area, and reimported duty free (or duty only paid on the value-added to the cut-outs during their temporary sojourn in a labor-intensive country). It is typical of 'maquiladora' activity, where the production process is divided up into labor and capital-intensive segments, and located, respectively, in low and high-wage areas.

The A2, B2 box is also occupied by firms/products that are sophisticated, high tech, and differentiated. So specialized, in fact, that they rely on subcontractors for most or all of their physical production. They may be located in only one place, but they possess global reach. They concentrate on R&D, design, finance, logistics and marketing—not on physical production. This type of firm may interact internationally with the specialized A1, B2 firm examined earlier.

In terms of the economics of agglomeration, a successful agglomeration may have fallen victim to growing congestion, poaching, and ever higher prices for the relatively immobile factors. These constitute diminishing returns and entrepreneurs start to look for alternatives: 'younger' agglomerations, new locations, new management strategies. Mobile factors are 'pushed' from one, and 'pulled' to the other. The old agglomeration gives birth to new ones, all over the world.

This phenomenon has given rise to a new profession—international supply-chain management. In June 1998 *The Economist* carried a story[6] about the Hong Kong firm Li & Fung, which has a network of 7,500 regular suppliers all over Asia, employing an average of 200 workers each (representing about 1.5 million workers). Li & Fung take orders from foreign companies to make anything, from ball-point pens to computers. Their people scout around for the best place for every operation—but they don't have to scout far. The 7,500 companies keep product development and engineering offices in Hong Kong (maintaining a credible level of competence), as well as marketing and distribution facilities (keeping in touch with demand, drawing attention to their abilities, and generally participating in the flow of specialized and informal information so crucial to a successful agglomeration). It is they, not Li & Fung, which manage the middle, more labor-intensive, manufacturing parts of the chain. As a result, says Mr Fung: 'we are lining up factors of production so that we can cut lead times from three months to five weeks' (p. 20). And what firm can boast of 1.5 million workers spread over dozens of countries?

The same survey also cites the example of Hana Technologies, which specializes in putting microchips into other parts of all sorts of products. This is high-precision work that needs sophisticated machinery and constant retraining of operatives for each new thing that arrives. Hana Technologies keeps this sophisticated operation in Hong Kong until it is running smoothly, then moves it to China or to Thailand, along with the just-acquired specific production knowledge and know-how. In short, Hong Kong is now a knowledge exporter.

4. Fragmentation Trends

4.1. *Trends in the Spatial Dimension*

According to every available study, our economies are becoming more and more global. *The World Trade Organization's (WTO's)* annual study of world trade[7] shows, year after year, that trade grows faster than GNP. For example, from 1990 to 1996 world manufactured goods trade grew by 6 percent per year in real terms, as compared with 1.5 percent per year for world GNP,[8] while services trade grew by about 10 percent a year from 1994 to 1996.[9] UNCTAD's annual study of foreign direct investment[10] shows that, though more volatile, FDI grows even faster than trade (it doubled from 1992 to 1995).[11] Finally, the Bank for International Settlements, which tries to keep track of international capital movements and portfolio investments, provides data which suggest that these have grown even faster—by a factor of 3.5[12]—over the same time-period.

This process has been driven partly by technological change which radically reduces transport and communication costs, by liberalization and deregulation (ranging from classical trade-barrier reduction in the WTO, to the unilateral abolition of exchange controls on capital movements) and by a sort of *pax mercatoria* which has greatly reduced the political risk of doing business abroad at the dawn of the twenty-first century. The wave of deregulation of public utilities which started in the 1980s in the United States has since spread. It has also played a part in pushing previously local activities into the international arena.

4.2. *Trends in the Specialization Dimension*

The trend for firms to 'downsize', 're-engineer', and 'rationalize' is pushing them ever further out toward specialization (A2 in terms of our fragmentation box), while global competition is forcing them to seek for cheaper sources of production (B2 in terms of Fig. 6.3). We have already noted that the conglomerate of yesterday is an endangered species (US General Electric does not make toasters any more: it is into space rockets and jumbo-jet aero engines). But even specialized firms are becoming more specialized. Why is this?

A good starting-point is Adam Smith's 200 year-old observation that specialization is limited by the extent of the market. As markets grow, so ever-increasing specialization is possible. That specialization brings net social gains in the form of lower costs and lower prices is one of those facts of life which is encapsulated in Ricardo's theory of comparative advantage, but it also contains dynamic elements in the shape of scale economies, learning curves, and agglomeration externalities. Firms which ignore these facts go bankrupt.

Take the example of an airline. Most airlines started out with their own catering departments. Now only Air France (still heavily subsidized) bothers. Aircraft catering has become a separate, competitive business because there are so many meals to be prepared (the market has grown so much) that at one moment the airline has to decide which business it is in: flying people around the world, or feeding them while up in the sky? Today, even internal service functions, like billing or accounting, can be hired on a contractual basis. In short, a growing market provides new opportunities for firms to split like amoebae, offering downstream firms cheaper and more varied inputs.

Why do they do so? Why don't firms just grow and grow? The answer to this question is given by Ronald Coase.[13] Coase asked why in some circumstances the economy admits of the coordinating functions of the entrepreneur and his management team, and in others, coordination is the work of open markets and the price mechanism. Under which conditions is the one to be preferred to the other? Broadly speaking, the market is an efficient coordinating and monitoring system, but it has its drawbacks—among them transactions costs. A business can economize on transactions costs by internalising them—but only up to a point. It tends to internalize familiar, repetitive transactions, but novel, complex decisions take a great deal of management time. There are limits to what the entrepreneurs (or even the modern MBA-trained manager) can effectively coordinate, and diminishing returns to management set in. At one moment the saving on transactions costs is just equal to the cost of management. It is the moment to split, to outsource.

The cost of coordination through management or through the market can be related to the number of transactions (decisions) along the lines suggested in Figure 6.4. The '*management cost*' (MC) coordination function within the firm is non-linear, high for few, one-off transactions, falling as the number of transactions increases, and rising again as the sheer number of transactions increases the complexity, and thus the cost, of management. The *transaction costs of market coordination* (TC) function is also non-linear. It is low for few, one-off transactions, rising as the number of repetitive decisions (transactions) increases, but falling again, as large numbers of new decisions have to be taken. This suggests that the market is efficient at both ends of the transactions spectrum, and firms are efficient between the two extremes.

The trend which concerns us here is the fact that trade liberalization, the fall in transport costs, and the development of cheap and reliable electronic communications, and the Internet in particular, are in the

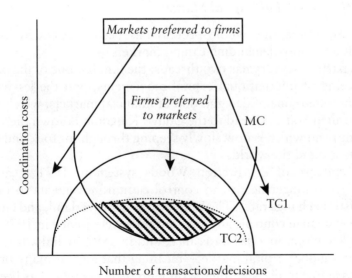

FIG. 6.4. Management or market?

process of radically reducing transactions costs. The search for relevant market information has become easier than before. Internet pages for every business sector imaginable provide online all the press releases by all the firms, every day. A business executive will know, as never before, what is available, at what price, in what quantity, to what quality, when and where—at a click of a button. America's Big Three auto companies have started a system on the Internet known as the Automotive Network Exchange. Any firm wishing to supply them can know at any time exactly what is needed, what price is offered, and what the competition is doing.[14] According to the Coasian approach, such a drop in market transactions costs will reduce the advantage of internalizing activities within the firm, and therefore reduce its size, forcing it to 'outsource' all but its core activities. In terms of Figure 6.4, the TC function shifts downwards (dotted line) to TC2, decreasing the area over which markets are efficient and reducing the scope for coordination by management (shaded area).

We would hypothesize further that *international* outsourcing is also contributing to shifting TC downwards by offering radically lower prices for inputs. We would guess that in many parts of the developing world, as well as in certain transition economies, 'young' industrial agglomerations have emerged which now offer the cost-cutting benefits of growing positive externalities along with much lower factor prices.

4.3. *Effect of Global Capital Markets*

In the meantime, the whole process has been accelerated by more efficient and more demanding capital markets.

This particular story has two threads: the familiar one of the progressive freeing of international capital movements, and the less obvious (but connected) one of deregulation of financial markets, which started in the United States, spread to the United Kingdom (known there as the Big Bang) and which is now slowly seeping through to stock and capital markets around the world.

The collapse of the Bretton Woods system in 1971 meant that countries no longer needed to control capital movements to prop up unrealistic exchange rates. The United States, Switzerland, and Germany had no exchange controls anyway, but they were joined in 1979 by the United Kingdom, in 1990 by France, and in 1992 by Italy. It is fair to say that a global capital market—meaning that a great many ordinary people are free to do what they wish with their savings—has been fully operational since about the mid-1980s.

In the meantime, domestic financial deregulation brought competition into a highly regulated and cartelized service industry. Not only did bankers have to try to offer better service, but they had to try to avoid being short-circuited by stock markets, which offered borrowers much more capital at a much lower cost. As companies flocked to sell stock and raise capital (which flowed in from every corner of the earth), they escaped the steely embrace of their bankers only to find that shareholders were just as bad, or even worse. They became slaves to 'stockholder value' (and stock options made managers very happy slaves).

There was a time when a reasonably successful firm (call it X-Co.) would operate a dozen divisions, only one of which really made money. The others would just cover their costs, or even lose money. Management consultants even invented names for these various situations: there would be 'cash cows' (i.e. profitable segments), 'stars' (possibly profitable sometime in the future), 'dogs' (kept for sentimental reasons, but losing money all the time), and 'black holes' (best not described). The cash cows would cross-subsidize both the past and the future of the company, which would make a modest return—nothing spectacular!—for its shareholders, who did not expect anything better.

Since these easygoing times, X-Co. has either fallen victim to a corporate raider, who split the business up and kept only the profitable cash cow, or has reached this painful decision itself, and has 'downsized'. If it has survived to tell the tale, X-Co. is now ready for a horizontal merger with a similar company. The end-result is a large, oligopolistic, but oh-so specialized firm which radically increases shareholder value through economies of scale. This, incidentally, is the main reason for the longest uninterrupted rise in stock markets ever recorded. Lazy cross-subsidization is gone forever, burnt away by efficient capital markets. In the meantime, *'Enterprise Resource Planning'* (ERP) software programs have been designed to let a company know, at any time, exactly how well each person, machine, or area of office space is performing. Bottlenecks, imbalances, and inefficiencies show up immediately.[15] Charlie Chaplain's classic 'Modern Times' is a pale image of the stress with which today's employees live.

The trend along the B-dimension is reinforced by the fact that customers are more and more demanding. They want their product 'to be enhanced by some individual variation, or some special service'.[16] They are not content with mass-production uniformity. They do not like to wait. The solution, according to *The Economist*, lies in 'mass customization', which means making basically similar products in hundreds, even thousands, of variations to suit specific customers' needs.

A single firm trying to manage such complexity would drown in coordination problems. It hits the wall of diminishing marginal returns to internalized coordination sooner than before (when consumers accepted undifferentiated products). Only markets and arm's-length transactions can handle such a degree of specialization and differentiation. And only mass specialization and ownership fragmentation permit costs to fall and stay low through competition. This is possible only if parts and components can be turned into commodities that can be bought and sold on the open market, in large numbers, and in many varieties. This, as we have just seen, is exactly what the Internet permits.

In terms of Figure 6.4, this trend could be represented by a shift to the left of the right-hand side of the MC function (not shown): managerial costs start rising at a lower level of transactions, reducing the area over which firms are more efficient than markets as coordinators of human action.

In the meantime, technological change seems to be favoring smaller batches of differentiated products. Electronic design, tooling, and retooling make it possible to reap the benefits of scale and customization at the same time. Shortening delivery times means saving on inventory tied up in the long chain of production. All these factors point to the increasing importance of small, specialized, and efficient firms, efficiently coordinated by industrial agglomerations which cut down on transport and inventory costs and keep information flowing smoothly through the system. Agglomerations of specialized firms combine the best of the coordinating functions of management with those of the market and may become an alternative for scale effects.[17] In terms of Figure 6.4, this trend could be represented by a shift to the left of the left-hand side of the MC function (not shown), again reducing the area over which internalization by firms is more efficient than coordination by markets.

The shortening of the technology life-cycle also points in the direction of smaller, less costly units, since there is less and less time in which to recoup any given investment and the response to change must be swift.

5. Fragmentation and Employment

As the modern world pushes advanced economies ever further along both dimensions of fragmentation, more and more people have good reason to fear the process. As basic manufacturing functions move abroad, many staple blue-collar jobs are lost in traditional activities.

As big firms downsize, some lost jobs may be saved in the smaller, rationalized offshoots, but not if cost-cutting is the driving motive. As firms rationalize through mergers, every press release is accompanied by estimates of the savings that will be made from the expected joint job redundancies. Share prices shoot up, jobs are lost, much to the disgust of media commentators. Privatization of monopolized public utilities threatens life-long employment of almost *fonctionnaire* quality. Deregulation challenges sleepy cartels and threatens jobs.

What must not be forgotten, however, as firms pursue growing markets and specialize, is that many firms will now do the work of one. It is by no means obvious that employment as a whole will drop, especially as the process reduces costs, and therefore prices, thus stimulating demand directly, or for other things, via real income growth. This is well known. But what is less frequently acknowledged is that the demand for managerial (and entrepreneurial) functions will increase, because there are many more firms to be managed. Thus the fall in transactions costs which makes specialization fragmentation attractive does not *substitute* markets for managers in the coordination function, as Coase would argue, but increases the need for both. This point has been made by Demsetz:

specialization theory, analyzing a reduction in transaction cost, views the interposition of a market between activities previously carried on within one firm, not as the substitution of market for firm, but as the substitution of two firms for one. Assuming that specialization is productive, this substitution can increase ... the total output of the economy ... Reliance on markets also increases, but not by eliminating firms. The number of firms and the degree to which they sell to ousiders increase, as does reliance on markets. The importance of firms and of markets in the economy correlates positively.[18]

It follows from this insight that we can look forward to an increasing number of smaller firms. In terms of Figure 6.4, the shaded surface beneath the dotted TC2 curve suggests that smaller firms are efficient over a smaller number of decisions/transactions, but as the total number of transactions increases over the whole economy, the total number of firms will rise.

Furthermore, there is no reason to believe, a priori, that modern technologies require ever more skilled and knowledgeable people to operate them. On the contrary, as Sowell has pointed out,[19] thanks to markets and specialization, modern people, individually, can afford to know less and less about more and more because they benefit hugely from the knowledge of others. The cleverness is in the machine, so to speak, not in the head of the person using it. It follows from this that the process of fragmentation does not require of the working population an inhuman level of effort to 'retool' for the modern world. It also means that more and more people in the developing world can enter the modern age at lower costs than ever before. But this enlarges markets, and so the process continues.

6. Fear of Fragmentation

Despite these trends, fear of fragmentation makes good headlines. Globalization is blamed, by the public, for all the stress which accompanies the restructuring processes just described, and even more besides. For instance, an international best-seller entitled *The Global Trap: Globalization & the Assault on Democracy & Prosperity*[20] which has been translated into twenty languages and sold a quarter of a million copies, paints a horrifying picture of social decay in the United States ('homeland of the capitalist counter-revolution'),[21] where crime has reached epidemic proportions, expenditure on prisons exceeds that on education and 10 percent of the population lives in guarded homes, spending twice as much money on private security guards as the government does on the police.

According to this thesis, globalization is to blame for all our social ills because it is responsible for dividing society into winners and losers. As the losers become ever more numerous, globalization 'turns out to be a trap for democracy itself'.[22] Even the Davos 2000 meeting was devoted to the theme of 'Globalization and the threat to democracy'.

The argument is simple. The ever-more numerous victims of globalization are turning to extreme right-wing parties to express their deep frustration—in the United States, France, Austria, Italy, and even Germany. Democracy will fail unless something is done quickly to spread the gains from globalization more fairly, and to slow down the pace of globalization itself.

In this debate it is of some importance that trends highlighted above suggest more, and smaller firms, and more competition rather than less. The public may not believe theorizing by economists, but the reality of the benefits of globalization will be difficult to set aside. The vast majority of people benefit not just from globalization, but also from the market-driven process of fragmentation just described. We tend to believe that these forces are moving us toward more efficient forms of production, more firms, more competition, more jobs, better and cheaper goods, more choice generally, and a growing range of options as consumers and factor owners. There are losers, of course, since no social process is ever an unalloyed gain for all. But if permanent restructuring did not take place, there would be even more losers and much lower incomes all around.

One cannot really single out for blame from the complex set of market forces pushing our societies into new economic structures just the geographic dimension. What is really being expressed by anti-WTO demonstrators is fear of market forces in general, not just globalization. In the old days, the victims of capitalism could take refuge in Communism and the far left. Nowadays, this alternative has lost credibility. We certainly would agree with the analysis outlined above that the stress engendered by market forces encourages political extremes in a democracy and that since the far left is no longer credible, the far right has replaced it. However, it seems to this author that the claims of impending demise of democracy are much overdone. First, because political extremism as a whole has not increased—the far right has risen at the expense of the far left. And secondly, because rising incomes permit societies to offer compensation to the losers—in fact, this is a familiar feature of modern democracy. The famous 'third way' is today hugely popular.[23] In the United States, the 'third way' is slightly more inclined to rugged individualism and letting market forces get on with the job than in Europe, but even here both federal and state governments are entrusted with smoothing the worst and harshest aspects of capitalism. In Europe the 'third way' goes much further to shield people from the consequences of technological change, deregulation, competition, and globalization. It perhaps grows more slowly as a result, but it is quite wrong to think that we have no choice in the matter. A certain amount of income redistribution makes economic change more politically and socially acceptable, and the latter pays for the former.

7. Conclusion

Our study of the origins of fragmentation suggests that it is being driven by many factors: wider markets, greater specialization, lower transport and communications costs, lower transactions costs, technological progress, lower efficient minimum scale of operations, more demanding consumers, more numerous agglomerations generating greater externalities before getting congested, more efficient and demanding international capital markets. There is no single driving force, but a conjunction of many forces acting simultaneously.

Our study of the effects of fragmentation points in the direction of higher employment through growth, more numerous and smaller firms, and a weakening of giant, unfocussed MNCs. This conclusion runs counter to the popular view that the world is increasingly dominated by 'uncontrollable, quasi-monopolist, transnational corporations'[24] and puts a more optimistic interpretation on the process of globalization. Although it should be a matter of simple empirical observation and verification to determine which view is correct, we suspect that the debate will continue for many years to come for lack of an agreed method for measuring the relative size of firms.

It is also an open question, in the aftermath of the failed WTO Ministerial Meeting in Seattle, whether the trends outlined above are likely to be halted by a rising tide of protectionism, or whether the process of globalization and fragmentation will continue to spread modern methods of production across the globe.

It seems to this author that even if the public does not buy all the standard economic arguments on the positive welfare effects of trade and economic change, events so far suggest that people generally support the kind of compromise which allows for economic change to occur. If this were not the case, there would be no fragmentation story to tell.

NOTES

1. Fujita and Thisse (1996) provide an excellent summary of the literature.
2. See *L'Expansion* (1995).
3. Scitovsky (1954).
4. Hymer (1976) was the first to point out that a multinational firm needed a proprietary advantage over local firms in order to succeed abroad. This idea is still retained in the foreign direct investment literature. See Dunning (1988).
5. Dunning (1997).
6. *The Economist* (1998).
7. World Trade Organization (1997).
8. ibid. 9.
9. ibid. 2.
10. UNCTAD (1997).
11. ibid. 263.
12. Bank for International Settlements (1998).
13. Coase (1937).
14. *The Economist* (1998: 14).
15. ibid. 11.
16. ibid. 10.
17. Dumont and Meeusen (1999).

18. Demsetz (1997).
19. Sowell (1980).
20. Martin and Schumann (1997).
21. ibid. 9.
22. ibid. 10.
23. Dionne (1998) captures the attractions of the middle ground for voters in the United States, Britain, France, Italy, Portugal, the Netherlands, and Germany (perhaps) which are 'supporting parties that propose to put some limits on the free market and to offset some of the inequities it creates' while at the same time making 'large accommodations to the market-place and entrepreneurial capitalism'.
24. Goldsmith (1999).

REFERENCES

Bank for International Settlements (1998). *68ᵗʰ Annual Report*, June (Basle: BIS), 143.

Coase, R. H. (1937). 'The Nature of the Firm', *Economica*, 4: 386–405.

Demsetz, H. (1997). *The Economics of the Business Firm: Seven Critical Commentaries* (Cambridge: Cambridge University Press), 10.

Dionne E. J. (1998). 'Third Way is in Vogue on Both Sides of the Atlantic', *International Herald Tribune*, 11 Aug. 6.

Dumont, M., and Meeusen, W. (1999). 'The Impact of the RTD Policy of the EU on Technological Collaboration: A Case Study of the European Telecommunications Industry', in W. Meeusen (ed.), *Economic Policy in the European Union: Current Perspectives* (Cheltenham: Edward Elgar), 135–56.

Dunning, J. H. (1988). *Explaining International Production* (London: Unwin).

—— (1997). 'The European Internal Market Programme and Inbound Foreign Direct Investment', *Journal of Common Market Studies*, 35 1 (Mar.), 1–30.

The Economist (1998). 'Manufacturing Survey' (20 June), 1–22.

Fujita, M., and Thisse, J.-F. (1996). 'Economics of Agglomeration', *Journal of the Japanese and International Economies*, 10: 339–78.

Goldsmith, E. (1999). 'Is Free Trade Working for Everyone?' An exchange of letters with Jagdish Bhagwati, *Prospect* (Dec.), 16–20.

Hymer, S. (1976). *The International Operations of National Firms: A Study of Direct Foreign Investment* (Boston: MIT Press).

L'Expansion (1995). 'Le Triomphe des réseaux á l'Italienne', No. 505 (10–23 July), 88–91.

Martin, H. P., and Schumann, H. (1997). *The Global Trap: Globalisation & the Assault on Democracy & Prosperity* (London and New York: Zed Books Ltd; 1st pub. in German in 1996).

Scitovsky, T. (1954). 'Two Concepts of External Economies', *Journal of Political Economy*, 62: 143–51.

Sowell, T. (1980). *Knowledge and Decisions* (New York: Basic Books), 6–8.

UNCTAD (1997). *World Investment Report 1997* (Geneva: United Nations).

World Trade Organization (1997). *Annual Report 1997*, i and ii (Geneva: WTO).

7

(OECD)

Just How Big is Global Production Sharing?

ALEXANDER J. YEATS

F14 F13
F23 L23

1. Introduction: Basic Issues

Historically, the development of international production-sharing activities has been a major and evolving process.[1] In one of its earliest forms, this process involved the production of primary commodities in developing countries, shipment of these goods to industrial nations for further processing, and then the re-exportation (in part) of the processed product back to the primary-commodity-producing country. As an example, iron ore might be mined in Mauritania, shipped to Europe for processing into iron and steel products—some of which were then re-exported to Mauritania. In part these 'production-sharing' trade flows were based on comparative advantage (some commodity processing, such as the fabrication of metals from ores or petroleum refining, is highly capital intensive), but other factors such as 'escalation' in industrial countries' trade barriers also contributed to this exchange pattern.

In the mid-1960s a different form of production sharing between developing and industrial countries began to emerge. This involved the development of specialized labor-intensive production activities within vertically integrated *international* manufacturing industries. As an example, semiconductors, valves, tuners, and other components began to be assembled for international electronics firms in Hong Kong, Thailand, Malaysia, and Singapore. Wearing apparel and leather goods were also assembled in the Dominican Republic, Jamaica, and the Philippines for transnational firms. Among the many other industries where parts of a production process were transferred to developing countries were those making television and radio receivers, sewing machines, calculators and other office equipment, electrical machinery, power tools, machine tools and parts, typewriters, cameras, optical equipment, watches, brass valves, aircraft parts, telecommunications equipment, chemicals and synthetic fibers, and musical equipment.

How important in the aggregate have these overseas production arrangements now become? What are their characteristics, and is co-production a universal phenomenon spread evenly over countries and products? Secondly, what caused the growth in this exchange and can particular characteristics of products and policies that were instrumental in promoting these opportunities be identified? Thirdly, what have been the effects of overseas production on home and host economies? In particular, have these operations resulted in sizeable employment losses in high-wage countries, or have they actually been a source of net job creation in the industries manufacturing and exporting production inputs? These are among the crucial questions relating to international production-sharing operations. The present chapter will focus almost entirely on the first: just how big is current global production sharing and has its relative importance been growing or declining?[2]

A major difficulty one previously faced in attempting to assess the magnitude and nature of global production sharing is that international trade data generally have not differentiated between components and assembled products. Identification of the former is crucial since these items are being shipped from one country to another for further processing. With this the case, it was not possible to determine the actual location where components and parts were being produced, the direction and composition of their exchange, or the magnitude of this trade. However, revisions to the *Standard International Trade Classification* system (*SITC*—both Revision 2 and 3) now make it somewhat easier to tabulate intra-industry trade in components within several broad industry groups. A second source is data compiled in connection with the use of special OECD tariff provisions that provide for preferential access for the re-entry of domestically produced components assembled abroad. Using these data sources jointly one can provide some estimates of the importance of global production sharing in international trade.

2. The Evidence from Trade in Components

In its original form the SITC classification system did a very inadequate job of distinguishing between trade in final goods and trade in components. At the lower (five-digit) level the SITC Revision 1 identified about 800 individual products—10 of which consisted only of 'parts' or components. However, in the late 1970s and early 1980s many countries shifted to the SITC Revision 2 system which greatly expanded the number of product groups composed solely of components. The coverage of these items was most complete within the machinery and transport equipment group (SITC 7) where about 50 individual three, four, and five-digit groups consist solely of components of other manufactured equipment.[3] Outside this sector the SITC still fails to differentiate sufficiently between assembled goods and components, so meaningful tabulations of the magnitude of trade in parts cannot be made. Furthermore, many developing countries did not shift to the SITC Revision 2 trade classification system until the early or mid-1980s so it was not possible to fully monitor non-OECD exports of components outside the recent period.

Table 7.1 utilizes this new data source to show the composition and relative importance of individual SITC 7 product groups, which consist solely of parts and components. The table identifies each product group by SITC (Rev. 2) number, it provides a description of each item, and also indicates the 1995 value of OECD imports. To help assess the relative importance of each product, its share in all parts and component imports is also shown. Appendix 7.1 provides similar statistics for OECD exports of these goods. Finally, the table also provides a measure of the net OECD trade balance for each individual item. The latter has been computed as the difference between OECD exports and imports of each good expressed as a percentage of OECD exports.[4]

Perhaps a key feature of this trade is that imports (and exports—see App. 7.1) are concentrated in a relatively few product groups. Specifically, Table 7.1 shows that 4 of the 44 SITC product groups account jointly for over 70 percent of total trade in components with parts of motor vehicles alone (SITC 784) accounting for over $91 billion, or about one-quarter of the total exchange in these goods. Outside this one group, parts of office machinery (SITC 759) and of telecommunications equipment (SITC 764) jointly account for about 35 percent of total trade with parts of switch gear (SITC 773) adding a further 10 percent. Outside these four groups the largest remaining products generally account for no more than 1 to 5 percent of the total (parts of aircraft, parts of internal combustion engines, and so on) with a few items, like parts of internal combustion engines, parts of wire-making machinery, or parts of grain-milling machinery representing less than one-tenth of a percent of total trade in these goods. Table 7.5 (see below) provides more information on the relative importance of trade in more aggregate two-digit SITC product groups.

TABLE 7.1. The 1995 value and share of OECD imports of parts and components
identified in the SITC Revision 2 system

SITC (Rev. 2)—Description		Trade balance (%)*	1995 Value of imports ($ million)	Share of total (%)
711.9	Parts of steam boilers and auxiliary plants	66.5	464.2	0.13
713.19	Parts of aircraft internal combustion engines	21.4	281.5	0.08
713.9	Parts of internal combustion engine, nes	27.2	13,142.2	3.59
714.9	Parts of engines and motors, nes	14.8	12,343.5	3.37
716.9	Parts of rotating electric motors	39.3	2,315.1	0.63
718.89	Parts of water turbines and hydraulic motors	69.4	126.1	0.03
721.19	Parts of cultivating equipment	−16.3	563.8	0.15
721.29	Parts of harvesting machinery	−10.3	1,054.2	0.29
721.39	Parts of dairy machinery	7.1	459.0	0.13
721.98	Parts of wine-making machinery	50.0	14.8	0.00
721.99	Parts of other agricultural machinery, nes	26.1	310.6	0.08
723.9	Parts of construction machinery	75.2	1,440.2	0.39
724.49	Parts of spinning and extruding machinery	45.8	921.2	0.25
724.69	Parts of looms and knitting machinery	29.0	1,245.7	0.34
724.79	Parts of textile machinery, nes	24.3	576.4	0.16
725.9	Parts of paper-making machinery	34.2	1,917.6	0.52
726.89	Parts of bookbinding machinery	−4.0	182.1	0.05
726.9	Parts of printing and typesetting machinery	20.8	1,710.2	0.47
727.19	Parts of grain-milling machinery	37.2	117.7	0.03
727.29	Parts of food-processing machinery	−300.0	32.2	0.01
728.19	Parts of machine tools for special industries	22.5	695.7	0.19
728.39	Parts of mineral-working machinery	48.2	995.2	0.27
728.49	Parts of machines for special industries, nes	38.1	6,078.9	1.66
736.9	Parts of machine tools for metal working	26.2	3,084.8	0.84
737.19	Parts of foundry equipment	39.6	391.8	0.11
741.49	Parts of refrigerating equipment	19.8	1,425.4	0.39
742.9	Parts of pumps for liquids	13.5	3,423.0	0.94
743.9	Parts of centrifuges and filters	23.9	4,851.9	1.33
744.19	Parts of fork-lift trucks	53.3	70.3	0.02
744.9	Parts of lifting and loading machines	22.6	9,025.7	2.47
745.19	Parts of power hand tools	−5.3	516.2	0.14
749.99	Parts of non-electric machinery, nes	49.9	1,694.4	0.46
759	Parts of office and adding machinery	−12.7	68,964.4	18.85
764	Parts of telecommunications equipment	19.0	64,874.2	17.73

TABLE 7.1. *Continued*

SITC (Rev. 2)—Description	Trade balance (%)*	1995 Value of imports ($ million)	Share of total (%)
771.29 Parts of electric power machinery	47.1	1,388.1	0.38
772 Parts of switch gear	23.0	37,822.1	10.34
775.79 Parts of domestic electrical equipment	1.2	641.0	0.18
778.29 Parts of electric lamps and bulbs	30.9	399.6	0.11
778.89 Parts of electrical machinery, nes	24.4	3,624.8	0.99
784 Parts of motor vehicles and accessories	16.7	91,611.0	25.04
785.39 Parts of carriages and cycles	2.3	3,625.7	0.99
786.89 Parts of trailers and non-motor vehicles	−4.8	1,867.3	0.51
791.99 Parts of railroad equipment and vehicles	16.2	1,860.1	0.51
792.9 Parts of aircraft and helicopters	27.1	17,656.3	4.83
All above items	17.2	365,806.0	100.00

Note: *Exports of the item less imports divided by exports and multiplied by 100.

Overall, Table 7.1 shows that OECD countries generally record a positive trade balance for almost all of the individual product groups with total OECD exports of components ($442 billion) exceeding imports ($365 billion) by about 17 percent. This pattern is not unexpected since most assembly operations are labor intensive in nature and non-OECD (developing) countries generally have a comparative advantage in this type of activity. In only 6 of the 44 product groups is this trade pattern reversed with the most noteworthy exception occurring for office and adding machine parts (SITC 759) where OECD imports ($69 billion) exceed exports by about 13 percent.

A key question relating to these data is how great is the relative importance of trade in parts and components within several broader product groups. Table 7.2 provides some evidence on the importance of trade in components within the entire machinery and transport (SITC 7) sector. The top half of the table shows the global export value of parts and components of machinery and transport equipment for selected years from 1978 to 1995. The lower half shows the share of these items in all SITC 7 exports for each year. Both sets of figures testify as to the global importance of this exchange. In 1995 OECD exports of transport and machinery components and parts surpassed $440 billion, which was about 30 percent of all traded SITC 7 products.[5] Although US exports of these goods ($102 billion) were about one-half those of the EU, their share (about 40 percent) was considerably higher than in either the EU

TABLE 7.2. The direction of trade for OECD countries' exports of parts and components

Exporter	Partner	Year			
		1978	1985	1990	1995
		(Values in US$ millions)			
OECD	World	84,418	142,704	293,499	441,531
	OECD	54,327	100,219	221,111	298,829
	Non-OECD	30,091	42,485	72,387	142,701
EEC12	World	43,554	60,891	139,656	199,941
	OECD	28,915	43,889	112,928	147,502
	Non-OECD	14,640	17,002	26,729	52,439
Japan	World	8,850	21,617	49,104	81,442
	OECD	3,970	13,464	32,329	44,982
	Non-OECD	4,880	8,152	16,775	36,459
USA	World	21,705	40,992	68,187	102,009
	OECD	13,204	26,552	45,228	61,140
	Non-OECD	8,501	14,440	22,959	40,869
Memo Item: intra-RTA					
EEC12	EEC12	20,483	28,817	81,390	102,525
NAFTA	NAFTA	31,634	64,915	103,753	188,667
EFTA	EFTA	3,642	4,713	9,773	11,332
		Percentage of total SITC 7			
OECD	World	26.1	28.9	28.9	30.0
	OECD	26.5	28.2	28.7	29.8
	Non-OECD	25.4	30.6	29.2	30.6
EEC12	World	26.2	28.7	27.0	27.9
	OECD	25.8	27.3	26.9	27.2
	Non-OECD	27.0	33.2	27.4	29.9
Japan	World	15.2	18.1	24.2	26.2
	OECD	13.2	17.4	24.8	27.6
	Non-OECD	17.3	19.5	23.3	24.7
USA	World	36.6	43.5	39.5	39.8
	OECD	40.0	44.5	39.9	41.4
	Non-OECD	32.3	41.6	38.9	37.6
Memo Item: intra-RTA					
EEC12	EEC12	26.3	28.1	27.1	26.8
NAFTA	NAFTA	38.5	37.9	37.1	32.6
EFTA	EFTA	26.0	26.3	28.6	34.6

Source: Computed from United Nations COMTRADE database.

or Japan. Japan, however, had the most rapid growth in the relative importance of these exports with their share increasing from about 15 to 26 percent over the 17 year period.[6]

What role did regional economic groupings like the European Union or EFTA play in the growth of this exchange? The preferential reduction of trade barriers in regional arrangements may have caused trade in components to rise faster than in trade with third countries. Also, because of the formal regional arrangements, trade with other member countries might be viewed as being somehow more 'secure' or less likely to encounter disruptions or new restrictions than trade with non-members. If 'risk' considerations are a major factor in the decision as to where to 'source' basic industry components, this could have favored intra-block trade in these goods. However, if this exchange is primarily motivated by considerations such as wage differentials, rising costs (particularly in Europe) could be a factor working against increased intra-block production sharing.

The data in Table 7.2 (see the memo item) show that in 1995 intra-block trade of the three regional groups accounted for 69 percent ($302.5 billion) of the total OECD exports of components to all destinations—up from about 66 percent in the late 1970s. However, the data do not indicate that there are important differences in the share of components in trade within or outside the regional blocks. For example, in 1995, 27.9 percent of EC global exports of transport and machinery products consisted of components and parts as opposed to these products' 26.8 percent share in intra-EU trade.

Overall, Table 7.2 shows that the share of components in total OECD SITC 7 exports has steadily increased over the period 1978 to 1995 and, at 30 percent, now stands about four percentage points above its earlier levels. Although the available data do not allow one to accurately track trends in developing countries' exports of these products during the 1980s, the available information indicates they were growing rapidly and were of major importance by the beginning of the 1990s. In 1995 shipments of components from developing countries exceeded $100 billion (this was about one-quarter of the total value of exports of these goods from the OECD), with Singapore having exports of $22 billion and Taiwan (China), Republic of Korea, Malaysia, and Mexico all having shipments in excess of $10 billion. These trends clearly signal the increasing interdependence of production-sharing operations in the whole machinery and transport sectors, as industries in one country become increasingly reliant on suppliers in another for essential manufacturing inputs.

TABLE 7.3. The major destinations of OECD countries' exports of parts and components

Importing country	1978		1995	
	Value ($ million)	Share	Value ($ million)	Share
United States	9,753.3	11.55	66,046.7	14.96
Germany	22,820.4	27.03	37,460.6	8.48
United Kingdom	4,135.7	4.90	29,616.1	6.71
Canada	7,203.9	8.53	27,029.6	6.12
France	5,282.0	6.26	24,558.1	5.56
Netherlands	3,074.9	3.64	15,648.3	3.54
Belgium	4,033.7	4.78	14,747.8	3.34
Mexico	1,851.7	2.19	13,377.6	3.03
Spain	1,342.1	1.59	12,195.7	2.76
Italy	2,533.6	3.00	11,947.9	2.71
Japan	1,099.5	1.30	11,717.4	2.65
China	193.3	0.23	10,668.0	2.42
Singapore	863.1	1.02	9,735.9	2.21
Korea	1,362.6	1.61	9,463.3	2.14
Hong Kong	553.9	0.66	8,553.6	1.94
Sweden	1,706.7	2.02	8,018.3	1.82
Taiwan (China)	927.3	1.10	7,734.4	1.75
Thailand	395.7	0.47	7,196.6	1.63
Switzerland	1,242.7	1.47	6,514.5	1.48
Australia	1,478.4	1.75	6,211.1	1.41
Austria	1,160.4	1.37	5,943.2	1.35
Malaysia	324.7	0.38	5,917.2	1.34
Brazil	1,398.7	1.66	5,150.1	1.17
Indonesia	463.7	0.55	4,617.5	1.05
South Africa	1,351.2	1.60	4,007.1	0.91
Ireland	495.4	0.59	3,718.9	0.84
Denmark	861.3	1.02	3,352.8	0.76
Norway	812.5	0.96	3,084.4	0.70
Saudi Arabia	1,893.3	2.24	3,037.8	0.69
Finland	549.0	0.65	2,879.8	0.65

Source: Computed from United Nations COMTRADE database.

Table 7.3 offers a different perspective on the OECD trade in components by identifying the 30 largest destinations for this exchange in 1995. For comparison, similar statistics on these countries' imports are also reported for 1978.[7] Germany and the United States were by far the largest markets for these goods in the earlier period when they received about 40 percent of all shipments, although their combined share fell

TABLE 7.4. The relative importance of parts and components in individual countries' imports

Country	1995 imports in US$ million				Share of parts and components in		
	Parts and components	Transport and machinery (SITC 7)	All manufactures	All goods	Total imports	Imports of manufactures	Transport and machinery
High income countries							
Canada	30,191	84,551	135,703	164,327	18.4	22.2	35.7
Singapore	22,528	71,992	103,285	124,503	18.1	21.8	31.3
Ireland	5,106	13,650	24,483	32,322	15.8	20.9	37.4
Oman	645	1,672	2,896	4,249	15.2	22.3	38.6
United Kingdom	37,317	107,874	209,214	262,572	14.2	17.8	34.6
Sweden	8,250	24,321	50,382	64,446	12.8	16.4	33.9
Australia	7,174	26,939	49,133	57,423	12.5	14.6	26.6
United States	94,597	357,625	607,992	770,822	12.3	15.6	26.5
Spain	13,374	40,284	80,235	113,399	11.8	16.7	33.2
Hong Kong	22,793	71,542	170,630	196,072	11.6	13.4	31.9
Norway	3,754	12,307	25,973	32,706	11.5	14.5	30.5
Finland	3,348	11,415	21,867	29,520	11.3	15.3	29.3
Germany	47,497	152,151	324,068	443,224	10.7	14.7	31.2
Austria	6,356	23,529	51,385	62,009	10.3	12.4	27.0
France	27,768	96,726	208,091	273,387	10.2	13.3	28.7

Netherlands	15,209	51,947	113,405	157,929	9.6	13.4	29.3
Portugal	3,212	11,327	24,169	33,565	9.6	13.3	28.4
Kuwait	745	3,213	6,294	7,790	9.6	11.8	23.2
Denmark	3,974	13,806	31,362	41,626	9.5	12.7	28.8
Israel	2,624	9,611	23,147	28,344	9.3	11.3	27.3
Other countries							
French Guinea	153	330	575	783	19.6	26.7	46.5
Thailand	11,408	33,730	56,993	71,156	16.0	20.0	33.8
Mexico	11,496	31,693	59,246	73,993	15.5	19.4	36.3
Indonesia	6,037	16,257	29,506	40,629	14.9	20.5	37.1
Malaysia	10,853	46,078	64,382	77,046	14.1	16.9	23.6
South Africa	3,715	12,143	21,081	27,737	13.4	17.6	30.6
Argentina	2,622	8,931	17,186	20,122	13.0	15.3	29.4
China	15,585	52,436	103,652	132,084	11.8	15.0	29.7
Philippines	3,130	9,238	16,462	28,487	11.0	19.0	33.9
Cent. Afr. Rep.	29	112	171	265	11.0	17.1	26.0
Brazil	5,865	21,020	38,160	53,737	10.9	15.4	27.9
Colombia	1,474	5,171	10,768	13,863	10.6	13.7	28.5
Czech Republic	2,591	9,108	19,582	25,303	10.2	13.2	28.4
Honduras	172	503	1,270	1,728	9.9	13.5	34.2
Algeria	954	2,990	6,353	9,831	9.7	15.0	31.9

Note: Countries have been ranked on the basis of the share of 'parts and components' in total imports of all goods.
Source: United Nations COMTRADE statistics.

to about 23 percent in 1995. However, the trend for the United States differed from that of Germany—US imports of components rose about sixfold over the period 1978 to 1995 while those going to Germany expanded at a far slower pace. The appreciation of the German mark, along with rapidly rising labor costs, were undoubtedly factors slowing the assembly of components in Germany.

A further point evident in Table 7.3 is how important international trade in components has become to some developing countries. Developing countries constitute 11 of the 30 largest markets for these goods with 1995 combined imports of Mexico and China being approximately $25 billion. The growth of this exchange in China's trade is the fastest of that for any of the major countries (i.e. Chinese imports of components rose from just under $200 million in 1978 to $10.7 billion in 1995— a compound annual growth rate in excess of 26 percent).

Table 7.4 provides a different perspective on the relative importance of individual countries' imports of SITC 7 parts and components in: (i) imports of all goods (that is, SITC 0 through 9); (ii) all manufactured goods (SITC 5 through 8 less 68); and (iii) all transport and machinery products (SITC 7). The table shows the value of each country's imports of each group as well as the share of parts and components within each total. The reader should again recall that the SITC does not do an adequate job of identifying 'parts' outside SITC 7 so the comparisons with total imports, and with imports of all manufactures, clearly understate the true importance of this exchange.

For each of the 35 countries listed in Table 7.4, components accounted for at least 27 percent of total SITC 7 exports which, with the exception of Israel, represents 10 percent or more of total imports of all goods. Imports of components account for 30 percent or more of total transport and machinery imports for about one-half of the countries in the table and reach a high of 46 percent for French Guinea. Appendix 7.2 provides similar statistics for individual OECD countries' exports.

What major individual product groups are of primary importance in trade in components? Table 7.5 provides some additional aggregated information by tabulating the 1978 and 1995 value of component product exports within each of the two-digit SITC subgroups which constitute all machinery and transport equipment (SITC 7)—see Table 7.1 for underlying data for individual products. Road motor vehicles parts account for over one-quarter ($115 billion) of the total exchange followed by telecommunications and office machinery ($61 billion) whose share is 18 percent.[8] With an annual growth rate of 16 percent, component exports of the latter subgroup expanded at an annual rate that was

TABLE 7.5. The composition of OECD countries' exports of parts and components

Parts and components group	1978		1995		Compound growth rate(%)
	Value ($ million)	Share (%)	Value ($ million)	Share (%)	
Power generating equipment	9,906	11.7	38,496	8.7	8.3
Machines for special industries	9,830	11.6	30,480	6.9	6.8
Metalworking machinery	1,219	1.4	4,832	1.1	8.4
General industrial machinery	5,080	6.0	27,797	6.3	10.5
Office machinery	4,943	5.9	61,172	13.9	15.9
Telecommunications equipment	12,364	14.6	79,101	17.9	11.5
Electrical machinery	9,428	11.2	57,753	13.1	11.3
Road vehicles	26,694	31.6	115,449	26.1	9.0
Other transport equipment	4,954	5.9	26,450	6.0	10.3
All above components groups	84,418	100.0	441,531	100.0	10.2
Memo item					
All transport and machinery (SITC 7)	323,925		1,470,292		9.3
Components share of total	26.1		30.0		

Source: Computed from United Nations COMTRADE database.

6 percent higher than that for all components and parts, and 7 percent higher than that for the total SITC 7 group.

3. Tariff Provisions for Offshore Assembly

A second source of information on international production sharing is statistics on tariff-induced *offshore assembly processing (OAP)* activity in international trade.

Specifically, most industrial countries' tariff schedules provide special favorable treatment for domestically produced components that are shipped abroad for further processing and then reimported into the home country (see App. 7.3). Data compiled by the US International Trade Commission indicate that the value of these goods ($74 billion) accounted for about 16 percent of all US imports in 1989, but there are various reasons why the recent available data understate the importance of this exchange.[9] Specifically, a considerable volume of US imports are already exempt from customs duties under special programs like the *Generalized System of Preferences (GSP)* or *Caribbean Basin Initiative (CBI)*. In these cases, foreign suppliers have no incentive to apply for the special tariff treatment so any production sharing in goods receiving these preferences would go unreported. Similarly, the United States recently negotiated a free trade arrangement with Mexico and Canada (NAFTA) that allows imports from these countries to enter the United States free of tariffs. Again, in this case, Mexican and Canadian suppliers would have no incentive to apply for this special OAP treatment. As such, there is reason to believe that the available data considerably understate the magnitude and importance of production sharing that occurs under these special tariff provisions.[10]

Table 7.6 employs the available US data sources on this OAP activity to examine the composition of 1993 and 1994 imports of assembled goods in terms of major product categories. About 40 percent of this exchange consists of road motor vehicle parts assembled abroad ($23 billion in 1994) followed by microelectronic components (such as assembled circuit boards—$8 billion) and apparel ($6 billion).[11] The fact that reported assembled road motor vehicle imports declined by about $2.2 billion is likely due to a loss of accuracy in the underlying statistics. The decline seems largely attributable to the fact that Canadian assemblers had no incentive to report this trade under the special US OAP tariff provisions when these goods became duty free under the US–Canadian free trade arrangement.

TABLE 7.6. United States 1993 and 1994 imports under HTS provision 9802.00.80 by major industry groups

Industry group	Value($ million)			Share of total
	1993	1994	1993–94 change	
Auto, trucks, and buses	25,315.5	23,095.4	−2,220.1	39.3
Microelectronic components	6,555.4	8,226.4	1,671.0	14.0
Apparel	5,034.1	6,029.9	995.8	10.3
Auto parts including engines	3,290.6	3,066.7	−223.9	5.2
Wiring harnesses for vehicles	1,973.9	2,861.3	887.4	4.9
Television receivers	2,254.5	2,607.1	352.6	4.4
Radio, TV, and phone equipment	1,415.6	1,807.4	391.8	3.1
Medical and scientific instruments	1,302.2	1,425.9	123.7	2.4
All other manufactures	1,526.9	1,349.1	−177.8	2.3
Computers	1,692.9	1,306.9	−386.0	2.2
Footwear	1,134.5	1,142.7	8.2	1.9
Other transport equipment	1,388.4	1,141.3	−247.1	1.9
Heating and air conditioners	877.3	1,047.4	170.1	1.8
Other machinery	855.4	800.8	−54.6	1.4
Electrical motors	585.9	717.0	131.1	1.2
Filtering equipment	362.9	705.9	343.0	1.2
Motor vehicle seats	120.5	640.1	519.6	1.1
Transformers	551.9	486.9	−65.0	0.8
Other textile articles	276.6	292.8	16.2	0.5
Total	56,515.1	58,750.9	2,235.8	100.0
Memo item				
Total US imports of selected products				
Auto, trucks, and buses	63,948	72,968	9,021	
Apparel	35,822	38,861	3,040	
Television receivers	2,800	3,632	832	
Footwear	11,183	11,697	514	
Medical and scientific instruments	14,161	16,556	2,395	

Source: Compiled from official statistics of the Department of Commerce and UN COMTRADE database.

Table 7.6 also illustrates the overall importance of production sharing by comparing the value of OAP imports of selected product groups with the total value of all imports of these same goods (see the memo item). For example, in 1993 OAP imports of automobiles and trucks ($25.3 billion) accounted for 40 percent of the total US imports ($63.9 billion) of these goods while 14 percent of all US clothing imports were from domestically produced components assembled abroad. However, OAP activity is actually involved in $2.6 billion of 1994 imports of television receivers which represents over 70 percent of the total imports of this one product group.

Table 7.7 provides a different view on the importance of this special tariff-induced OAP trade—this time from the perspective of individual exporting countries that utilize these tariff provisions. Specifically, the second and third columns of the table show the value and share of components in all US imports of foreign-assembled goods from individual developed and developing countries. This share ranges from a high of 80 percent for Jamaica down to about 2 percent for Sweden, Germany, or Belgium.[12]

Quite obviously, tariff savings are not the key factor motivating trade with the latter three OECD countries—non-tariff-related cost saving or other technical aspects of production were certainly at work, as well as the necessity of establishing a physical presence in foreign markets in order to properly service domestic customers.[13] Finally, the three right-hand columns are designed to indicate the importance of this trade to the exporting countries. Specifically, these columns show: (i) the total US import value of OAP goods, (ii) the total value of all US imports from each country, and (iii) the share of OAP products in total imports.

The major point evident in Table 7.7 concerns the importance of assembly operations in the total exports of some of the (primarily developing) countries. Over 50 percent of Haitian, Dominican Republic, and El Salvador's exports to the United States consist of assembled products—the share is over 40 percent in the case of Jamaica and Mexico. Perhaps the most surprising point emerging from Table 7.7, however, is the importance of OAP activity in the total exports from some of the *industrial* countries. Specifically, between 16 and 18 percent of all US imports from Sweden and Germany involve the return of domestically produced components which have been assembled in these countries. As previously noted, this is likely associated with the need for transnational firms to establish a presence in the major markets they serve. In doing so there may be advantages in utilizing components produced in the country where sales of the final good are made.

4. Some Perspectives on South–North Production Sharing

What factors contributed to the development of North–South production sharing (OAP) activity reflected in the previous tables? This exchange has been especially important for many developing countries in that it provided a far easier means for implementing 'outward-oriented'

TABLE 7.7. The importance of offshore assembly processing (OAP) activity in US imports and trading partner exports in 1994

Exporter	US content of foreign assembled goods		Imports from trading partner		
	Value ($ million)	Share of assembled goods (%)	Value of assembled goods ($ million)	Imports of all products ($ million)	Share of assembled goods in all imports (%)
Haiti	25	71.4	35	62	56.5
Dominican Rep.	1,109	65.0	1,707	3,166	53.9
El Salvador	175	54.3	322	635	50.7
Jamaica	306	80.5	380	790	48.1
Mexico	11,508	50.2	22,944	50,280	45.6
Honduras	326	72.1	452	1,175	38.5
Costa Rica	411	66.0	623	1,767	35.3
Guatemala	219	48.6	451	1,386	32.5
Philippines	640	46.5	1,377	6,025	22.9
Germany	121	2.1	5,857	32,685	17.9
Sweden	17	2.0	859	5,243	16.4
Belgium	16	1.6	1,018	6,861	14.8
Malaysia	968	49.9	1,940	14,415	13.5
Japan	472	4.5	10,481	122,466	8.6
Korea	479	27.8	1,723	20,374	8.5
Singapore	335	27.3	1,229	15,651	7.9
Colombia	147	58.3	252	3,386	7.4
Thailand	353	59.4	594	10,799	5.5
United Kingdom	109	9.0	1,211	25,811	4.7
Taiwan (China)	372	32.0	1,161	27,940	4.2
France	78	11.0	708	17,316	4.1
Austria	24	40.0	60	1,811	3.3
Hong Kong	135	41.0	329	10,141	3.2
Spain	18	15.5	116	3,810	3.0
Indonesia	47	22.9	205	7,020	2.9
Netherlands	38	23.9	159	6,358	2.5
Ireland	17	25.8	66	2,953	2.2
Brazil	17	11.6	147	9,265	1.6
China	73	12.1	601	41,364	1.5
Australia	3	7.3	41	3,423	1.2
Canada	456	35.3	1,292	130,405	1.0
India	4	8.0	50	5,663	0.9
Italy	12	17.4	69	15,440	0.4
Other developing	93	47.4	196	n/a	n/a
Other developed	14	14.6	96	n/a	n/a
Total	19,137	32.6	58,751		

growth strategies, since an associated firm, located in an industrial country, handles marketing and distribution functions. Evidence compiled by the US International Trade Corporation suggests four factors contributed to this production sharing.

4.1. *The Influence of OECD Trade Barriers*

In the 1960s there was general pessimism concerning the ability of many developing countries to expand foreign exchange earnings due to poor prospects for traditional commodity exports and OECD trade barriers against exports of labor-intensive manufactures. For example, in the late 1960s industrial countries' tariffs on exports from countries like the Republic of Korea, Hong Kong, Singapore, and Taiwan (China) averaged about 17 percent, reaching a high of 19.5 percent in the United Kingdom (see Table 7.8). OECD tariffs also discriminated against developing countries, as reflected in the higher than average tariffs on their exports. In addition, GSP schemes had not yet been adopted, so Mexico, the newly industrialized Asian and the Caribbean countries—where production sharing made its earliest appearance—had to compete with other suppliers on an equal most-favored-nation basis.

In this environment developing countries had major incentives to adopt measures favoring labor-intensive activities. Furthermore, many developing countries realized OECD firms which stood to benefit from such production sharing would have a major incentive to help resist demands for new protection against goods manufactured in such a production-sharing arrangement.[14] This led to active involvement by

TABLE 7.8. Average levels of OECD countries' tariffs in the mid-1960s

Import market	Mid-1960 tariff averages on total imports of manufactures	Mid-1960 tariff averages on imports of manufactures from developing countries
United States	11.5	17.9
United Kingdom	15.2	19.5
European Community	11.0	14.3
Sweden	6.6	9.8
Japan	16.1	18.0
All industrial countries	10.9	17.1

Source: UNCTAD, *The Kennedy Round Estimated Effects on Tariff Barriers* (TD/6/Rev. 1) (New York: United Nations, 1968).

developing countries' governments in efforts to attract this type of activity (see Section 4.4) and involvement on the part of transnational firms to promote tariff-induced OAP development.

4.2. *Labor Costs*

One major factor that facilitated the early development of OAP production sharing was marked differences in wage rates between developed and developing countries. In the 1970s wages in most of the Caribbean countries, Mexico, and Latin America ranged between 60 and 80 percent below those in the United States. By drawing on these foreign labor sources US corporations could both enhance their own profitability from domestic sales and also increase their ability to compete in third markets due to lower overall production costs.

Recent production sharing in Europe appears to have been driven by similar economic incentives—often involving wage differentials—and considerations such as those motivating earlier production sharing in North America. To remain competitive in international markets, manufacturers in high labor cost regions of Europe moved some of their more labor-intensive production and assembly operations to neighboring countries with lower labor costs (see Table 7.9). In addition to low labor costs, factors such as labor skills and education, adequate transportation and financial infrastructure, and technical training were important in determining the magnitude and direction of this OAP activity in Europe. Moreover, EU firms have used offshore processing to gain access to new markets, particularly in Central Europe. In addition to geographic proximity, Table 7.9 suggests that the combined effect of low wages and high literacy rates may have helped the former socialist countries in Europe attract most of the European Union's new OAP processing contracts during the period 1991 to 1994.

4.3. *Transport and Distance*

Products that have high value relative to their bulk, and therefore have transport costs which make up a very small proportion of their total value, are the most suitable for assembly abroad. Although international freight and insurance charges average about 5 to 6 percent of the value of all US imports (Yeats, 1989), the rates ranged from about 2 percent on watches and jewelry to 20 to 40 percent for furniture and some wood manufactures. Other studies also found that major differences

TABLE 7.9. Hourly compensation, GDP per capita, and literacy rates in European and Central European countries

Country	Hourly wage costs (US dollars)	GDP per capita (US dollars)	Literacy rate (%)
Top five EU OAP importers			
Germany	25.70	16,500	99
France	16.23	18,200	99
Italy	16.00	16,700	97
Netherlands	19.95	17,200	99
United Kingdom	12.76	16,900	98
Average	18.13	17,100	98
Leading five non-OECD sources			
Poland	1.10	4,680	98
Hungary	1.48	5,500	99
Czech Republic	1.23	7,200	97
Romania	n/a	2,700	98
Slovenia	n/a	7,600	98
Average	1.27	5,536	98

Source: USITC Publication 2966. *Production Sharing: Use of U.S. Components and Materials in Foreign Assembly Operations, 1991–94* (Washington: USITC, May 1996)

often exist in nominal freight rates for similar goods shipped from different countries and have a major impact on the competitive position of exporters. As an example, Yeats (1981) determined that transport costs for apparel exports from Indonesia to the United States were about 25 percent higher, on average, than those on similar products shipped from Malaysia. This point is important since even small variations in international transport costs can have an important influence on the location of global production and export volumes.[15]

Adverse transport costs appear to be one reason why sub-Saharan Africa has generally failed to participate in OAP activity—in spite of the very low prevailing wages. For example, Table 7.10 reports international transport charges for all 1993 sub-Saharan African exports to the United States. Individual product freight rates for all export items were ranked in ascending order and their quartile values computed. In addition, freight costs for shipments of the same goods from other suppliers were computed in order to determine how much extra Africa pays above other exporters.

Specifically, the table shows that half the nominal vessel freight rates for middle-income West Africa (10 percent) are about 2 percentage points higher than those paid by other exporters of the same goods.[16] To

TABLE 7.10. Level, distribution, and range of African freight costs for exports to the United States, 1993

Region[a]	Transport mode	Nominal freight rates for African exports (%)				African transport cost margin (median[a]—percentage points)
		Quartile values			Range	
		First	Median	Third		
All sub-Saharan Africa	Air	5.3	14.1	26.5	0.5–87.4	3.5
	Vessel	4.6	7.5	13.8	0.2–56.1	1.1
Low-income East and Southern Africa	Air	3.7	9.2	23.6	0.7–56.9	4.4
	Vessel	4.2	7.1	13.8	0.2–55.9	1.2
Low-income West Africa	Air	3.7	20.5	35.6	0.4–92.6	7.4
	Vessel	3.5	9.3	19.4	0.2–89.7	1.1
Middle-income East and Southern Africa	Air	2.5	8.0	16.4	0.9–29.7	0.9
	Vessel	3.8	6.2	8.9	0.7–17.5	0.8
Middle-income West Africa	Air	7.3	13.3	24.2	0.4–43.1	3.0
	Vessel	4.9	10.0	12.8	2.3–50.6	1.9

Note: Trade flows of less than $50,000 have been excluded from these comparisons. See World Bank (1995) for a listing of the African countries included in each region while Amjadi and Yeats (1995) describe the procedures used in estimating these freight costs.
[a] Median transport costs are the difference between African freight rates and those on competitors' products. Positive values reflect adverse African transport costs.
Source: US Department of the Census data.

put this in perspective, the Uruguay Round achieved an average 2.4 percentage point reduction in industrial country tariffs. Moreover, in every instance there is a larger adverse margin for air freight than for vessel shipments. African air transport, at first glance, appears to be relatively less cost efficient than vessel freight. Finally, the third-quartile values indicate that some African exports encounter very high transport costs. About 25 percent of Africa's air exports have freight rates exceeding 26 percent and a quarter of low-income West Africa's vessel shipments have nominal rates of more than 19 percent. These comparisons clearly show that international transport costs have a significant adverse impact on the region's ability to participate in international production sharing.[17]

4.4. *Governmental Influences*

As previously noted, governmental policies have a major impact on the location and extent of production sharing between developed and developing countries. Specifically, special OECD tariffs for foreign-assembled goods played a major role in stimulating this exchange (see App. 7.3).[18] However, developing countries' own governmental policies are almost certainly more important. Special incentives are frequently offered to industrial exporters by the governments of the less developed countries which have taken the form of tax holidays, credits, and rebates; subsidized credit, rent, and other infrastructure; direct and indirect export subsidies of various types; freedom from import duties or exchange controls. Indirect governmental policies that improved literacy rates and the quality of the workforce, or which promoted the development of adequate transport and communications systems may be equally important (Apps. 7.4 and 7.5 provide an assessment of the role these measures played in promoting OAP activity in the Caribbean).

Risk is a further factor contributing to decisions as to where production-sharing activity will be located. Risks include all of the usual dangers for foreign investors—exchange risk, nationalization without adequate compensation, political disruptions, and so forth. To these must be added risks resulting from the decision to separate production processes from one another in those circumstances where this has not previously been the practice. The international vertical integration of industry increases the risk associated with supply disruption in a single overseas location, for it can bring the entire international production to a halt. Such disruptions could be the product of shipping delays, political disturbances, strikes, or take the form of loss of quality control. Disruption of component supplies is apparently perceived by potential

TABLE 7.11. 1995 imports of parts and components as a share of production and apparent consumption of machinery and transport equipment in the EU, Japan, and United States

Market	Sector	Components imports as a share of (%)	
		Apparent consumption	Production
European Union	Transport and machinery	15.6	14.1
Japan	Transport and machinery	8.4	6.7
North America	Transport and machinery	10.6	11.6

investors of this type as the primary risk.[19] Appendix 7.5 examines the extent to which these factors have influenced the location of production sharing and manufacturing activity within the Caribbean region. This information is intended to show why some countries participated while others did not and how important the overall extent of this activity has been.

5. How Big is Global Production Sharing?

If, at this point, one returns to the question of how big is global production sharing, the answer clearly is 'very big'! The available data on trade in machinery and transport equipment components showed these items comprised about 30 percent of the total exchange and that trade in these goods was growing at a faster pace than the overall SITC 7 total. Various 'yardsticks' are available for measuring the importance of international production sharing. For example, the 1994 UNCTAD *Handbook of International Trade and Development Statistics* estimates that North American (United States plus Canada) apparent consumption (defined as production less exports plus imports) of machinery and transportation came to $1,175,636 million. Data produced in this report showed that Canadian and US imports of parts and components totaled $124,788 million or about 10.6 percent of apparent consumption. Using the UNCTAD estimate, one can derive North American production of these goods (defined as consumption less imports plus exports) which totaled $1,064,806 million.

   Imports of parts and components stood at about 11.6 percent of this production base. As the above table indicates, imports of parts and components accounted for almost 16 percent of apparent consumption of transport and machinery products in the European Union and a slightly smaller share of total production of these goods.

How important is production sharing outside the machinery and transport equipment group? Data collected in connection with the use of special OECD tariff provisions for the reimport of components assembled abroad suggest production sharing is a key factor in the manufacture of textiles and clothing, leather goods, footwear, and other labor-intensive manufactures. However, again it is recognized that these data likely incorporate a downward bias as to the extent to which this type of production sharing occurs. Special tariff treatment for goods exchanged within *free trade areas (FTAs)* and schemes like the generalized system of preferences, as well as the low average level of most-favored-nation tariffs in OECD countries, all reduce the incentive for countries to utilize these tariff provisions, so much of this OAP trade goes unreported. Even so, the reported data show this exchange still accounts for 40 percent or more of the total manufactures exports of some developing countries.

Given the available statistics, and their limitations, it appears the 30 percent share of parts and components in total SITC 7 exports also constitutes a reasonable estimate for the production-sharing component of all manufactured goods trade. One reason is that the transport and machinery product group by itself accounts for more than one-half of all trade in manufactures and marked differences would have to exist in the composition of trade of other manufactured products for the overall share to deviate significantly from the 30 percent average. The available data relating to OECD tariff provisions for reimported components suggest this is not the case—production sharing frequently occurs and is of major importance in other sectors. The implications are that at least $800 billion of world trade in manufactures—which totaled approximately $2.7 trillion in the early 1990s—consisted of some form of global production-sharing operation.

Appendix 7.1. Parts and Components Identified in the SITC Revision 2 Classification System and the 1995 Value of OECD Exports of these Goods

SITC (Rev. 2)—Description	1995 Value of exports ($ million)	Share of total (%)
711.9 Parts of steam boilers and auxiliary plants	1,386.9	0.31
713.19 Parts of internal combustion engines for aircraft	358.7	0.08
713.9 Internal combustion engine parts, nes	18,042.8	4.09
714.9 Parts of engines and motors, nes	14,485.4	3.28
716.9 Parts of rotating electric motors	3,811.7	0.86
718.89 Parts of water turbines and hydraulic motors	411.6	0.09
721.19 Parts of cultivating equipment	485.4	0.11
721.29 Parts of harvesting machinery	955.7	0.22
721.39 Parts of dairy machinery	494.3	0.11
721.98 Parts of wine-making machinery	29.5	0.01
721.99 Parts of other agricultural machinery, nes	421.2	0.10
723.9 Parts of construction machinery	5,797.1	1.31
724.49 Parts of spinning and extruding machinery	1,698.0	0.38
724.69 Parts of looms and knitting machinery	1,756.3	0.40
724.79 Parts of textile machinery, nes	760.9	0.17
725.9 Parts of paper mill and paper-making machinery	2,915.2	0.66
726.89 Parts of bookbinding machinery	175.0	0.04
726.9 Parts of printing and typesetting machinery	2,159.0	0.49
727.19 Parts of grain-milling machinery	188.1	0.04
727.29 Parts of food-processing machinery	7.6	0.00
728.19 Parts of machine tools for special industries	897.9	0.20
728.39 Parts of mineral-working machinery	1,921.4	0.44
728.49 Parts of machines for special industries, nes	9,818.0	2.22
736.9 Parts of machine tools for metal working	4,183.4	0.95
737.19 Parts of foundry equipment	649.2	0.15
741.49 Parts of refrigerating equipment	1,776.6	0.40
742.9 Parts of pumps for liquids	3,957.6	0.90
743.9 Parts of centrifuges and filters	6,376.7	1.44
744.19 Parts of fork-lift trucks	149.9	0.03
744.9 Parts of lifting and loading machines	11,667.3	2.64
745.19 Parts of power hand tools	490.4	0.11
749.99 Parts of non-electric machinery, nes	3,379.1	0.77
759 Parts of office and adding machinery	61,172.3	13.85
764 Parts of telecommunications equipment	79,103.4	17.92
771.29 Parts of electric power machinery	2,621.6	0.59

APPENDIX 7.1. *Continued*

SITC (Rev. 2)—Description		1995 Value of exports ($ million)	Share of total (%)
772	Parts of switch gear	49,113.7	11.12
775.79	Parts of domestic electrical equipment	648.7	0.15
778.29	Parts of electric lamps and bulbs	578.5	0.13
778.89	Parts of electrical machinery, nes	4,792.7	1.09
784	Parts of motor vehicles and accessories	109,966.9	24.90
785.39	Parts of carriages and cycles	3,709.5	0.84
786.89	Parts of trailers and non-motor vehicles	1,781.8	0.40
791.99	Parts of railroad equipment and vehicles	2,219.8	0.50
792.9	Parts of aircraft and helicopters	24,231.1	5.49
All above items		441,548.0	100.00

Note: nes = not elsewhere specified.

Appendix 7.2. The Relative Importance of Parts and Components in Individual Countries' Exports

Reporter	1995 exports in US$ million				Share of parts and components in		
	Parts and components	Transport and machinery (SITC 7)	All manufactures	All goods	Total exports	Exports of manufactures	Transport and machinery (SITC 7)
United States	102,009	256,256	417,443	546,442	18.7	24.4	39.8
Japan	81,442	310,708	421,428	442,937	18.4	19.3	26.2
Singapore	21,532	77,568	99,013	118,263	18.2	21.7	27.8
Taiwan (China)	19,420	53,493	103,306	111,343	17.4	18.8	36.3
Sweden	13,843	35,972	68,235	79,917	17.3	20.3	38.5
Malaysia	10,521	40,673	55,131	73,778	14.3	19.1	25.9
United Kingdom	33,627	102,470	195,680	239,948	14.0	17.2	32.8
Germany	69,548	251,866	446,023	508,508	13.7	15.6	27.6
Hong Kong	4,070	8,809	28,019	29,946	13.6	14.5	46.2
French Guiana	21	52	79	158	13.5	26.9	40.9
Israel	2,547	5,107	16,978	19,047	13.4	15.0	49.9
Ireland	5,823	15,127	31,116	43,790	13.3	18.7	38.5
Finland	5,301	14,264	33,658	40,409	13.1	15.8	37.2
Mexico	10,367	41,634	61,643	79,489	13.0	16.8	24.9
France	33,093	112,492	218,358	284,046	11.7	15.2	29.4
Thailand	6,193	19,052	41,418	56,655	10.9	15.0	32.5
Barbados	18	30	99	168	10.9	18.5	61.6
Austria	5,724	20,555	46,643	52,807	10.8	12.3	27.8
Canada	20,626	75,081	119,660	192,161	10.7	17.2	27.5

Reporter	1995 exports in US$ million				Share of parts and components in		
	Parts and components	Transport and machinery (SITC 7)	All manufactures	All goods	Total exports	Exports of manufactures	Transport and machinery (SITC 7)
Czech Republic	2,296	6,336	17,703	21,686	10.6	13.0	36.2
Rep. of Korea	12,553	65,625	114,387	125,056	10.0	11.0	19.1
Switzerland	7,760	25,624	76,072	81,641	9.5	10.2	30.3
Italy	21,610	86,706	206,321	231,346	9.3	10.5	24.9
Spain	8,225	37,970	69,780	89,616	9.2	11.8	21.7
Denmark	3,926	12,248	29,152	47,222	8.3	13.5	32.1
Slovenia	640	2,613	7,442	8,316	7.7	8.6	24.5
Netherlands	13,358	47,166	110,697	177,626	7.5	12.1	28.3
Philippines	1,129	3,800	7,054	17,174	6.6	16.0	29.7
Brazil	2,992	8,837	24,679	46,505	6.4	12.1	33.9
China	9,000	31,297	124,871	148,780	6.0	7.2	28.8
Belgium	9,602	45,012	125,887	165,173	5.8	7.6	21.3
Croatia	249	777	3,415	4,633	5.4	7.3	32.1
Nicaragua	25	31	103	509	5.0	24.6	81.6
Guadeloupe	8	59	76	162	4.7	10.1	13.0
Australia	2,326	5,080	12,194	50,357	4.6	19.1	45.8

Note: Countries have been ranked on the basis of the share of 'parts and components' in total exports of all goods.
Source: United Nations COMTRADE statistics.

Appendix 7.3. Tariff Provisions for International Production Sharing

From 1963 through 1988 statistics on the value of products assembled abroad from US manufactured components and then returned under tariff items 806.30 and 807.00 were compiled by the US International Trade Commission. After 1988 this tariff treatment was continued with some modification in US tariff schedule provisions 9802.00.60 and 9802.00.80.

US imports qualifying for this special treatment enter almost entirely under tariff provision 9802.00.80. Such products are subject to duty at the full imported value of the good less the value of the US-produced components. To qualify for this treatment imports must require no further processing in the United States and only 'operations incidental to the assembly process' (but not manufacturing) may occur abroad. Tariff provision 9802.00.60 provides similar treatment for metals that are manufactured in the United States, exported for further processing, and then returned.

European Community tariff schedules contain provisions similar to those of the United States. These provisions, known as 'outward processing relief arrangements', allow EC components to be exported for further processing or assembly. Upon reimport, products may be exempted totally or partially from duties. The types of activities that may qualify for this special EC tariff treatment include fitting, assembling, processing, or repairing goods.

EC production-sharing provisions apply equally to goods exported by one member country and returned as well as to triangular trade in which goods are exported from one EC country and returned to another member after foreign processing. Authorization to engage in outward processing is allowed on either a special or general basis, but only when customs officials can clearly determine that EC-produced components have been incorporated in imported products. An application to engage in outward processing may be denied if evidence indicates it could damage EC processors.

Despite general similarities, differences in the EC and US provisions exist with the most important being the method used for calculating the tariff on assembled goods returned. Under US provisions, the applicable duty is applied to the full value of the article as imported, less the value of the US components. However, the method used by the EC is a 'differential taxation' method based not only on the value added outside the EC but also on changes in applicable rates of duty on the foreign processing and assembly. That is, the duties are applied to both the value of the component products originally *exported from* the EC as well as the final good. The EC provisions also differ from those of the United States in that such transactions must have the prior approval of the member country into which the final goods are imported. US regulations have no such provisions.

Source: United States International Trade Commission.

Appendix 7.4. Production Sharing in the Caribbean

Most US apparel imports from the Caribbean come from the Dominican Republic, Costa Rica, Haiti, and Jamaica and are the result of offshore assembly operations. The USITC indicates the growth of US imports of Caribbean apparel is due largely to increased foreign investment. Because of US *Multifiber arrangement* (MFA) quotas on Hong Kong, Korea, and Taiwan (China), producers in those countries, as well as the United States, have invested in the Caribbean as a site for export-oriented production aimed primarily at the US market. Although US investment has been dominant, Asian investment has also been strong. US investment has been concentrated mainly in activities that use US components while Asian investment has focused on cut, make, and trim production utilizing Asian fabrics. Jamaica has been particularly attractive to Asian investors because its exports receive preferential access to EC markets under the Lome Convention.

One principal attraction for foreign investors in the Caribbean is the relatively low labor costs. In 1989, hourly wages in the Dominican Republic and Haiti were $0.61 and $0.58 respectively. Average productivity in the four leading Caribbean countries ranges between 80 and 90 percent of that in the US, with Haiti the lowest and Costa Rica the highest. Extended social benefits and a better educated workforce account for Costa Rica's relatively higher wages of $1.07 per hour. However, these higher wages are offset by the ability of Costa Rican firms to handle a full range of production and style changes.

Political stability and a healthy business environment have played major roles in attracting foreign investment. Costa Rica, in particular, has been a leader in production of offshore assembly goods due to its history of political stability and its well-developed infrastructure and communications network. Haiti, although the fourth largest producer of these goods, has comparably low foreign investments as a result of political instability, unreliable energy sources, and health concerns. In fact, much of the OAP activity is by locally owned producers rather than with foreign-owned manufacturing activities.

The Caribbean countries have established programs to attract potential investors through various government incentives such as tax breaks and free zones. All the major Caribbean suppliers established free zones, which provide investors with production sites and substantial tax and duty exemptions. The Dominican Republic has 18 free zones from which the majority of its apparel exports originate. The Caribbean also indirectly benefits from other US programs. Section 936 of the Internal Revenue Code provides a tax break to US companies that operate 'twin' or complementary plants in Puerto Rico and Caribbean Basin Initiative beneficiary countries. This program has further increased the attraction of investment in sewing operations in the region.

The Caribbean Basin countries not only offer low-cost labor, but their proximity to the United States also allows US firms greater control over production and delivery times than do Asian nations. The competitive position of US producers increasingly depends on their ability to react quickly to changes in consumer requirements. Reduced duties resulting from trade agreements as well as unilateral market reforms in Caribbean countries have enabled US apparel and other firms producing labor-intensive products to improve their ability to compete against low-cost imports from Asia, while maintaining US production of components that are used in these assembly operations and retaining US production that would otherwise be lost to foreign producers.

Appendix 7.5. OAP and the Caribbean's Expanding Manufactures Trade: Who Participated, Who did Not?

While all Caribbean exports of manufactures to the OECD more than doubled over the 1986–92 period, different trends are evident in some of the individual country statistics. As indicated below, the rapid growth was largely confined to six countries: Antigua and Barbuda, the Bahamas, Dominican Republic, Grenada, St Lucia, and St Vincent and the Grenadines. After declining by more than 25 percent from 1980 to 1986, exports of manufactures from Jamaica more than doubled over the next six years. In contrast, manufactures exports from the rest of the Caribbean were stagnant or even declined (Barbados, Dominica, Guyana, and Haiti).

TABLE A7.1. Trade growth in Caribbean manufactures

Exporting country	OECD imports of manufactures (US$ 000)			1980–92 growth rate (%)
	1980	1986	1992	
All Caribbean	1,678,456	2,185,972	4,483,058	8.5
Antigua and Barbuda	47	229	6,320	50.4
The Bahamas	166,428	276,348	707,548	12.8
Barbados	67,077	118,068	41,956	−3.8
Belize	16,895	21,840	20,837	1.8
Dominica	14,819	3,743	5,595	−7.8
Dominican Republic	294,893	594,529	2,155,229	18.0
Grenada	151	503	6,320	36.5
Guyana	34,089	15,624	21,289	−3.8
Haiti	230,744	374,684	122,538	−5.1
Jamaica	479,481	352,817	779,819	4.1
St Kitts and Nevis	17,708	61,456	19,859	1.0
St Lucia	345	534	36,926	47.3
St Vincent and Grenadines	650	1,509	18,201	32.0
Surinam	238,337	148,491	260,600	0.7
Trinidad and Tobago	116,792	215,598	280,021	7.6

What caused this markedly different performance of the Caribbean countries? Clearly, one factor accounting for the superior performers' success was the incentives to attract OAP activity. These include speed and simplicity in processing investment applications, the relative absence of foreign-exchange restrictions on OAP investors, factors influencing the general industrial relations climate, differences in the productivity of domestic labor, relatively low international transport costs and the absence of policies that impede transport operations, and the absence of major supply bottlenecks. Similarly, several specific negative factors contributed to the other Caribbean countries' poor export performance, that is, political instability (Haiti), foreign-exchange restrictions (Guyana—until 1989, Dominica in the 1990s, Barbados since 1989, and so on), an 'unfriendly' business environment (Guyana), or lack of adequate air transport (Dominica).

What emerges from this assessment? The key point is that Caribbean countries' success or failure as exporters has in large part been determined by these nations' own domestic policies. Those that adopted 'outward-oriented' trade policies have generally succeeded while those that pursued more restrictive 'inward-looking' trade regimes have generally failed.

NOTES

The views expressed in this chapter are those of the author and need not reflect those of the World Bank, its staff, or its member countries.

1. Production sharing is defined as the internationalization of a manufacturing process in which several countries participate in different stages of the manufacture of a specific good. The process is of considerable economic importance since it allows stages of production to be located where they can be undertaken most efficiently and at the lowest cost. Furthermore, if production sharing is increasing in relative importance, this implies that countries are becoming more interdependent on each other.

2. A trend toward an international 'slicing up of the value' chain in manufacturing would be important for the development process for several reasons. First, by increasing the set of internationally traded goods, it increases opportunities for developing countries to benefit from the gains from trade by allowing them greater room for specialization in the labor-intensive stages of manufacturing processes (which as a whole might be technology or capital intensive). Also, by broadening the scope for gains from trade, it would render protectionist, import substitution or anti-foreign-investment policies even less sensible or attractive than before. In addition, given that these kinds of production and trade tend to occur within tightly knit 'just in time' global networks, it attaches added importance to improving the efficiency of transportation and communications infrastructure and a generally low-cost, hassle-free, and predictable business environment.

3. The tabulations in this study are based solely on these SITC groups which are identified as consisting solely of components. This clearly causes the estimates of the level of international production sharing to be downward biased. Specifically, some other SITC 7 product group exports (like television picture tubes) may be used for further assembly operations in the importing countries. However, given the nature and limitations of the available trade data, it is not possible to determine whether, and to what extent, these items are used for further assembly or are traded as finished goods for final consumption.

4. That is, if Oxj and Oij represent total OECD exports and imports of SITC product j, respectively, then the trade balance measure (Bj) is derived from

$$Bj = ((Oxj - Oij)/Oxj) \times 100.$$

5. A recent estimate placed world trade in all manufactures at about $2.7 trillion. As such, the components trade reported in Table 7.1 alone would constitute about 16 percent of this total exchange. However, as noted, two deficiencies in the SITC system may cause these data to seriously under-report the true importance of this exchange. First, some products in the machinery and transport group are exported, at least in part, for further assembly abroad. Since their actual end-use could not be determined from the SITC data they were excluded from the tabulations. Secondly, it was not possible to identify SITC groups that consisted solely of components in other manufactures groups—yarns and textile fabrics were almost certainly employed in this manner—so these had to be excluded from the tabulations.

6. The rapid expansion of Japanese components exports is largely concentrated in trade with the United States which received $27.6 billion (34 percent) of all such shipments

in 1995. Motor vehicle components dominated this exchange, accounting for about three-quarters of all exports. Aside from the United States, Japanese exports of components were largely directed at Asian markets as Taiwan (China), Thailand, Singapore, Hong Kong, and Korea each received about 5 percent of total Japanese exports of these goods.

7. The fact that Table 7.3 shows the seven largest markets for components are developed countries may come as something of a surprise. A detailed analysis of the underlying trade data (see also Table 7.4) shows that differences in factor intensities do not appear to be playing a major role in the direction of this exchange—rather the trade flows appear often to consist of high-tech products where skill factors may play a major role in the location of production facilities across countries. No doubt, discriminatory trade barriers like those applied in EFTA, the European Union, or in the Canadian–American free-trade agreement, were also a factor contributing to the high share of intra-OECD trade in this exchange.

8. The available data do not allow one to distinguish between trade in automotive components that are intended for further assembly as opposed to those that are intended for repair or replacement purposes. In any case, the growth in this exchange signals a growing interdependence in international operations—either on the part of assembly operations or on the part of service industries which handle repair or replacement services.

9. Commission staff have routinely monitored the effect of production sharing on US industry and maintain regular contact with US companies that use foreign assembly as part of their competitive strategy. The effects of these production-sharing tariff provisions and the use of assembly in Mexico's maquiladora industry on the US economy were the subject of a USITC (1988) investigation. In that study, the Commission surveyed over 300 companies in industries making use of foreign assembly. According to these responses, use of foreign assembly and the production-sharing tariff provisions has: (1) improved the overall competitiveness of US firms; (2) reduced fixed costs and improved profitability; and (3) increased US employment. Most of the respondents indicated that were it not for the production-sharing tariff provisions, the firms would have lost market share to foreign producers that do not use US-made components. See Grunwald and Flamm (1985), Drucker (1987), and Echeverri-Carroll (1988) for other analyses of the impact of foreign assembly on the competitiveness of US industry.

10. European Union statistics on this type of activity almost certainly suffer from the same type of bias. In addition to the GSP, the EU provides many developing countries with manufactured exports preferences under the Lomé Convention. Recipient countries would have no incentive to apply for OAP tariff concessions if the processed goods are already duty free under these programs. Similarly, the EU has negotiated free trade arrangements with EFTA, Turkey, Israel, and a number of North African countries. OAP exports from these sources would likely go unreported if they are not subject to import duties.

11. The European Union has a production-sharing tariff provision comparable to that of the United States (see App. 7.3) but it appears to be far less extensively used. The principal imports of the EU under the European OAP tariff provision were apparel and other textile articles, which accounted for 43 percent ($6 billion) of the total. Germany accounted for over two-thirds of the EU production-sharing imports of

apparel in 1994. Textile and apparel producers in Germany ship fabric mostly to Central Europe where it is cut and sewn into garments.

12. The OAP trade between the US and other industrial countries may be due, in part, to the fact that companies 'rationalize' production by consolidating the manufacture of a particular product or component in a limited number of locations. Plants that may have diversified products become specialized in the production of fewer goods. This can lead to greater efficiency and economies of scale, and to interdependency between plants requiring coordination of production planning.

13. Department of Commerce data show that US multinationals tend to sell most of what they make abroad to customers in the foreign markets where their subsidiaries are located. Even in developing countries, more than 60 percent of the production by foreign affiliates of US multinational manufacturers is sold locally. A portion of the intra-OECD countries' trade reflected in Table 7.5 is the shipment of resident firms' domestically produced components and parts to supply their foreign subsidiaries. These shipments may be very important to the economy of the country where the parent corporation is located since the job-creating effects of the production and export of components may be sizeable.

14. Aside from wage differences, other cost considerations helped promote the development of North–South production sharing. While many new transnational firms' production processes are often quite costly, this was not the case for OAP activity. All that normally was required was the allocation of some research on the *identification* (within their existing operations) of labor-intensive activities which were potentially transferable to low-wage countries. That is, new technologies were not needed as it was generally a matter of identifying those existing (fixed coefficient) activities which might be located abroad.

15. In a Nobel symposium on the location of international economic activity, Assar Lindbeck argued that 'given other costs, firms chose between alternative international locations in order to minimize transport costs. These costs, therefore, may become low precisely because they have been highly important for location—high transport cost locations are avoided if other costs are equal'. Similarly, Jagdish Bhagwati observed that 'even if transport costs for any alternative location were a small proportion of total product price, they could still affect location if they varied geographically more than other costs of production' (Ohlin *et al.*, 1977: 276).

16. These statistics exclude port and inland transport costs which may be very high for some African countries. The importance of the latter in Africa should not be underestimated. For example, World Bank data compiled by Tyler Biggs show port charges for clearing a 20-ft. container in Abidjan and Dakar are $1,100 and $910 respectively. In contrast, the ocean freight cost for shipping the container to Hamburg or Le Havre ranges between $1,350 and $1,430.

17. This raises two key questions. What factors account for the adverse African transport costs and what corrective policy measures are available? Evidence suggests that the anti-competitive cargo reservation policies adopted by most African governments have had a major adverse influence on freight costs. The OECD provides an assessment of these anti-competitive practices and the current situation regarding shipping in West and Central Africa:

> In 1992, West and Central African states showed no indication of liberalizing their protectionist shipping policies based largely on the unilateral interpretation

of certain provisions of the UN Liner Code Convention. On the contrary there were various moves towards enacting existing, but not yet implemented restrictive policies. These attempts met with opposition by OECD member countries and their shipping lines which considered this as both protectionist and discriminatory. However, the operation of some 50 shipping lines offering regular services to West Africa from most ports of the world was not only hampered by protectionism. Civil unrest, economic depression, a sharp increase in criminal activities towards vessels together with poor port management and severe and often discriminatory customs regulations were factors shipping lines had to struggle with. (OECD 1992: 43)

So, the answer is clearly deregulation. World Bank studies show deregulating and stimulating competition for shipping services may reduce liner freight rates by as much as 50 percent (Bennathan, 1989).

18. These tariff provisions are available not only to US manufacturing firms but also to jobbers and to non-US producing firms. Thus they, like all others, do not affect the extent of protection offered to US-*owned* firms but only that offered to US-*located* ones. Items 806.30 and 807.00 encourage the location of particular types of activity outside the United States; or, more appropriately, the repeal of these thoroughly rational provisions would discourage non-US locations. At the same time, however, these provisions increase the competitiveness in the American market of many US-based (and presumably US-owned) firms. They can also be viewed, then, as a device to encourage the use of US raw materials and early stage processing in US-based metal-finishing operations and in all foreign-based assembly which caters to the US market.

19. These risks can be lowered through geographic diversification of the portfolio of component investments. In considering the risk involved in any particular overseas investment, what is relevant is the marginal change in the riskiness of the entire overseas and domestic investment portfolio and not merely the riskiness of that particular investment itself. There is survey evidence that international firms prefer not to place more than one plant in one country, but rather to spread the risks somewhat, even if it involves them in more transport and management costs.

REFERENCES

Amjadi, A., and Yeats, A. (1995). 'Have Transport Costs Contributed to the Relative Decline of Sub-Saharan African Exports?' World Bank Policy Research Working Paper No.1559 (Washington: World Bank, Dec.).

Bennathan, E. (1989). 'Deregulation of shipping: what is to be learned from Chile?' *World Economic Record*, 58/160: 73–81.

Echeverri-Carroll, E. (1988). 'Maquilas: Creating Jobs in Texas and in Mexico', *Texas Business Review* (Feb.).

Drucker, P. (1987). 'The Changed World Economy', *Journal of the Flagstaff Institute* (Feb.).

Grunwald, J., and Flamm, K. (1985). *The Global Factory: Foreign Assembly in International Trade* (Washington: The Brookings Institution).

OECD (Organization for Economic Co-operation and Development) (1992). *Maritime Transport Review* (Paris: OECD).

Ohlin, B., Hesselbom, P. -O., and Mijkman, P. M. (1977). *The International Allocation of Economic Activity* (London: Macmillan Press).

USITC (United States International Trade Commission) (1988). *The Use and Economic Impact of TSUS Items 806.30 and 807.00* (Washington: USITC Publication 2953, Jan.).

World Bank (1995). *Global Economic Prospects and the Developing Countries 1995* (Washington: World Bank, Apr.).

Yeats, A. (1981). *Shipping and Development Policy: An Integrated Assessment* (New York: Praeger Press).

—— (1989). 'Shifting Patterns of Comparative Advantage: Manufactured Exports of Developing Countries', *The Developing Economies* (Summer).

8

Globalization and Fragmentation: Evidence for the Electronics Industry in Ireland

FRANCES RUANE AND HOLGER GÖRG

1. Introduction

This chapter looks at fragmentation and globalization in the context of the electronics sector in Ireland. We focus on the electronics sector for several reasons. First, it is a sector which is expanding rapidly and whose effects are permeating the production structures of virtually every activity in the manufacturing and service sectors. Recent data for the sector in Table 8.1 show that its growth rate in the period 1995 to 1997 continues to exceed the growth in real GDP worldwide and in the United States and Europe. Secondly, electronics is a sector where there are increasing returns to scale at the firm level, as has been found by Pratten (1988) for the EU and O'Malley (1992) for Ireland. This implies that firms may be able to exploit significant scale effects by the increased level of specialization brought about by fragmentation. Thirdly, electronics appears to be a sector in which the process of fragmentation has been quite dramatic, especially over the past twenty years—as evidenced by the 'downsizing' and increasing specialization of the world's largest electronics producers, such as IBM. Fourthly, it is a sector that in principle has a high level of globalization potential. Its production is effectively footloose, being virtually independent of resources other than capital, for which there is now a global market, and labor, both skilled and unskilled. Finally, because of the relative weightlessness of many of the products of the sector, transportation costs, which can often play a vital role in linking production to consumption, are a trivial part of total costs. For these reasons, differences in factor costs, effectively the costs of skilled and unskilled labor, can drive the global production location decisions for different fragments in the production process.

TABLE 8.1. Overview of the electronics industry world-wide

	1995	1996	1997
Real growth of electronics industry (production)			
World	3.8	5.9	3.4
United States	4.0	7.2	5.3
Europe	1.0	3.7	4.1
Ireland	35.0	10.0	20.0
Growth of real GDP			
OECD	2.2	2.6	3.0
United States	2.0	2.4	3.6
EU	2.4	1.6	2.3
Ireland	10.3	7.3	6.7

Source: Calculated using data from Reeds Electronics Research, Yearbook of World Electronics Data, 25th edn. (1998) and 26th edn. (1999), and OECD, Economic Outlook 61 (June 1997).

Ireland is chosen to illustrate how the fragmentation process has developed over the past two decades. As the electronics industry has developed globally over the past decade, Ireland has become a significant production base for this sector worldwide, despite its small size (population of 3.5 million and GDP of ECU 61.3 billion), and its peripheral location. As Table 8.1 shows, the growth rate in production in the electronics sector in Ireland has exceeded the growth rate in electronics in the aggregated country groupings. Ireland now accounts for 1 percent of total world electronics production and almost 5 percent of electronics production in Western Europe. It hosts the European base of two of the key enabling technology companies, namely, Microsoft and Intel, as well as a battery of major companies from many subsectors within electronics. *Multinational companies* (*MNCs*) locating in Ireland have been mainly responsible for developing this sector, supported by Ireland's industrial development policy which recognized in the 1970s that the growing fragmentation within this sector could provide a role for indigenous Irish-owned firms, acting as sub-suppliers of fragmented parts of the final or intermediate products (see Killeen, 1975 and White, 1982).

Section 2 discusses the issues arising in applying concepts of fragmentation generally and in the context of the electronics sector. Section 3 presents some background on the evolution of the electronics sector in Ireland, while Section 4 presents the empirical evidence for fragmentation in the Irish electronics industry. Finally, Section 5 summarizes and draws some conclusions from the analysis.

2. Applying Concepts of Fragmentation

Fragmentation, as discussed in some detail in the contribution by Ronald Jones and Henryk Kierzkowski in this volume, refers to the breaking up of vertically integrated production processes into various components. Different stages of production do not need to take place under one roof in the same plant but may be contracted out to different plants of either the same firm or of altogether different firms. While this process of itself is long recognized in the industrial economics literature,[1] what is new is the global scope of the fragmentation that is taking place in this decade, and the consequent implications for the international distribution of production, for international trade and capital flows, and for income distribution (both national and international).

Continuing advances in production and telecommunication technology, together with reductions in transport and telecommunication costs as well as in barriers to trade (especially services trade), underlie the dramatic development of globalized, fragmented production. As evident in the chapters in this volume, the literature on fragmentation has focused on a range of different aspects of its relationship to globalization. In addition to explaining why fragmentation takes place, this literature examines the welfare effects of increased fragmentation, the differences in industrialization between core and peripheral countries (Krugman and Venables, 1995), and the distribution of income among skilled and unskilled workers following the sourcing of low-skill intensive inputs from developing countries (see, for example, Jones and Engerman, 1996, and the literature cited by Sugata Marjit (1998)).

Two conceptual distinctions are particularly appropriate when applying the concept of fragmentation. First, fragmentation can take an intra-firm or inter-firm form.[2] In the case of the former, plants belonging to the same firm but operating at different locations specialize in the production of different components, which are then brought together for final assembly. On the other hand, where different firms engage in such specialization, sometimes as part of a production network or an industry agglomeration and at other times as suppliers of standardized components to a globalized market, fragmentation can be said to be 'inter-firm'. This type of fragmentation is also frequently referred to as 'outsourcing'.

Secondly, fragmentation can take place across borders or within the same country. While international fragmentation arguably offers more possibilities for exploiting differences in comparative advantages across countries, fragmentation within the same economy may, on the other hand, involve lower transaction costs.[3] Where this process is intra-firm and takes place across borders, we are effectively dealing with MNCs, where production units specialize in different stages of the production process.[4] Global sub-supplying, either inter- or intra-firm, is most likely to happen among countries which have factor costs differences and when fragments of production involve different factor intensities.

Firms engage in fragmented production processes when it is profitable for them to do so. As the technological possibilities of fragmentation emerge, a firm, which is currently engaged in integrated production and opts for fragmentation, will choose between intra- and inter-firm fragmentation in response to the particular transaction costs involved.[5] These costs include the direct transaction costs of fragmented production as well as the risk costs of undesired spillovers of proprietary capital.

In the case of intra-firm fragmentation, the transaction is internal to the firm which precludes any negative external market effects which could occur due to, for example, the transfer of technology or know-how to the intermediate-producing plant. This is likely to be more important when the fragmented product is non-standard. However, intra-firm fragmentation may involve diseconomies of scope, that is, the attempt to produce all necessary components of the good within the same firm may lead to higher costs. This is especially likely to happen when products are complex and there are large information costs associated with producing at each level of the production chain. Also, sunk costs involved with setting up an own plant in another location (possibly abroad) may be substantial, such that economies of different locations, for example, low wages in developing countries, may not be fully exploited if a firm engages in intra-firm fragmentation. Furthermore, an exclusive intra-firm strategy will preclude the firm from readily multi-sourcing, thereby leaving itself exposed to possible sub-supply risks, for example, a strike at a particular plant or a national disaster at the location of such a plant.

In the case of inter-firm fragmentation, a firm is free to choose from where to source intermediate inputs and may, therefore, be able to reap the benefits of international specialization more fully. However, in addition to the possible negative external effects noted above, there may also be additional transaction costs where a firm outsources intermediates, especially from abroad. Communication and transportation costs may be higher and, while new technologies have led to a reduction of these cost factors, differences in culture (both firm and national) and, not least, language may impose additional costs on the firm engaging in global fragmentation.

There are many case-study examples of the apparent successes and failures of fragmentation in the electronics industry, from the perspective of an individual firm. For example, IBM experienced the possible negative external effects of inter-firm fragmentation in the 1980s when it produced *personal computers (PCs)* assembled using various components from intermediate producers. The 'open architecture' technology allowed competitors (starting with Compaq) to engage in 'backward engineering' and produce machines similar to IBM's at substantially lower costs. However, IBM also experienced the possible diseconomies of scope associated with intra-firm fragmentation in the production of mainframe computers in the 1980s. The production of all parts in-house appears to have led to an X-inefficient and inflexible organizational structure.

The electronics industry also provides ample evidence of across-border fragmentation, with PC producers such as Compaq, Dell, and Gateway 2000 using monitors, keyboards, hard-disks, and so on which are all produced by different firms across a range of countries according to those countries' comparative advantages. Much of this fragmentation is inter-firm, involving standardized parts, which are sourced from a low-cost location. There are also examples of intra-firm cross-border fragmentation, like Intel, which produces silicon wafers at its plant in Ireland, using skill-intensive and capital-intensive production methods, while the cutting of such wafers into individual microprocessors, which is highly labor intensive, is undertaken by an Intel plant in Malaysia.

3. Growth of the Electronics Industry in Ireland

Before discussing the development of the electronics industry in Ireland it is necessary to define what we consider to be part of this industry. There is no single definition of what comprises the electronics industry and our data, coming from widely different sources, relate to several different definitions. In this section, overall employment data coming from Forfás, the policy and advisory board for industrial development in Ireland, relate to three manufacturing sectors, namely, computers, office machinery, and electrical engineering (NACE Rev. 1 30–1). Trade data from the *Central Statistics Office (CSO)* relate to the office machines and *automatic data processing (ADP)* machines and units sectors (SITC section 75), while the capital expenditure data from the US Department of Commerce are for the electric and electronic equipment sector (SIC code 36). Even though the data are based on different definitions, they

TABLE 8.2. Development of the electronics industry in Ireland

(i) Employment by nationality of firm ownership

	1974	1979	1984	1989	1994	1997
Irish	238	180	897	1,810	2,163	3,236
Foreign	766	3,263	6,427	7,423	9,525	19,497
Total	1,004	3,443	7,324	9,233	11,688	22,733

(ii) Trade in electronics as percentage of total trade*

	1974–8	1979–83	1984–8	1989–93	1994–7
Imports	5.21	4.91	10.40	10.19	16.49
Exports	5.15	9.24	19.00	17.93	20.83

(iii) Ireland's Share of US Capital Expenditures in the EU* (%)

1974–8	1979–83	1984–8	1989–93	1994–5
2.12	4.01	5.75	13.63	25.08

*Averages.
Source: Calculated using data from (i) Forfás, (ii) Central Statistics Office, and (iii) US Department of Commerce.

indicate a consistent pattern and give a reasonably good indicator of the overall development of the electronics industry in Ireland over time.

Regardless of the data source used, it is obvious that the development of the Irish electronics industry is a relatively recent phenomenon. As the employment figures in Table 8.2 show, employment in the manufacturing electronics sector accounted for only 1,000 employees in 1974 but grew to 22,700 in 1997; that represents an annual average increase of 13.7 percent, compared with an annual average increase in total employment in Ireland of 1.5 percent during the same period. The figures also indicate that this development has been driven by foreign-owned multinationals locating in Ireland; the increase in employment in these companies in the late 1970s is seen to have had positive effects on the development of indigenous firms.[6]

For example, Cogan and Onyemadum (1981), in their analysis of the emergence of indigenous firms in the Irish electronics industry, also provide evidence for such a positive effect of foreign MNCs on indigenous firms. They argue, based on a small case-study survey of a number of Irish-owned firms in the electronics sector, that foreign MNCs act as 'incubators' for indigenous firms with previous employees of MNCs acting as the main initiators for a number of Irish-owned electronics firms.

The trade data in Table 8.2 also indicate the increasing significance of the electronics industry for the Irish economy. In the context of Ireland's having a very open economy, we note that the share of imports and exports attributed to the electronics industry rose from roughly 5 percent in the mid-1970s to 16 percent and 21 percent for imports and exports respectively in the mid-1990s. The significant and growing gap between the export and import figures indicates the development of Ireland as a manufacturing base for electronics.

As the data in Table 8.2 indicate, most of the employment in the electronics industry is in foreign-owned firms and inspection of the data on capital expenditures by US MNCs indicates that Ireland appears to be a particularly attractive location for US companies. In the mid-1990s, around 25 percent of all capital expenditures made by US electronics companies in the EU were in Ireland, while Ireland's share of EU GDP in the same period was around 1 percent. Many reasons have been suggested in the literature as to why Ireland attracts such a high level of foreign investment. The most frequently discussed reasons are Ireland's membership of the EU, its relatively cheap and well-skilled labor force, and the fiscal and financial supports available to foreign investors (discussed below). A further reason why Ireland has been so attractive as a base for US firms is the common language and relatively similar culture (see, for example, Krugman, 1997 and McAleese, 1998). The common language and culture effectively reduce substantially the transaction costs of international fragmentation for firms compared to, for example, a location in Eastern Europe where English, while becoming more and more common especially among younger people, is by no means as widely spoken.

These factors alone, however, would not be sufficient to explain why Ireland has been an extremely attractive base particularly for investment in the electronics sector.[7] Krugman (1997) links this phenomenon to the 'changing geography of the world economy'. His arguments suggest that industries which have negligible transportation costs are more likely to move to peripheral countries than other heavy industries and, as pointed out by Quah (1997), the electronics industry is such an industry where transportation costs do not play an important role (see also Görg and Ruane, 2000). In this context, it is perhaps less surprising that Ireland, given its other location advantages, has been attractive to firms in the electronics industry.

In any evaluation of the factors which have contributed to Ireland's success over the past decade in attracting *foreign direct investment* (*FDI*) from foreign MNCs, particularly in the electronics sector, the role of policy is clearly important. Any review of Irish industrial policy over the past forty years would identify it as being *pro-globalization*, that is, pro-trade and pro-FDI, and *proactive*, that is, supportive of industrial expansion in an interventionist manner.[8] Pro-globalization policy is evident in Ireland's trade policy, its policy towards MNCs, and the freedom of capital movements. Proactive policy is evident in Ireland's having stable low corporate tax rates for *internationally traded* goods and services for more than two decades and the use of grants and other financial instruments to support investment in these traded activities. The low corporate tax rate is available to all firms *automatically* while the grants and other financial supports are *discretionary*. The grants, linked to a combination of capital and labor, are available up to certain maxima (determined by legislation) and implemented at the discretion of the *Industrial Development Authority (IDA)*, Ireland, on the basis of a formal project evaluation.

In effect, industrial policy in Ireland for over forty years has operated at project level and it has become increasingly proactive and selective since the 1980s. While good projects in virtually all sectors of internationally tradable economic activity are in principle eligible for financial support, not only has the level of grant support varied, but personnel resources have been increasingly deployed to distinguish suitable international projects on a market-driven basis, that is, where market growth potential is greatest, projects are footloose and transportation costs relative to product values are low. This has typically meant projects with significant EU markets. The precise pattern of MNC projects which come to Ireland is thus strongly influenced by this process, which could be described as 'market-led intervention'.[9]

In the mid-1970s the IDA identified the electronics sector as providing the most promising opportunities for foreign investment projects for Ireland.[10] The very fact that production processes in this sector were becoming highly fragmented contributed to its attractiveness to the policy-makers as it was seen that Ireland could, over a period of time, move up the spectrum of product quality and product complexity. Thus production started with simple labor-intensive sub-assembly activities in the early 1970s, based on assembling complete component kits, sourced globally by the headquarters of the electronics firms in the United States. Even at this stage in the evolution of the industry it was not possible for Ireland to compete in the production of many types of passive components which, because of unit labor costs, could only be produced profitably in really low-wage countries in Asia. However, certain parts of the components industry could be sourced in Ireland, and an indigenous sub-supply industry did develop during this period.

During the 1980s as the mini-computer industry went into decline with the growth in the PC market, the sector had to restructure. A crucial element of policy was to attempt to attract key companies, with crucial enabling technologies, to establish their European bases in Ireland. This succeeded with the establishment of the sole European outlets for Microsoft and Intel at the end of the 1980s, leading rapidly to the location of a wide range of commercial electronics industry activities in Ireland during the 1990s. The range excludes (i) activities which required very low-cost labor (in particular, passive components, especially in consumer electronics), (ii) instrumentation, where Ireland was perceived as having no comparative advantage because of the absence of a military industry, and (iii) for the most part, high R&D-intensive activities.[11] Furthermore, the domestic potential associated with the fragmentation of the sector was recognized by policy-makers in increasing the likelihood of linkages between domestic and foreign firms which occurred in practice (see Crowley, 1996 and Görg and Ruane, 1998). The United States was identified as the most likely market source for such projects, both because of its leadership role in the sector (compared with European countries) and because of the common language which reduces the costs of operating complex and fragmented inter- and intra-firm production processes.

In the context of the fragmentation literature, it is perhaps interesting to note that by the late 1970s, the policy-makers had developed their objective for the sector as creating industrial clusters in particular subsectors of electronics. They set out to attract large industrial players in these subsectors, using the presence of one player to support the attraction of another. In some instances, the basis for the attraction has been the direct trade facilitated by these companies; more often, it has been the creation of a pool of skilled labor which has attracted new investors.

It has been argued recently (Barry and Bradley, 1997; Krugman, 1997; McAleese, 1998) that one of Ireland's advantages for MNCs is the existence of agglomeration economies, particularly in the electronics sector. Barry and Bradley (1997) argue that, for foreign firms, the 'location decision is now strongly influenced by the fact that other key market players are already located in Ireland' (p. 1804). This point was also taken up by Krugman (1997), who referred to this as 'Demonstration Effects and Cascades' (p. 49). For example, computer firms located in Ireland include Apple, Compaq, Dell, Gateway 2000, Hewlett-Packard and IBM, while the silicon-chip manufacturers Intel and NEC, as well as software companies, such as Microsoft, Lotus, and Oracle, also have significant production facilities in Ireland. At this point, it appears that the Irish policy of creating clusters in the electronics sector has been successful.

4. Evidence of Fragmentation in the Electronics Industry in Ireland

In this section we present some empirical evidence on the extent of fragmentation in the Irish electronics industry. In looking at the evidence, we attempt to provide answers to a set of questions related to fragmentation in the electronics sector in Ireland. We attempt to establish whether Ireland is a base for fragmented production in electronics and whether fragmentation is relatively more important in Ireland than in the rest of the EU. Given the concern in the literature that fragmentation leads to the location of low-skilled production in the country in which fragmented production is located, we attempt to shed some light on this issue for the Irish electronics sector. A related question is whether Ireland has maintained its competitiveness in terms of labor, which is, as pointed out above, the crucial local factor for the location of electronics firms. Furthermore, we investigate whether there is any evidence to show that local fragmentation takes place in the electronics sector and we examine in some more detail whether there is evidence of local fragmentation taking place in the computer sector, a sector where one would a priori expect a high level of fragmentation to occur.

One way of establishing whether projects in an EU country are involved in global fragmentation is to examine the level of *outward or inward processing trade (OPT/IPT)* in the country. OPT are goods which are temporarily exported to a country outside the EU for processing and are subsequently reimported for sale on the EU market. As such, OPT indicates whether a country is a source for fragmentation. IPT are imports that enter an EU country for the sole purpose of being processed and subsequently re-exported to another destination outside the EU. To analyze Ireland's importance as a base for fragmentation, we examine the extent of IPT, which gives a good indication of the extent of fragmentation across borders. Unfortunately, we cannot infer from these data whether this fragmentation is inter- or intra-firm. Our benchmark for Ireland is its IPT compared with the EU average, both for manufacturing overall and for electronics. To analyze IPT we use data available from the Eurostat Comext database; the data for the electronics sector relate to the ADP machines and parts sector (combined nomenclature sections 8471 and 847330).

The data presented in Table 8.3 indicate that IPT going into Ireland increased roughly fourfold between 1988 and 1997, compared with a doubling of IPT in the EU overall over the same period. IPT in the electronics sector in Ireland increased sixfold between 1988 and 1997, compared with an increase of less than twofold for the total EU. This

TABLE 8.3. Inward processing trade (imports) in Ireland

	1988	1990	1992	1993	1994	1995	1996	1997
Value of IPT (million ECU)								
IRL total	588.6	808.4	895.9	1,366.7	2,125.6	2,849.9	2,917.1	3,057.9
EU total	24,601.6	27,743.2	28,434.5	31,361.5	37,063.1	37,903.4	45,055.2	48,093.6
IRL electronics	207.4	242.6	297.5	497.5	988.9	1,467.2	1,550.8	1,464.6
EU electronics	2,348.3	2,726.0	2,801.2	3,469.9	4,584.7	5,803.3	6,566.1	6,488.7
IPT in Ireland as percentage of total EU								
Total IPT	2.4	2.9	3.2	4.4	5.7	7.5	6.5	6.4
Electronics	8.8	8.9	10.6	14.3	21.6	25.3	23.6	22.6
IPT as percentage of total imports								
IRL total	3.8	4.4	4.1	—	7.4	8.5	7.8	6.6
EU total	2.7	2.6	2.5	—	2.9	2.7	3.0	2.8
IRL electronics	20.4	17.9	23.0	—	38.0	37.4	38.2	29.2
EU electronics	6.6	6.3	5.9	—	8.4	9.4	9.9	8.1
IPT in electronics as percentage of total IPT								
IRL	35.2	30.0	33.2	36.4	46.5	51.5	53.2	47.9
EU	9.5	9.8	9.9	11.1	12.4	15.3	14.6	13.5

Source: Eurostat: intra- and extra-EU trade (combined nomenclature). CD rom.

indicates the increasing importance of IPT in Ireland, and its being a relatively attractive destination for IPT in the EU. In 1997, 6.4 percent of total IPT entering the EU went into Ireland, and this share is 22.6 percent in the electronics sector. The importance of IPT for Ireland is also mirrored in terms of total Irish imports; in 1997, almost one-third of imports in the electronics sector were IPT imports. These IPT data clearly suggest that fragmentation is highly important for production in the Irish electronics sector, and this conclusion is substantiated further by the fact that almost half of total IPT into Ireland in 1997 were IPT electronics imports, compared with under 15 percent for the total EU.

As pointed out above, fragmentation can lead to a shift of low-skilled production into the country in which fragmentation takes place. We have available some firm-level data to examine whether that is what has been happening in the Irish electronics sector. Our data here cover both manufacturing and service activities (including software) and are taken from the Employment Survey, which is an annual survey of all manufacturing and internationally traded services firms in Ireland, collected by Forfás, the policy and advisory board for industrial development in Ireland. The data are classified into twelve electronics subsectors, which we have aggregated according to their level of skill intensity into low-, medium- and high-skill intensive.[12] There is only one sector operating in Ireland categorized as low-skill intensive, namely, peripherals and media. As shown in Table 8.4, seven sectors are defined as medium-skill intensive, while four sectors, namely, semiconductors, IT-related services, software development, and software production are said to be high-skill intensive.

The figures in the first part of Table 8.4 suggest that since 1986 employment in the high-skill intensive sectors has been growing faster than the average rate of growth for electronics, in the case of both Irish and foreign firms. However, foreign firms also enjoyed faster growth in employment in the low-skill intensive sectors. This suggests that Ireland attracts investment projects for different reasons. One possibility is that firms in the low-skill sectors may be seeking a European base, and that in this context they find Irish labor costs relatively low compared with other European locations.[13] By contrast, low-skill activities, which do not require a European base, may choose to locate in lower-wage countries, for example, in South East Asia. High-skill-intensive sectors are attracted to Ireland because of the existence of skilled labor at relatively low wages and agglomerations of firms in the Irish electronics sector.

TABLE 8.4. Employment in the electronics industry

	Irish firms			Foreign firms		
	1982–5	1986–90	1991–5	1982–5	1986–90	1991–5
Employment growth (averages) (%)						
Peripherals and media	354.8	−34.3	16.9	41.5	51.2	60.7
Components	124.0	50.9	40.0	75.2	28.5	0.0
Computers	173.9	−32.9	37.0	154.3	−8.9	−19.3
Consumer electronics	−29.7	−24.0	28.9	23.9	41.8	7.0
Instrumentation	21.9	41.2	13.9	25.3	53.7	11.6
Networking/data communication	433.3	59.4	4.5	28.3	54.1	237.2
PCBA	284.9	7.4	−9.2	1416.7	286.7	82.1
Telecommunications	53.5	−1.0	128.6	52.9	28.2	−9.9
Medium skill	42.4	9.7	29.6	85.4	23.8	5.1
Semiconductors				67.4	29.1	25.0
Services	94.1	73.2	61.8	40.5	24.1	26.8
Software development	239.6	160.0	85.5	13.2	95.3	72.9
Software production	—	219.0	131.3	395.0	665.6	65.6
High skill	157.9	138.5	84.8	40.1	72.8	49.9
Total	59.2	28.4	45.5	66.4	39.8	27.3
Employment shares (averages) (%)						
Peripherals and media	4.2	3.2	1.7	12.1	11.6	13.8
Components	11.8	14.2	14.7	14.1	13.8	9.9
Computers	2.5	1.9	0.9	24.2	21.7	11.2
Consumer electronics	31.6	14.7	13.7	6.7	5.1	7.3
Instrumentation	8.7	10.8	10.2	5.2	6.0	5.1
Networking/data communication	1.9	2.9	2.8	2.2	2.2	1.7
PCBA	18.6	18.4	11.5	0.8	2.8	4.3
Telecommunications	11.4	9.8	11.2	9.5	7.3	7.8
Medium skill	86.5	72.7	65.0	62.6	58.9	47.4
Semiconductors	0.0	0.0	0.0	9.3	9.0	10.3
Services	4.7	5.3	5.6	6.0	6.7	6.0
Software development	4.6	17.5	24.2	9.5	10.7	14.4
Software production	0.0	1.3	3.5	0.5	3.0	8.1
High skill	9.3	24.1	33.3	25.3	29.5	38.8
Total	100.0	100.0	100.0	100.0	100.0	100.0

Source: Calculated from Forfás Irish Economy Expenditure Survey data.
Note: PCBA = printed circuit-board assembly.

These results are mirrored in the data in the second part of Table 8.4 which show the share of employment in each subsector. While medium-skill-intensive sectors still account for the highest share of employment, it is apparent that this share has declined since 1981, as the share of the high-skill-intensive sectors has risen. In the early 1990s, 33 and 39 per-cent of employment in the electronics sector was in high-skill-intensive industries in Irish and foreign firms respectively, compared with 9 and 25 percent respectively in the early 1980s. Thus, our results seem to indi-cate that there is a shift toward high-skill-intensive production in Ireland, although we note that low-skill production still occurs, especially in the foreign-owned sector.[14]

If production in Ireland develops toward high-skill-intensive sectors using highly skilled labor, one would expect wages to rise as highly skilled workers are being paid their marginal product. This begs the question as to whether this has happened in Ireland and, if so, whether Ireland will be able to maintain its competitiveness in terms of labor costs. While the data on hourly compensation costs for manufactur-ing workers in the 'electronic and electrical equipment' sector, available from the US Department of Labor, indicate that the absolute level of compensation in Ireland has risen, Figure 8.1 shows that the costs in Ireland relative to other countries, which may be seen as Ireland's com-petitors in attracting foreign investment in electronics, have not. Irish hourly compensation costs in the electronics sector are lower than in the UK and Germany and the ratio remained virtually constant between 1975 and 1994. The picture is even starker if one compares Ireland with one of its competitors in South East Asia. The ratio of Irish to

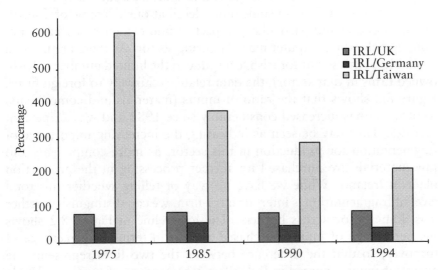

FIG. 8.1. Comparison of hourly compensation costs in electronics

Source: US Department of Labor, *Hourly Compensation Costs for Production Workers in Manufacturing* (June 1996).

Taiwanese costs has decreased considerably since 1975; while Irish costs were almost six times as high as Taiwanese costs in 1975, they were only twice as high in 1994.[15] This indicates that Ireland, despite the massive influx of foreign investment in the electronics sector, seems to have been able to maintain its competitiveness which must be in large measure due to the fact that labor has been in relatively abundant supply in Ireland, because of its exceptionally high unemployment rates and the increasing participation of women in the workforce.

Looking at the electronics sector overall, we can find evidence of domestic fragmentation among Irish-owned firms and MNCs producing intermediate components, in the evolution of their domestic sales ratios. If the intermediate goods produced in these firms are directed to the domestic market, this may be interpreted as evidence that there is fragmentation taking place *within* the economy. Most of this fragmentation can be expected to be inter-firm as there are few Irish multi-plant firms. Table 8.5 presents data on the percentage of domestic sales, which suggest that fragmentation occurs in some of the sectors. A number of sectors, including both Irish and foreign-owned firms, have increased their domestic sales ratios, such as Irish firms producing components and foreign firms producing components and semiconductors as well as foreign firms engaging in *printed circuit-board assembly* (PCBA). This suggests that there has been a relative increase in domestic fragmentation compared with cross-border fragmentation in these subsectors.

We now turn to look in some more detail at one example of a sector in which one would particularly expect to find evidence of fragmentation, namely, the computer manufacturing sector. As there are no data available on this sector for Irish firms (due to the limited number of Irish-owned firms in that sector), the data relate exclusively to foreign firms. Figure 8.2 shows that the ratio of inputs (materials and components) to turnover has increased considerably since 1982 and was 71 percent in 1995. This may be seen as indicating the increasing importance of fragmentation for production in this sector, as more components and raw materials are purchased for further processing in the production plant in Ireland. While we have no way of telling whether this total level of fragmentation is inter- or intra-firm, we can distinguish whether it is domestic or across borders. The lower line in Figure 8.2 shows the percentage of inputs purchased abroad in terms of percentage of turnover, so that the difference between the two lines represents the extent of inputs sourced in Ireland as a percentage of turnover. While the percentage of imported inputs increased between 1982 and 1995 and reached 53 percent in 1995, locally purchased inputs increased at

TABLE 8.5. Domestic sales ratios in the electronics industry (averages)

	Irish firms (%)			Foreign firms (%)		
	1982–5	1986–90	1991–5	1982–5	1986-90	1991–5
Peripherals and media	0.0	5.0	14.3	1.8	10.1	23.2
Components	7.7	32.8	39.8	3.9	5.7	10.9
Computers	—	—	—	0.7	1.0	2.8
Consumer electronics	14.8	34.4	47.2	8.8	7.0	5.1
Instrumentation	—	—	35.4	2.8	0.8	0.9
Networking/data communication	—	56.9	68.6	—	0.3	0.3
PCBA	85.8	36.4	48.1	0.0	13.7	47.3
Telecommunications	86.0	38.8	4.1	12.7	9.5	5.2
Medium skill	48.6	39.9	40.5	4.8	5.4	10.3
Semiconductors	—	—	—	0.1	0.0	2.7
IT services	—	9.4	15.7	0.0	1.9	15.6
Software development	—	—	40.3	42.8	65.2	6.6
Software production	—	—	35.0	—	1.0	1.2
High skill	—	9.4	30.4	14.3	17.0	6.5
Total	27.4	37.6	33.6	3.9	3.0	6.4

Source: Calculated from Forfás Irish Economy Expenditure Survey data.
Note: PCBA = printed circuit-board assembly.

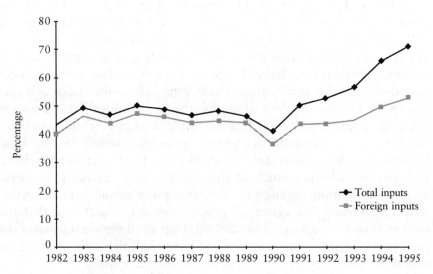

FIG. 8.2. Inputs as percentage of turnover in computer manufacturing sector
Source: Calculated from Forfás Irish Economy Expenditure Survey data.

an even faster rate and amounted to 18 percent of turnover in 1995.[16] As most MNCs located in Ireland have only one production plant in the country, we may infer that this domestic fragmentation is inter-firm fragmentation. The increased level of local fragmentation provides support for the responsiveness of firms to the potentially lower service costs associated with fragmentation within rather than across country boundaries, as foreign firms have increased their purchases from firms located within Ireland.[17]

5. Conclusions

The growth in the possibilities of fragmentation in production have greatly increased the potential for the globalization of industries, as different segments of production can be better matched to the factor supplies of individual locations. Such globalization has maximum potential in the situation where the industry concerned is internationally footloose in production terms, that is, factor requirements are such that it can potentially locate anywhere, and whose value to volume ratio is high, that is, relative transportation costs are low.

In this chapter we have looked at the electronics sector, arguably the manufacturing sector which has greatest potential to fragment and to globalize. Looking at the development of this sector in Ireland, we found empirical evidence of fragmentation in a number of data sources. IPT data indicate that production in the Irish electronics sector is globally fragmented, and that the scale of such fragmented production is growing. Furthermore, Ireland's share of fragmentation is rising faster than that in the EU generally and most especially in the electronics sector. Other firm survey data show that the scale of local fragmentation has risen relative to global fragmentation as firms in different Irish intermediate-goods-producing sectors trade increasingly on the local Irish market. Since there are few multi-plant firms located in Ireland, we can conclude that much of this trade is inter- rather than intra-firm. Looking more specifically at the computer manufacturing sector, we find evidence of fragmented production in this sector in that the ratio of bought-in materials to total sales has risen significantly over the past decade. Furthermore, as this has happened, the scale of domestic fragmentation has risen relative to global fragmentation.

Are there any lessons to be learned from the Irish analysis? Clearly globalization through fragmentation has been very positive for Ireland, in allowing the development of an entirely new sector. Furthermore, following on from global fragmentation has come the opportunity for local fragmentation, giving domestic firms an opportunity to act as sub-suppliers to local MNCs. In addition, Ireland has attracted investment both in high-skill and low-skill-intensive sectors and appears to be managing to move up the skill spectrum, by moving from lower to higher-skill segments of the fragmented production structure. This raises the issue of whether or not it can continue this progression over time.

Any evaluation of the Irish case needs to take account of the fact that Ireland has actively promoted MNC investment since the early 1950s and established itself as a strong base for multinational production in Europe. Furthermore, the strategy which it formulated back in the 1970s anticipated the development of electronics as a fragmented production structure and attempts were made to match over time the skill intensity of the sector with the domestic skill supply. The fact that English is the spoken language in this sector which is so clearly globalized undoubtedly assisted in the process and enhanced the potential of Ireland as a beneficiary of the process of fragmentation.

NOTES

We are grateful to Adrian Redmond of the Central Statistics Office, and Niall O'Donnellan and Dennis Slater of Forfás for help with the data used. We are particularly indebted to Frank Ryan and Peter Lillis of IDA Ireland for providing a valuable insight into the historic development of the electronics sector in Ireland. Finally, our thanks for valuable comments are due to participants at the conference on 'Globalization and International Trade' in Bürgenstock in July 1998 and especially to Ron Jones, Henryk Kierzkowski, and Sven Arndt. Financial support from Forfás is gratefully acknowledged.

1. These ideas, though with an altogether different focus, are implicit in Coase (1937) and more explicit in Williamson (1975), as well as discussions of post-Fordism in the business management literature.
2. See also Sect. 4 of Ch. 12.
3. As Jones and Kierzkowski in this volume argue, fragmentation is made possible due to the utilization of services (for example, transportation and communication), and costs for these services can be assumed to be lower if fragmentation takes place nationally rather than internationally.
4. Global MNC activities do not necessarily indicate fragmentation as plants in different countries may simply replicate plants elsewhere and be independent of their production activities. This is especially likely to be the case where transportation costs are high and where production is driven by establishing behind tariff barriers.
5. See Williamson (1975).

6. Such a process has recently been formally modeled by Markusen and Venables (1999). They argue that, if there are backward and forward linkages between foreign and indigenous firms, foreign firms can foster the development of indigenous firms in the same or in related sectors. Görg and Strobl (1999) provide econometric evidence that the presence of MNCs has had a positive effect on the entry of indigenous firms in Irish manufacturing as a whole.

7. As pointed out above, Ireland received, on average, 25 percent of US capital expenditures in the EU in the electronics sector between 1992 and 1995, compared with 5 percent in total manufacturing.

8. There are various extant reviews of Irish policy toward foreign investment, the most recent substantial ones being found in Foley and McAleese (1991). Other recent commentaries include O'Sullivan (1995), Ruane (1991), and Ruane and Görg (1999).

9. IDA Ireland personnel have described this as a 'fast-follower' approach.

10. Ireland had a very limited electronics sector in the 1960s and its potential was not recognized at this point. Key MNCs, such as General Electric and Westinghouse had plants in Ireland in the 1970s based primarily on Ireland's low labor costs. According to IDA personnel, the training of Irish management by these companies turned out to be crucial in the 1970s in the development of the mini-computer industry (Digital, Wang, etc.) and in the growth of the PC industry in the 1980s. This echoes the findings of Cogan and Onyenadum (1981) in their survey referred to above.

11. Exceptions are certain R&D activities currently being established by IBM and Xerox. The recent establishment of the Microsoft R&D facility in Cambridge UK, leaving the European localization facility in Ireland, has increased the emphasis among policy-makers on marketing Ireland as a base for higher-skill-intensive activities.

12. This aggregation is based on the views of industry specialists. Sectors are classified as low-skill intensive if less than 30 percent of their employees are graduates; medium skill if the graduate content is more than 30 but less than 50 percent, and high-skill intensive if the graduate content is 50 percent or more.

13. In effect, for such projects, Ireland is competing for investment projects only with other European countries and not globally.

14. One needs to exercise caution in interpreting these results as there may be skill differences within sectors which are hidden from our analysis. Kearney (1997) and Figini and Görg (1999) find that multinationals seem to increase the demand for skilled labor in Ireland, a result that also indicates that production by multinationals uses high-skilled rather than low-skilled labor.

15. Of course, this is for the most part due to the rapid increase in hourly compensation in Taiwan, particularly over the last decade.

16. In their econometric analysis of linkages in the Irish electronics industry, Görg and Ruane (1998) find that, at individual firm level, domestic sourcing of inputs has also increased in the total electronics sector.

17. These firms include both Irish-owned firms or other MNCs located in Ireland. Unfortunately none of our data sets allow us to distinguish how much is inter-MNCs and how much is between MNCs and Irish-owned companies.

REFERENCES

Barry, F., and Bradley, J. (1997). 'FDI and Trade: The Irish Host-Country Experience', *Economic Journal*, 107: 1798–811.

Coase, R. H. (1937). 'The Nature of the Firm', *Economica*, 4: 386–405.

Cogan, D. J., and Onyenadum, E. (1981). 'Spin-off Companies in the Irish Electronics Industry', *Irish Journal of Business and Administrative Research*, 3: 3–15.

Crowley, M. (1996). *National Linkage Programme: Final Evaluation Report* (Dublin: Industry Evaluation Unit).

Figini, P., and Görg, H. (1999). 'Multinational Companies and Wage Inequality in the Host Country: The Case of Ireland', *Weltwirtschaftliches Archiv*, 135/4.

Foley, A., and McAleese, D. (eds.) (1991). *Overseas Industry in Ireland* (Dublin: Gill and Macmillan).

Görg, H., and Ruane, F. (1998). 'Linkages between Multinationals and Indigenous Firms: Evidence for the Electronics Sector in Ireland', Trinity Economic Papers, Technical Paper No. 98/13. Trinity College, Dublin.

—— —— (2000). 'European Integration and Peripherality: Lessons from the Irish Experience', *The World Economy*, 23/3 (Mar.), 405–21.

—— and Strobl, E. (1999). 'Multinational Companies and the Entry of Indigenous Firms: Panel Data Evidence for Ireland', Centre for Economic Research Working Paper WP99/8. University College, Dublin.

Jones, R. W., and Engerman, S. (1996). 'Trade, Technology and Wages: A Tale of Two Countries', *American Economic Review*, 86: 35–40.

Kearney, I. (1997). 'Shifts in the Demand for Skilled Labor in the Irish Manufacturing Sector: 1979–1990', Working Paper 83. Economic and Social Research Institute, Dublin.

Killeen, M. J. (1975). 'Contribution to the Symposium on Increasing Employment in Ireland', *Journal of the Statistical and Social Inquiry Society of Ireland*, 23/3: 50–64.

Krugman, P. R. (1997). 'Good News from Ireland: A Geographical Perspective', in: A. W. Gray (ed.), *International Perspectives on the Irish Economy* (Dublin: Indecon), 38–53.

—— and Venables, A. J. (1995). 'Globalization and the Inequality of Nations', *Quarterly Journal of Economics*, 110: 857–80.

McAleese, D. (1998). 'Global Integration, Factor Mobility and EMU: Implications for the Irish Economy', Trinity Economic Papers, Policy Paper No. 98/1. Trinity College, Dublin.

Marjit, S. (1998). 'Globalization and Wage Inequalities in the Emerging Markets', mimeo.

Markusen, J. R., and Venables, A. J. (1999). 'Foreign Direct Investment as a Catalyst for Industrial Development', *European Economic Review*, 43: 335–56.

O'Malley, E. (1992). 'Industrial Structure and Economies of Scale in the Context of 1992', in J. Bradley, J. Fitzgerald, and D. Mccoy (eds.), *The Role of the Structural Funds: Analysis of Consequences for Ireland in the Context of 1992* (Dublin: Economic and Social Research Institute), 203–49.

O'Sullivan, M. (1995). 'Manufacturing and Global Competition', in J. W. O'Hagan (ed.), *The Economy of Ireland: Policy and Performance of a Small European Economy* (Dublin: Gill and Macmillan), 363–96.

Pratten, C. (1988). 'A Survey of Economies of Scale', *Economic Paper No. 67*. Directorate-General for Economic and Financial Affairs (Brussels: Commission of the European Communities).

Quah, D. T. (1997). 'Increasingly Weightless Economies', *Bank of England Quarterly Bulletin* (Feb.), 49–56.

Reeds Electronics Research (1998). *Yearbook of World Electronics Data 1998*, i and ii (Surrey: Reeds Electronics Research).

Ruane, F. (1991). 'The Traded Sector: Industry', in J. W. O'Hagan (ed.), *The Economy of Ireland: Policy and Performance*, 6 edn. (Dublin: Irish Management Institute), 345–77.

—— and Görg, H. (1999). 'Irish FDI Policy and Investment from the EU', in R. Barrell and N. Pain (eds.), *Investment, Innovation and the Diffusion of Technology in Europe* (Cambridge: Cambridge University Press), 44–67.

White, P. A. (1982). 'A Concept of Industrial Development in the 1980s', *Journal of the Statistical and Social Inquiry Society of Ireland*, 24/5: 51–9.

Williamson, O. E. (1975). *Markets and Hierarchies: Analysis and Antitrust Implications* (New York: The Free Press).

9

Foreign Direct Investment and International Fragmentation of Production

LEONARD K. CHENG, LARRY D. QIU, AND GUOFU TAN

1. Introduction

Recently, increasing attention has been given to the phenomenon of international fragmentation of production and its impact on international trade, wage, employment, and welfare. International fragmentation arises when the multiple stages of a good's production take place in two or more countries. It is similar in meaning to globalization, outsourcing, and intra-product specialization. The high costs of international coordination, communication, and transportation were crucial obstacles to international fragmentation in the past, and technological improvements in these areas are widely recognized as an important reason for the recent surge in fragmentation.

We would like to point out another important reason for the rapid increase in international fragmentation—*foreign direct investment (FDI)*. Liberalization of FDI in many developing countries in the last twenty years has been one of the most important international policy changes. The speed of FDI liberalization in these countries, especially in East and South East Asia, even outpaces trade liberalization. Ever since the mid-1980s, international capital flows in general and FDI in particular have grown much faster than trade flows.

Furthermore, there is a close connection between FDI and trade flows. An example of FDI is that of outsourcing, that is, a *multinational corporation (MNC)* from a developed country establishes a subsidiary in a developing country, producing labor-intensive and material-intensive intermediate goods, which are then shipped back to its home base for assembly. Depending on profitability, an MNC decides whether to concentrate the whole process of production in one country (i.e., without international fragmentation) or break the process into several steps to be undertaken in different countries (i.e., with international fragmentation). As part of the global production, cross-country technology transfer occurs as the subsidiary brings in new technologies and better managerial skills.

The literature on international trade is largely concerned with trade in final goods. There is a small but fast growing literature on international fragmentation of production, including contributions from Dixit and Grossman (1982), Sanyal and Jones (1982), Arndt (1997, 1998), Deardorff (1998), Harris (Ch. 4, this vol.), and Jones and Kierzkowski (1990, 2000). They have focused on two central issues, namely the pattern of production and the welfare implications of fragmentation. It has been generally established that, in the multiple stages of production leading to a final product, a country will engage in the production of the range of parts and components in which it has comparative advantages, in the sense of Ricardo or Heckscher–Ohlin. In general, there are few surprising or conflicting results about the pattern of trade. In contrast, different models result in different welfare implications of international fragmentation. Wage and employment may rise or fall in a country that has lost some labor-intensive production to other countries as the result of fragmentation.

The above-mentioned literature has not incorporated an important element of international fragmentation, namely FDI and the concomitant technology transfer, in its analysis. As a distinguishing feature of our chapter, we explicitly examine the impact of FDI on the international fragmentation of production, where FDI is taken as the primary vehicle of technology transfer.[1] We consider a framework in which there are two economies (regions), say Hong Kong and Guangdong, a province of China that is adjacent to Hong Kong. The production of a final product, y, requires skilled labor and the intermediate input, x. The production of x requires only unskilled labor. Assume that the technologies and endowments in the two regions enable both regions to produce x, but only Hong Kong can produce y. There are three possible scenarios: (i) no fragmentation—Hong Kong produces both x and y and Guangdong produces neither of them; (ii) partial fragmentation—Hong Kong produces both x and y and Guangdong produces x; and (iii) complete fragmentation—Hong Kong produces y and Guangdong produces x. We characterize the conditions (in terms of relative wages, technologies, transportation costs, and so on) for each scenario as an equilibrium outcome. One of the major results we obtain is that FDI makes complete fragmentation more likely to occur.

In this model, fragmentation, whether or not induced by FDI and technology transfer, definitely reduces unskilled labor employment but raises skilled labor employment in Hong Kong. However, the total employment of unskilled labor in Guangdong may increase or decrease. Our analysis also helps to predict which types of upstream firms (firms producing x) will relocate their production from Hong Kong to Guangdong.

Production fragmentation is an aspect of economic geography. The recent development in economic geography has been nicely surveyed and synthesized in Fujita *et al.* (1999). This new theory builds on models of increasing returns to scale and imperfect competition to explain the geographical concentration of economic activities. In contrast, the recent studies of international fragmentation of production explain how the different stages of a production process take place in different regions to exploit their comparative advantages. In our model, increasing returns to scale are absent and there is no inherent advantage in having production of the intermediate good x close to the production of the final good y. Consequently, there is an incentive to move intermediate goods production to the low-cost region.[2] We show that FDI reinforces this incentive and may even lead to complete fragmentation.

The chapter is organized as follows. In Section 2, we construct and analyze a model that allows possible international fragmentation but without FDI. In Section 3, FDI is incorporated into the model from which the main results of the chapter are derived. Section 4 describes the evolving integration of Hong Kong and Guangdong in recent years. It is a case of cross-border investment and production fragmentation.

2. A Partial Equilibrium Model without FDI

Consider two regions, Home and Foreign, denoted by H and F respectively. There is a final good, denoted by y, to be produced and sold to the world market at a given price, denoted by q. The production of y requires both skilled labor k and an intermediate good, x, which can be produced using unskilled labor l. Suppose that H and F have a comparative advantage in the production of the intermediate good, but the transportation costs of shipping x to the world market exceed the difference in production costs. Under this assumption, x is traded between H and F, but not between either region and the world market.

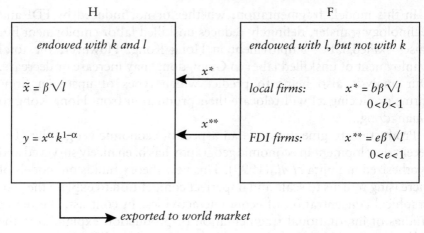

FIG. 9.1. A partial equilibrium model with FDI

To sharpen our analysis, consider the case where H has skilled laborers to produce the final good, but F does not. Since laborers are not mobile across regions, only H firms can produce the final good.

The production and trade relationships of the two regions are depicted in Figure 9.1.

Intermediate Good Production

In H there is a continuum of potential firms (entrepreneurs) facing the same technology in producing the intermediate good. However, each firm has a different ability to apply the technology. To capture this idea, let β within the unit interval denote an H firm's ability in producing the intermediate good according to the following production function:

$$\tilde{x} = \beta\sqrt{l}, \quad \beta \in [0, 1], \tag{9.1}$$

where $\tilde{x}$ is the supply of the intermediate good by firm β in H and l is the amount of unskilled laborers employed by the firm. A fixed cost, c, must be incurred by each firm that produces any positive quantity.

The intermediate input industry is one of many industries employing unskilled labor. Thus, the wage rate is fixed as far as the industry is concerned. We normalize H's wage rate to unity. The output price, denoted by p, is determined by aggregate supply and aggregate demand, but each firm takes it as given when making its decision on output and labor demand. Firm β chooses l to maximize its profit $p\beta\sqrt{1-l} - c$.

The solution for profit maximization is given by

$$l_\beta(p) = \frac{\beta^2 p^2}{4} \tag{9.2}$$

It follows that the firm's output and profit are given by

$$\tilde{x}_\beta(p) = \frac{\beta^2 p}{2} \quad \text{and} \quad \pi_\beta(p) = \frac{\beta^2 p^2}{4} - c \tag{9.3}$$

respectively. Firm β will only produce for the market if $\pi_\beta(p) \geq 0$, or equivalently

$$\beta \geq \underline{\beta}(p) \equiv m/p \tag{9.4}$$

where $m = 2\sqrt{c}$. The total supply of $\tilde{x}$ in H is

$$\tilde{x}(p) = \int_{\underline{\beta}}^1 \tilde{x}_\beta(p) \, d\beta = \frac{p^3 - m^3}{6p^2} \tag{9.5}$$

if $p \geq m$, and $\tilde{x}(p) = 0$ otherwise. Thus, there is a minimum price equal to m above which the most efficient H firm produces the intermediate good. The derived demand for unskilled labor in H is

$$l(p) = \int_{\underline{\beta}}^1 l_\beta(p) \, d\beta = \frac{1}{2} p \tilde{x}(p) \tag{9.6}$$

In F there is also a continuum of potential firms, β, facing the same technology to produce the intermediate good. However, in F firm β's production function is given by

$$x^* = b\beta\sqrt{l^*}, \quad 0 < b < 1 \tag{9.7}$$

where b captures the technology gap or management gap between H and F. It can be interpreted as either that F has the same technology as H but lower ability to apply the technology than H, or that both H and F have the same ability to apply the technology but H has better technology than F, or both. We assume in this section that there is no FDI, or equivalently technology transfer is not feasible. The assumption will be relaxed in the next section.

As a reflection of its more abundant supply of unskilled labor, the wage rate in F is fixed and is lower than that in H, that is, $w^* < 1$.

Shipping x from F to H is subject to an *ad valorem* tariff-cum-transport cost, t. Given the prevailing price p in H, firm β chooses l^* to maximize $pb\beta\sqrt{l^*}/(1+t) - w^*l^* - c^*$. If firm β decides to produce, its output and labor demand will be given by

$$x^*{}_\beta(p) = \frac{b^2\beta^2 p}{2(1+t)w^*} \quad \text{and} \quad l^*{}_\beta(p) = \frac{b^2\beta^2 p}{4(1+t)^2 w^{*2}} \tag{9.8}$$

respectively. Define $m^* = 2(1+t)\sqrt{(c^*w^*)}/b$. Firm β will produce for the market if $\pi_\beta{}^*(p) \geq 0$, or equivalently

$$\beta \geq \underline{\beta}^*(p) \equiv m^*/p \tag{9.9}$$

The total supply of x^* in F is

$$x^*(p) = \int_{\beta^*}^{1} x^*{}_\beta(p)\, d\beta = \frac{b(p^3 - m^{*3})}{6w^*(1+t)p^2} \tag{9.10}$$

if $p \geq m^*$, and $x^*(p) = 0$ otherwise. m^* is the minimum price for a positive supply. It decreases with b, but increases with t, c^*, and w^*. The smaller is m^*, the greater is the advantage of F firms over H firms in the production x.

The derived demand for unskilled labor in F is

$$l^*(p) = \frac{px^*(p)}{2(1+t)w^*} \tag{9.11}$$

Given p, the total supply of x from the two regions is $x_s(p) = \tilde{x}(p) + x^*(p)$. Notice that there is a minimum price equal to $\min\{m, m^*\}$ above which there is a positive and upward-sloping supply curve for the intermediate good.

Final Good Production

Consider a representative firm with *constant-returns-to-scale* (CRS) production technology

$$y = f(x, y) = x^\alpha k^{1-\alpha}, \quad \alpha \in (0, 1) \tag{9.12}$$

where k denotes skilled laborers. The firm takes as given the final good price q, intermediate input price p, and wage for skilled laborers r, and chooses a combination of inputs to maximize its profit function,

$qf(x, k) - px - rk$. The optimal demands for the intermediate good and skilled labor satisfy the following first-order conditions:

$$\alpha q \left(\frac{k}{x}\right)^{1-\alpha} - p = 0 \quad \text{and} \quad (1-\alpha) q \left(\frac{x}{k}\right)^{\alpha} - r = 0 \qquad (9.13)$$

It follows that the relative demand is given by

$$\frac{k}{x} = \frac{(1-\alpha)p}{\alpha r} \qquad (9.14)$$

Furthermore, the firm's choice is subject to the following zero profit condition

$$q \left(\frac{k}{x}\right)^{1-\alpha} - p - r \left(\frac{k}{x}\right) = 0 \qquad (9.15)$$

With CRS technology, a firm's output or input demand is indeterminate. However, as we will show below, in equilibrium the industry's total output is uniquely determined since, unlike individual firms, the industry faces upward-sloping supply curves of the intermediate input and skilled labor.

Market Equilibrium

We now determine the equilibrium prices and quantities in the markets for the intermediate good and skilled labor. Assume that the skilled labor supply is given by

$$k_s = v(r - r_0), \quad \text{for } r > r_0 \qquad (9.16)$$

where r is the wage rate of skilled labor and r_0 represents the reservation wage.

To explicitly derive the demand function for the intermediate good, we first substitute k/x from eqn (9.14) into eqn (9.15) and obtain

$$r = \theta p^{-\alpha/(1-\alpha)}, \quad \text{where } \theta \equiv \left[q\alpha^{\alpha}(1-\alpha)^{1-\alpha}\right]^{1/(1-\alpha)} \qquad (9.17)$$

We then combine the supply function (9.16) and demand function (9.14) to yield

$$px = \frac{\alpha}{1-\alpha} r k_s \qquad (9.18)$$

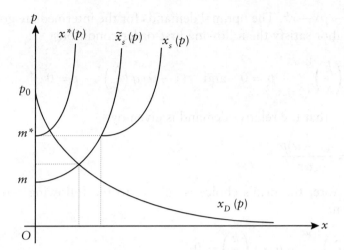

FIG. 9.2(i). No fragmentation

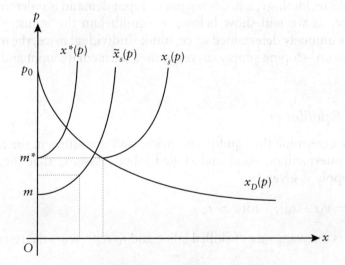

FIG. 9.2(ii). Partial fragmentation

It follows that demand for the intermediate good is

$$x_D = \frac{\alpha}{1-\alpha} v \left(\theta p^{-\alpha/(1-\alpha)} - r_0 \right) \theta p^{-1/(1-\alpha)} \qquad (9.19)$$

Define $p_0 = (r_0/\theta)^{-(1-\alpha)/\alpha}$ as the maximum price below which there is a positive demand for the intermediate good. As expected, p_0 depends

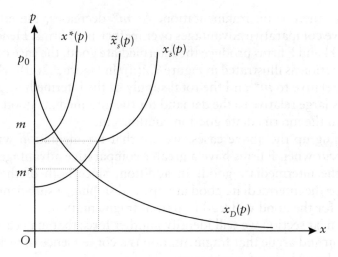

FIG. 9.2(iii). Complete fragmentation

positively on the price of the final good but negatively on the wage rate of skilled labor.

Finally, equating $x_s(p)$ and $x_D(p)$ determines the equilibrium price and quantity of the intermediate good. Clearly, there exists an equilibrium with a positive level of the intermediate good if and only if $\min\{m, m^*\} < p_0$. The equilibrium k and r of the skilled labor are determined accordingly. The following proposition summarizes the main features of the equilibrium.

Proposition 1: Suppose $\min\{m, m^*\} < p_0$. *Then in equilibrium the following holds.*

(i) *When* $m < m^* < p_0$, *the intermediate good is supplied only by H firms if* $x_D(m^*) \leq \tilde{x}(m^*)$ *and by both types of firms otherwise.*
(ii) *When* $m^* \leq m \leq p_0$, *the intermediate good is supplied only by F firms if* $x_D(m) \leq x^*(m)$ *and by both types of firms otherwise.*

Proposition 1 states that, depending on the values of the parameters, three scenarios may emerge: (*a*) complete fragmentation, that is, the final good is produced in H, but all of the intermediate input is produced in F; (*b*) partial fragmentation, that is, the intermediate input is produced in both regions; and (*c*) no fragmentation, that is, both the final good and intermediate input are produced in H. The demand and supply of the intermediate good under different conditions are illustrated in Figures 9.2(i)–(iii). Figure 9.2(i) illustrates the case in, which m^* is large relative to m, so in equilibrium only H firms produce the intermediate good and there is no fragmentation. As m^* decreases, the efficient F firms have comparative advantages over inefficient H firms. Hence, both efficient H and F firms produce the intermediate good, the case of partial fragmentation as illustrated in Figure 9.2(ii). In Figure 9.2(iii), where m^* is small relative to m^* and the total supply of the intermediate good by F firms is large relative to the demand for the intermediate good, F firms supply all the intermediate good in equilibrium.

Summing up the above cases, we see that fragmentation will more likely occur when F firms have a greater comparative advantage in producing the intermediate good. In addition, since both of the supply curves for the intermediate good are upward sloping, a sufficiently large demand for the good will lead to partial fragmentation.

In the next section we will identify another force that may cause fragmentation and argue that fragmentation is a consequence of technology transfer through direct investment.

3. A Partial Equilibrium Model with FDI

Now suppose FDI is allowed and is the primary vehicle for technology transfer from H's firms to their subsidiaries in F. There is, however, an efficiency loss when an H firm operates in F with its own technology and F labor. If e denotes the degree of efficiency retained under technology transfer, then an H firm of type β has the following profit from direct investment in F:

$$\tilde{\pi}_\beta = pe\beta\sqrt{l^{**}}/(1+t) - w^*l^{**} - c^{**}, \quad e \in (0,1) \tag{9.20}$$

where l^{**} is the H firm's hiring of labor in F and c^{**} is the fixed cost of direct investment.

We need to distinguish between two cases. In the first case, an H firm can produce in both regions, whereas in the second case an H firm can only produce in one region due to some constraints, say, limited supply in managerial talent.

Consider the first case. Similar to the analysis in Section 2, if an H firm of type β produces in F, its output and labor demand are given by

$$x_\beta^{**}(p) = \frac{\beta^2 e^2 p}{2(1+t)w^*} \quad \text{and} \quad l^{**}{}_\beta(p) = \frac{\beta^2 e^2 p^2}{(1+t)^2 w^{*3/2}} \tag{9.21}$$

respectively. Firm β will produce for the market if its profit is non-negative, or equivalently

$$\beta \geq \underline{\beta}^{**}(p) \equiv m^{**}/p \tag{9.22}$$

where $m^{**} = 2(1+t)\sqrt{(c^{**}w^*)}/e$. As in the case of F firms, the smaller is m^{**}, the greater is the advantage of H firms producing in F. Similar to the derivation in the previous section, the total supply of the intermediate good by the H invested firms is given by

$$x^{**}(p) = \frac{e(p^3 - m^{**3})}{w^*(1+t)p^2} \tag{9.23}$$

if $p \geq m^{**}$ and $x^{**}(p) = 0$ otherwise. The minimum price for a positive supply is m^{**}. The derived demand for unskilled labor in F is

$$l^{**}(p) = \frac{px^{**}(p)}{2(1+t)w^*} \tag{9.24}$$

Thus, the total supply of x from the two regions is $x_s(p) = \tilde{x}(p) + x^*(p) + x^{**}(p)$. The minimum price for a positive supply is equal to $\min\{m, m^*, m^{**}\}$. The new equilibrium price and quantity of the intermediate good is determined by equating the demand to the total supply. There exists a positive price if and only if $\min\{m, m^*, m^{**}\} < p_0$. The following proposition highlights the effect of technology transfer on the equilibrium.

Proposition 2: Suppose that H firms can produce in H and make direct investment in F. Then there exists a $\hat{m}$ such that in equilibrium some efficient H firms make direct investment in F if and only if $m^{**} < \hat{m}$. Furthermore, the equilibrium price of the intermediate good falls as a result of direct investment.

Proposition 2 says that the efficiency of technology transfer determines whether there will be direct investment in F. When e is very close to zero, m^{**} is large so in equilibrium there is no direct investment. As e increases, m^{**} decreases and the most efficient H firms will first cross the border to produce. The less efficient H firms will follow as m^{**} continues to decrease. Furthermore, an increase in e increases the total supply of the intermediate good, and consequently the equilibrium price of the intermediate good falls.

The pattern of direct investment and fragmentation is quite interesting. There are several cases to consider. For simplicity, here we focus on the case when m^* is relatively large. If direct investment is not allowed,

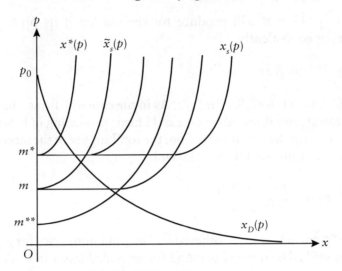

FIG. 9.3. FDI and fragmentation

then by Proposition 1 the intermediate good is supplied only by H firms and there is no fragmentation. If direct investment is feasible, Proposition 2 shows that as long as m^{**} is relatively small, some efficient H firms will produce in both regions while none of the F firms will produce. Thus, partial fragmentation occurs due to technology transfer. If m^{**} is small enough, none of H firms will produce in H, but the most efficient H firms will make direct investment and produce in F. The situation is illustrated by Figure 9.3.

Therefore, when the technology gap between the two regions is large and the cost of transferring technology from H to F is relatively small, complete fragmentation can arise. In addition to comparative advantage, the technology gap between the two regions and the cost of technology transfer are another source of fragmentation of production. This is the main point of our chapter.

We now turn to the second case where an H firm can either produce in H or F, but not in both regions because of constraints such as limited managerial talents. A representative H firm β chooses to produce in F if and only if

$$\pi_\beta^{**}(p) \geq \max\{0, \pi_\beta(p)\} \tag{9.25}$$

Similarly, it chooses to produce in H if and only if

$$\pi_\beta(p) \geq \max\{0, \pi_\beta^{**}(p)\} \tag{9.26}$$

Notice that the difference in profits between producing in H and in F is

$$\pi_\beta^{**}(p) - \pi_\beta(p) = \frac{\beta^2 p^2 (R_e^2 - 1)}{4} + c - c^{**} \tag{9.27}$$

where $R_e = e/[(1+t)\sqrt{w^*}]$. To simplify our analysis below, we assume $c^{**} < c$. The case in which $c^{**} \geq c$ can be analyzed similarly.

Case 1. Small efficiency loss in technology transfer. First, let us consider the case of a small efficiency loss in technology transfer, that is, $R_e \geq 1$. It follows that m^{**} is less than m. In this case, firm β never produces in H but will produce in F if $\beta \geq m^{**}/p$. That is, if the efficiency loss in transferring technology is small relative to the tariff-cum-transport costs and the wage in F, then all the firms that used to produce in H will now make direct investment and only produce in F. There are also some H firms (i.e., for β such that $m^{**}/p \leq \beta \leq m/p$) that did not produce in H before, but now produce in F.

An interesting question is whether, under the constraint that H firms cannot produce in both H and F simultaneously, direct investment by H firms raises the supply of the intermediate good. For all firms with $\beta \geq m/p$, their output from direct investment exceeds their former level of production in H, that is,

$$x_\beta^{**}(p) = \frac{e^2 \beta^2 p}{2(1+t)w^*} > \frac{\beta^2 p}{2} = \tilde{x}(\beta) \tag{9.28}$$

since $e^2 \geq (1+t)^2 w^* > (1+t)w^*$. For firms with β lying in the range $[m^{**}/p, m/p]$, they did not produce in H before but now produce in F. Therefore, the total supply of the intermediate good increases unambiguously due to technology transfer. Consequently, its equilibrium price drops.

Case 2. Moderate efficiency loss in technology transfer. Now consider the case of moderate efficiency loss in technology transfer in the sense that $\sqrt{(c^{**}/c)} \leq R_e \leq 1$. It is still the case that $m^{**} < m$. However, firm β produces in F only when $m^{**}/p \leq \beta \leq m'/p$, and produces in H only when $\beta > m'/p$, where $m' = 2\sqrt{(c - c^{**})}/\sqrt{(1 - R_e^2)} \geq m$. When the efficiency loss of technology transfer is moderate, the more efficient H firms have more to lose proportionally than the less efficient H firms. Thus, the former are less likely to transfer their technologies than the latter.

The supply curve is determined similarly. For those firms that remain in H, their output as a function of p does not change. For those firms that make direct investment $(m^{**}/p \leq \beta \leq m'/p)$, their total output is given by

$$x^{**}(p) = \frac{e^2}{6(1+t)w^*p^2}(m'^3 - m^{**3}) \tag{9.29}$$

The reduction in $\tilde{x}(p)$ due to the movement of some H firms that previously produced in H but now produce in F is given by

$$\Delta\tilde{x}(p) = \frac{m'^3 - m^3}{6p^2} \tag{9.30}$$

It can be shown that the difference, $x^{**}(p) - \Delta\tilde{x}(p)$, is positive. Thus, for any given p, the total supply for the intermediate good increases due to technology transfer.

Case 3. Large efficiency loss in technology transfer. Consider the case of a large efficiency loss in technology transfer, that is, $\sqrt{(c^{**}/c)} \leq R_e < 1$. In this case, none of the H firms produces in F and all of them produce in H whenever profitable. There is no direct investment and the supply curve is as given in Section 2.

Thus, the size of the efficiency loss in transferring technology relative to the wage in F and the tariff-cum-transport cost determines which H firm makes direct investment in F and which stays home to produce. Technology transfer increases the total supply of the intermediate good as long as $R_e \geq \sqrt{(c^{**})}/c$, which is equivalent to $m^{**} \leq m$.

The above results are summarized as:

Proposition 3: Suppose that H firms can either produce in H or set up production in F and that $c^{**} < c$. If $m^{**} \leq m$, then in equilibrium the H firms make direct investment in F if the efficiency loss in technology transfer is small and the more efficient H firms invest in F. If the efficiency loss is moderate then the more efficient H firms stay home, whereas the less efficient firms invest in F. So long as direct investment has taken place, the equilibrium price of the intermediate good falls as a result of direct investment.

Similar results can be obtained for the case of $c^{**} \geq c$. When the efficiency loss in technology transfer is large $(R_e \leq 1)$, no FDI occurs. However, when the efficiency loss is small or moderate, the efficient H firms make direct investment in F, thereby increasing the supply of the intermediate good and reducing its price.

A related question is how direct investment affects the labor demand in the two regions. First, notice that the total demand for unskilled labor in H is $l(p) = p\tilde{x}(p)/2$. FDI decreases the equilibrium price of the intermediate good and thus reduces the demand for unskilled labor in H. Secondly, the total demand for unskilled labor in F is $l^*(p)$ prior to FDI and $l^*(p) + l^{**}(p)$ after FDI. FDI increases the total demand for unskilled labor by $l^{**}(p)$ but $l^*(p)$ decreases it, so the effect on total demand is ambiguous.

4. A Case Study of the Investment–Trade Nexus between Hong Kong and the Chinese Mainland

In this section, we characterize some important features of the investment–trade nexus between Hong Kong and the Chinese Mainland. These features are directly related to the models developed and the results obtained in Sections 2 and 3.

Fragmentation of Production and Services

In our basic model, we can reinterpret x as the final product and y as trade services. Trade services help to deliver products to consumers. With this interpretation, a possible pattern of international fragmentation is when Hong Kong specializes in the export of products produced in the Chinese Mainland. Such exports are Hong Kong's re-exports. In reality, Hong Kong also takes up key production stages such as product design and quality control.

Hong Kong's re-exports really took off in the mid-1980s (see Table 9.1). As late as 1987, its re-exports grew by almost 50 percent over the previous year but still fell short of its domestic exports. While re-exports continued to grow in leaps and bounds in the next decade, domestic exports started to stagnate beginning in 1989, and experienced actual declines in nominal value in four out of the last five years. As a result of this divergent development, by 1997 Hong Kong's re-exports were almost six times its domestic exports.

The predominance of re-exports in Hong Kong's external trade is very much the result of China's open-door policy, in particular after China launched its new policy measures to attract FDI in 1986. Beginning in 1989, China supplied more than 50 percent of Hong Kong's re-exports and from 1986 onward it often absorbed more than 30 percent of Hong Kong's re-exports.

TABLE 9.1. Hong Kong's external trade

Year	Domestic Exports		Re-exports	
	Value (US$ bn.)	Growth rate from previous year	Value (US$ bn.)	Growth rate from previous year
1985	16.65	—	13.50	—
1986	19.74	18.56	15.71	16.41
1987	25.03	26.80	23.43	49.15
1988	27.91	11.48	35.31	50.68
1989	28.73	2.96	44.41	25.78
1990	28.96	0.79	53.08	19.51
1991	29.62	2.29	68.57	29.19
1992	30.02	1.33	88.57	29.17
1993	28.59	−4.74	105.54	19.16
1994	28.47	−0.42	121.53	15.15
1995	29.70	4.31	142.62	17.36
1996	27.20	−8.42	152.02	6.59
1997	27.10	−0.35	159.56	4.96

Source: Census and Statistics, *Hong Kong Monthly Digest of Statistics*, various issues.

From China's point of view, a large portion of its booming exports was handled by Hong Kong in the form of the latter's re-exports. As Table 9.2 shows, more then 40 percent of China's exports to the world market have been exported through Hong Kong since 1989. In absolute value, this rose from US$1.5 billion in 1981 to US$65 billion in 1995.

Foreign Direct Investment and Fragmentation

Ever since the adoption of China's open-door policy in 1978, Hong Kong has been the largest source of inward FDI in China. Due to many factors such as cultural and geographical proximity, Hong Kong's investment in China has concentrated in Guangdong province, especially in the *Pearl River Delta (PRD)*, the growth center of Guangdong.

Table 9.3 shows the amount and the share of realized FDI in Guangdong from Hong Kong. As the figures show, FDI from Hong Kong accounted for over 60 percent of total FDI in Guangdong in every single year since 1988. The number of Hong Kong-invested enterprises in the province rose from 6,438 in 1988 to 49,341 in 1995. The lion's share of Hong Kong's FDI went into manufacturing. Between 1985 and 1994 FDI in manufacturing was over 70 percent of Hong Kong's FDI in the province.

The bulk of Hong Kong's investment in Guangdong was aimed at taking advantage of the cheap labor and land. In addition, it was mainly

TABLE 9.2. China's indirect exports through Hong Kong, 1981–1995

Year	China's total exports (US$ bn.)[a]	Hong Kong's re-export of China's goods measured at China's export price (US$ bn.)[b]	Share of China's exports through Hong Kong (%)
1981	22.0	1.5	6.8
1982	22.3	1.7	7.6
1983	22.2	2.3	10.4
1984	26.1	3.2	12.3
1985	27.4	4.0	14.6
1986	30.9	5.9	19.1
1987	39.4	9.7	24.6
1988	47.5	15.1	31.8
1989	52.5	21.6	41.1
1990	62.1	26.3	42.4
1991	71.8	33.6	46.8
1992	84.9	42.1	49.6
1993	91.8	48.2	52.5
1994	121.0	56.0	46.3
1995	148.8	65.4	44.0

Source: [a]*Almanac of China's Foreign Economic Relations and Trade* (1991–96). [b]*Hong Kong Review of Overseas' Trade* (various issues), *Annual Review of Hong Kong External Trade* (various issues). The original data in the second column are given in HK$. We use HK$7.8/US$ in conversion. These figures are obtained by subtracting Hong Kong's re-export margin from the value of Hong Kong's re-exports of products originating from China. According to *Hong Kong Monthly Digest of Statistics* (Feb. 1996), the estimated rates of re-export margin from 1989 to 1995 are 11.5%, 17.4%, 20.5%, 22.9%, 26.1%, 24.9%, and 24.7%, respectively. We have no information about the rates before 1989. Thus, we use 11.5% for 1981 through 1988.

TABLE 9.3. Hong Kong's investment in Guangdong and Guangdong's exports, 1988–1996

Year	Guangdong's realized FDI from Hong Kong (US$ bn.)	Share of Hong Kong FDI in Guangdong (%)	Share of Guangdong's exports by foreign-funded enterprises (%)	Share of processing trade in Guangdong's total exports*
1988	1.48	61	16	5.4
1989	1.48	62	28	7.8
1990	1.26	62	35	6.3
1991	1.62	63	39	6.5
1992	3.45	71	44	5.9
1993	7.37	76	38	23.9
1994	8.70	76	40	28.3
1995	8.99	74	44	26.7
1996	9.39	68	51	27.2

Note: *The sudden increase of shares from 1992 to 1993 is due to the adoption of new statistical methods since 1993.
Source: *Statistical Yearbook of Guangdong* (various issues) and the authors' calculation.

export-oriented, that is, products were exported to Hong Kong or to the world market. The third column of Table 9.3 indicates the increasingly important role played by foreign-funded enterprises in the province's export growth. 'Foreign-funded enterprises' in China are enterprises wholly or partly owned by foreign investors. Moreover, the last column of the table shows that exports due to 'export processing' and 'compensation trade' accounted for an additional 27.2 percent of total exports in 1996. The case of Guangdong has demonstrated clearly that international fragmentation of production may take the form of FDI as well as international subcontracting, even though FDI's importance has grown over time. One can argue that if technology transfer is not essential to cross-border production (e.g., if production technology is identical across economies), then FDI is not a necessary element of production fragmentation at all. However, if there are substantial differences in production technology across economies, then cross-border production fragmentation and FDI tend to go together, because MNCs are generally regarded as the best vehicle for technology transfer.

According to a survey conducted by the Hong Kong Federation of Industries (1991), on average 40 percent of manufacturing firms in Hong Kong had their investment in the Pearl River Delta by 1990. The electronics industry had the highest percentage, 69.4 percent. Moreover, on average these firms' production in the PRD, either as finished or processed products, accounted for almost 75 percent of their total industrial production. In particular, manufacturers in the toys sector had 92.8 percent of their products finished or processed in their factories in the PRD. Table 9.4 shows the figures for selected industries.

The cross-border fragmentation in production has generated a large volume of trade between Hong Kong and southern China. Over 70 percent of Hong Kong's domestic exports and over 40 percent of its re-exports to the Chinese Mainland, and over 70 percent (since 1992) of its imports from the latter are related to Hong Kong's 'outward processing' activities in southern China.

Impacts of Fragmentation on Economic Structure

One of the predictions of our model about the consequences of FDI and international fragmentation is the increased employment in the production of x in F, decreased employment in the production of x in H, and increased employment in the production of y in H. If we identify H as Hong Kong and consider Hong Kong's re-exports as the final stage of

TABLE 9.4. Hong Kong's manufacturing firms in the Pearl River Delta (PRD), 1990

Industries	Percentage of firms having investment in PRD	Percentage of products finished or processed in PRD
Apparel	26.2	54.2
Electronics	69.4	78.9
Toys	58.3	92.8
Plastic, rubber, and leather products	48.1	72.5
Electrical and optical products	45.3	84.0
Textiles	18.5	69.6
Jewelry	30.8	68.6
Watches and clocks	46.2	68.8
Average	40.7	74.9

Source: Federation of Hong Kong industries (1991).

the production-service chain, we should expect the employment in trade-related services in Hong Kong (which in reality require both skilled and unskilled workers) to increase and its employment in manufacturing to decline.

As Hong Kong moved some of its manufacturing functions across the border to southern China, especially to the Pearl River Delta, and as the goods manufactured in China were exported back to Hong Kong or through Hong Kong to the world market, Hong Kong's own economic structure experienced dramatic structural changes as shown in Table 9.5. The most visible feature is the decline in the importance of manufacturing in Hong Kong's GDP and employment share. In 1987, manufacturing accounted for 22 percent of Hong Kong's GDP, but by 1996 the share declined to 7.2 percent. In terms of employment, manufacturing peaked in 1987 (in absolute terms) at 919,000, or 34.1 percent of total employment in that year. The employment figure has continued to decline ever since, and by 1996 it fell to 340,500, or 11.4 percent of total employment.

As a mirror image of the decline in its manufacturing activities, Hong Kong's trade-related activities have expanded. For instance, the category that includes 'import/export trades' increased its share in GDP from 22.3 percent in 1986 to 25.4 percent in 1996. The share for 'transport, storage, and communications' increased from 8.2 percent in 1986 to 10.2 percent in 1996. While these two categories included more than just external trade-related activities, they were indicative of the latter's growth. Moreover, much of the trade-related services in support of the

TABLE 9.5. Structural changes in Hong Kong's economy

Year	Share (%) in GDP			Share (%) in total employment		
	Manufacturing	Wholesale, retail, import/export trades, restaurants and hotels	Transport, storage, and communication	Manufacturing	Import/export trades	Transport, storage, and communication
1986	22.6	22.3	8.2	34.7	7.7	8.2
1987	22.0	24.3	8.6	34.1	8.3	8.3
1988	20.5	25.1	9.1	32.3	9.4	8.7
1989	19.3	25.0	8.9	30.4	10.3	9.1
1990	17.6	25.2	9.5	27.8	11.4	9.3
1991	15.4	25.9	9.6	24.5	12.7	9.4
1992	13.6	26.1	9.7	21.5	13.5	10.3
1993	11.2	27.0	9.5	18.4	14.9	10.9
1994	9.2	26.2	9.7	15.4	17.1	11.4
1995	8.3	26.6	10.0	13.4	17.6	11.0
1996	7.2	25.4	10.2	11.4	17.5	11.0

Source: Hong Kong Monthly Digest of Statistics, various issues.

Pearl River Delta's production and trade is provided by Hong Kong. The phenomenon is indicative of the scale economies in what Jones and Kierzkowski (1990) call service links.

As the fifth column of Table 9.5 shows, the share of employment in import/export trades rose steadily from 7.7 percent in 1986 to 17.5 percent in 1996. That is, the employment share more than doubled in a decade. Employment in this industry began to exceed that in manufacturing in 1994, and the gap has continued to widen ever since. Despite the drastic contraction of the manufacturing sector, total employment has been rising.

What has happened to employment in the Chinese Mainland (F in the model) by Hong Kong's firms? As of now, there are more than 40,000 Hong Kong companies in the Peal River Delta, employing up to 5 million people there,[3] in comparison with Hong Kong's total population of 6.2 million.

NOTES

We thank Professor Yun-Wing Sung for providing us with useful data and participants of the 'Globalization and International Trade' conference held in Burgenstock, Switzerland, and the 'International Trade, Factor Mobility and Asia' workshop held in Hong Kong for helpful comments.

1. FDI is traditionally regarded as an organic amalgamation of capital, technology, and management. With the increasing integration of the global capital market and the development of domestic capital markets in many host countries of MNCs, capital movement from the home countries of MNCs to the host countries seems to have become the least important ingredient of FDI (see Blomstrom and Kokko, 1994 and Krugman, 1998 for some empirical evidence). In contrast, technology and managerial skills have become the key ingredients of FDI. We (Cheng *et al.*, 2000) have developed general equilibrium models of international trade and FDI by taking FDI to be synonymous with the transfer of technology and managerial skills.
2. See chapter 14 of Fujita *et al.* (1999) for the economic geography approach to international specialization of production.
3. These figures come from an article written by Victor Fung, Chairman of Hong Kong Trade Development Council, in *Hong Kong Economic Journal*, 1 May 1998.

REFERENCES

Arndt, Sven W. (1997). 'Globalization and the Open Economy', *North American Journal of Economics & Finance*, 8/1: 71–9.

Arndt, Sven W. (1998). 'Globalization and the Gains from Trade', in K. J. Koch and K. Jaeger (eds.), *Trade, Growth and Economic Policy in Open Economies* (New York: Springer-Verlag).

Blomstrom, Magnus, and Kokko, Ari (1994). 'Home Country Effects of Foreign Direct Investment: Evidence from Sweden', NBER Working Paper No. 4639, National Bureau of Economic Research, Cambridge, Mass.

Cheng, Leonard K., Qiu, Larry D., and Tan, Guofu (2000). 'Technology Transfer, Foreign Direct Investment and International trade', mimeo, Department of Economics, Hong Kong University of Science and Technology.

Deardorff, Alan V. (1998). 'Fragmentation in Simple Trade Models', mimeo.

Dixit, Avinash K., and Grossman, Gene M. (1982). 'Trade and Protection with Multistage Production', *Review of Economic Studies*, 49.

Federation of Hong Kong Industries (1991). *Hong Kong's Industrial Investment in the Pearl River Delta* (Hong Kong: Federation of Hong Kong Industries).

Fujita, M., Krugman, P., and Venables, A. J. (1999). *The Spatial Economy: Cities, Regions and International Trade* (Cambridge, Mass.: MIT Press).

Jones, Ronald W., and Kierzkowski, Henryk (1990). 'The Role of Services in Production and International Trade: A Theoretical Framework', ch. 3 in Ronald W. Jones and Anne O. Krueger (eds.), *The Political Economy of International Trade* (Oxford: Basil Blackwell).

—— —— —— (2000). 'Globalization and the Consequences of International Fragmentation', forthcoming in Rudiger Dornbusch, Guillermo Calvo, and Maurice Obstfeld (eds.), *Money, Factor Mobility and Trade: A Festschrift in Honor of Robert A. Mundell* (Cambridge, Mass.: MIT Press).

Krugman, Paul R. (1998). 'Fire-sale FDI', found on his homepage.

Sanyal, Kalyan K., and Jones, Ronald W. (1982). 'The Theory of Trade in Middle Products', *American Economic Review*, 72 (Mar.).

10

F23 L23
F14
L60

Will Italy Survive Globalization?

ALBERTO PETRUCCI AND BENIAMINO QUINTIERI

1. Introduction

Globalization has brought about a very rapid growth of international trade in manufactured goods between industrialized and developing countries. Some of the major structural changes that have occurred recently in the advanced economies have often been associated with increased competition from the newly industrializing countries.

The standard model of international trade theory, that is, the two goods-two factors Heckscher–Ohlin–Samuelson model, is the most used tool to describe the effects of increased trade on goods and labor markets in industrialized countries. This theory provides very clear and straightforward predictions. Assume that the two goods are X and Y and that the two factors of production are unskilled (L) and skilled labor (H). Assume also that X is relatively unskilled-labor-intensive compared with good Y and that industrialized countries are relatively abundant in skilled labor compared with developing countries. The Heckscher–Ohlin–Samuelson model predictions for the industrialized countries, following increased competition from unskilled-abundant developing economies, are the following:

1. the relative 'world' price of X will fall;
2. the production of good X will fall and the full employment requirement will imply inter-sectoral substitution of production toward the less unskilled-intensive good Y;
3. as good X is relatively intensive in unskilled labor, imports from developing countries will negatively affect the demand for unskilled workers in the industrialized countries. This would result in a fall of relative earnings for the unskilled (the Stolper–Samuelson theorem);
4. the rise in the real wages of skilled workers and the reduction of the real wages of unskilled ones will be accompanied by an increase in the relative employment of unskilled workers in all sectors.

Is the empirical evidence in accordance with these theoretical predictions? As we shall see in the next section, recent trends in the patterns of trade between OECD countries and developing countries seem to confirm points 1 and 2. A large amount of evidence concerning point 3 is also available for almost all the industrialized countries, showing a deteriorated position for unskilled workers. There is, however, much debate on the impact of trade on the labor market.[1] Some studies have reached the conclusion that the labor market effects of trade are small and that technological change biased against the use of unskilled labor is the culprit of the fall in the relative wages of unskilled workers and/or of the increased unemployment of production workers. Other studies, however, have found evidence of a strong link between trade and labor markets. Finally, no evidence has been, so far, provided in favor of point 4.

Among the industrialized countries, Italy represents a very interesting and atypical case. Instead of retrenching under competition from developing countries, this country's unskilled-intensive sectors have been flourishing. At the same time, however, we observe increased wage differentials in favor of skilled workers and a fall in the employment of unskilled workers in the manufacturing sectors.

The aim of this chapter is to build a model capable of explaining the evolution of the international specialization observed in Italy and in some other industrialized countries and providing some links between trade and globalization that are not found in the traditional theory. The model is based on two main hypotheses. First, since the observed evidence shows that much trade is based on product differentiation, we postulate that (intra-industry) trade among countries with different factor endowments is based on goods having different qualities. We assume that differences in qualities are associated with differences in skill content, so that higher quality products require a higher content of skilled labor.

The second hypothesis considered is that skilled workers are not mobile among sectors as assumed by the Heckscher–Ohlin–Samuelson theory. In our view (much) of the skill 'embodied' in each worker is specific to the sectors in which the worker is employed, being the result of the experience accumulated 'on the job'. This implies that moving from one sector to another is 'costly' to the worker, as part of his skill is lost and with it part of his earning capability. This idea is incorporated in the model by making the extreme assumption that human capital is totally sector-specific. The two hypotheses are embedded into a specific-factors model with human capital and vertical product differentiation.

While most of the literature on intra-industry trade incorporates the assumptions of increasing returns based on monopolistic competition in the goods market and full factor mobility among sectors,[2] in the present chapter the explanation of intra-industry trade is based on vertical product differentiation obtained in a competitive environment with no economies of scale as we want to focus our attention on some sort of 'structural imperfections' of the labor market arising from the sectoral specificity of skilled workers.

The model provides an explanation of the effects of globalization based on the 'fragmentation' (meant to describe differences in quality) of output produced within a sector. In this regard we depart from the concept of fragmentation employed and developed in other chapters of the book, where it represents a process of trade in parts and components of products, that is, intra-product trade. Our idea of fragmentation is based on the fact that the production of a good is carried out along a vertical ladder and international trade involves different qualities of the same 'good'. Since the production of higher qualities requires a higher skill content, then each country will specialize in that part of the vertically differentiated good spectrum that suits its factor endowment and a geographical reallocation of trade flows will take place according to the world distribution of endowments.

2. Some Stylized Facts on the Italian Trade Structure

It has been argued that the fact that trade with emerging economies is relatively balanced and represents only a small share of total OECD trade rules out the possibility that such trade may have a significant labor market impact for industrialized countries. However, as predicted by theory, if the labor content of import-competing sectors is different from that of export sectors, relative factor prices will change as a result of increased foreign competitive pressures. Moreover, if workers do not easily move from import-competing sectors to export sectors, globalization may generate unemployment at least in the short run.

Table 10.1 provides a picture of trade patterns between the G7 countries and emerging economies. The first four columns show the main sectors that face import competition from the emerging economies. In these sectors, the value of imports exceeds the value of exports. There are only slight differences (with the exception of Italy) among the main industrialized countries as to the nature of the sectors which are typically above-average net importers from the emerging economies.

TABLE 10.1. Trade patterns with emerging economies

| | Sectors with a high incidence of net imports from emerging economies (EEs), 1993 Net imports from EEs as a percent of trade turnover[a] | | | | Earnings of import-competing sectors, 1990 | Evolution of trade prices, 1980–1990 Percentage changes | | |
| | Textiles, apparel, footwear and leather | Wood products | Rubber and plastics | Other manufacturing[b] | Average earnings of the sectors as a percentage of average manufacturing earnings | Import prices[c] | Export prices[d] | Trade price gap |
	(1)	(2)	(3)	(4)	(5)	(6)	(7)	(8) = (7) − (6)
France	9.1	6.2	6.4	14.1	89.1	20.9	38.0	17.1
Germany	14.9	5.6	6.5	14.6	79.5	20.2	40.4	20.2
Italy	1.1	1.8	4.7	1.8	87.0	24.0	32.7	8.7
United Kingdom	21.4	15.3	12.8	1.9	85.4	19.3	28.2	8.9
EU unweighted average	11.5	4.8	6.2	10.6	83.9	20.7	31.2	10.5
Japan	36.8	42.0	5.7	14.3	74.8	−7.5	43.2	50.7
Canada	34.8	0.6	10.8	22.6	86.1	14.0	38.0	24.0
United States	46.1	16.2	39.3	33.5	83.6	0.7	30.3	29.6
OECD unweighted average	17.4	7.9	10.5	15.1	84.8	18.0	29.5	11.5

Notes: [a]For each sector, the figures refer to imports from EEs minus exports to EEs expressed as a ratio of trade turnover (calculated as total exports of the sector plus total imports of the sector).
[b]The other manufacturing sector includes mainly consumer products.
[c]Import prices are average unit values of import-competing sectors.
[d]Export prices are average unit values of export sectors.
Source: OECD (1997).

What are the characteristics of 'import-competing' sectors? Is the production process of these sectors characterized by a high intensity of unskilled labor? Column 5 of Table 10.1 tries to answer these questions indirectly, showing that average earnings in import-competing sectors are lower than the average in the total manufacturing sector of the OECD countries. We interpret this as implying a lower-skill intensity. Columns 6 to 8 show the evolution of import prices of import-competing sectors and export prices of export sectors. Between 1980 and 1990 import prices rose cumulatively in all countries (with the exception of Japan), with an average increase for the OECD countries of 18 percent. During the same period prices in export sectors increased more rapidly in all the countries. As a consequence we can observe, for the industrialized countries, a decline in the relative price of import-competing sectors (column 8).

Overall, this evidence suggests that import-competing sectors are characterized by relatively low earnings and, presumably, a relatively high incidence of unskilled workers. Trade between industrialized countries and the emerging economies seems to be mainly of the inter-industry type. This fact highlights the role of the differences in resource endowments as one key determinant of trade between these two areas in line with standard Heckscher–Ohlin–Samuelson theory.

Italy represents an important departure from this general pattern: as shown in Table 10.1, this country has the lowest import intensities in the 'import-competing' sectors. In fact Italy shows a very atypical position in that, according to the predictions of theory, the 'traditional' sectors should have been sized down by increased competition from newly industrialized countries.

Table 10.2 offers some crude evidence of the relationship between the labor-skill content of production and the competitive position of the Italian industrial sector. In particular, we have considered two indicators: the *import–penetration ratio* (*IMPEN*) and the *normalized trade balance* (*NTB*). As skill indicators we have used, in addition to the more usual ratio between *white- and blue-collar workers* (*WB*), two other measures of the skill level within the two broad occupational categories. BC1 and WC1 are then defined, respectively, as the share of the most skilled blue- and white-collar workers with respect to total blue- and white-collar employment.

Table 10.2a reports the correlation coefficients between trade indicators and technological indexes based on different labor-skill measures. The most striking result for 1990 is the strong negative relationship between skill indicators and trade performance. The NTB appears to

Alberto Petrucci and Beniamino Quintieri

TABLE 10.2. Industry characteristics and trade
indicators (Italy 1990)

(*a*) *Correlation coefficients*

	Skill intensity			
	WB	BC1	WC1	R&D
NTB	−0.52	−0.03	−0.31	−0.16
IMPEN	0.46	0.19	0.39	0.44

(*b*) *Correlation coefficients*

Industries	Trade indicators		Skill composition of employment				
	NTB	IMPEN	WB	WC1	BC1	Blue collar	White collar
Traditional industries (A)	43.50	12.09	24.01	40.67	21.34		
Advanced industries (B)	−6.51	29.17	53.54	58.84	32.42		
Wage differentials between (B) and (A)						14.82	8.95

Notes: NTB = normalized trade balance; IMPEN = import penetration; WB = ratio between white- and blue-collar workers; WC1, BC1 = shares of, respectively, the most skilled white- and blue-collar workers with respect to white- and blue-collar employment; R&D = R&D expenditures/sales.
Source: Quintieri (1995), ch. 6.

be negatively correlated with all the skill indexes, showing that the most technologically intensive industries are relatively least successful on international markets. We reach somewhat similar results when we consider the usual indicators based on R&D expenditures.

In Table 10.2*b* we have grouped industries according to the taxonomy proposed by Pavitt and widely used to analyze the technological content of international trade. We have divided the manufacturing industries into two categories, 'traditional' industries and 'advanced' industries. What emerges are large differences in the skill composition of employment between the two groups of industries and a wage differential favoring the advanced industries, which, in the case of Italy, showed relatively weak performances on the international market.

The atypical position of Italy in international trade was intensified during the last two decades. This can be seen in Figure 10.1, which shows Italy's comparative advantages. Most of the industrial sectors are located in the upper-right-hand quadrant of the graph and below the diagonal, implying a persistent pattern of specialization in so-called traditional sectors.

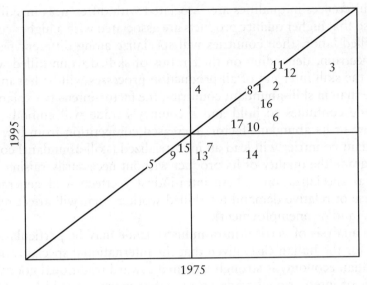

FIG. 10.1. Comparative advantages of Italy: normalized trade balances

Notes:

1. Leather and products;
2. Textiles;
3. Wearing apparel and clothing accessories;
4. Cork and wood manufactures;
5. Paper and products;
6. Polygraphy, publishing, and cinematography;
7. Basic metal industries;
8. Machinery;
9. Office machines and precision instruments;
10. Transport equipment;
11. Other metal manufacturing;
12. Non-metallic mineral products;
13. Chemical;
14. Petroleum and coal products;
15. Artificial and synthetic textile fibers;
16. Rubber;
17. Other manufacturing.

This picture appears to be in contrast with the effects of globalization predicted by the standard Heckscher–Ohlin–Samuelson model of international trade. What should be explained is the lock-in of sectoral specialization in the presence of the increased international competition that took place mainly in those sectors. Our hypothesis is that, at least for countries like Italy, the effects of globalization could be captured by looking at *intra-industry trade* (IIT) instead of inter-industry trade. Although intra-industry trade among similar countries is largely based on product differentiation and is a phenomenon of a horizontal specialization, IIT among countries with very different factor endowment can be based on goods with different qualities.

If differences in qualities are associated with differences in skill content, so that higher quality products are associated with a higher content of skilled labor, then countries will specialize along different parts of the spectrum, depending on their ratios of skilled to unskilled wages. Since the skill intensity of all production processes will be less in skill-scarce than in skill-abundant countries, the factor-intensity explanation of trade continues to hold and a country's trade will embody a net outflow of its abundant factor. Increased competition from low-skill-abundant countries will lead an industrialized (skill-abundant) country to upgrade the quality of its product without necessarily raising inter-sectoral specialization. These intra-industry effects will generate an increase of relative demand for skilled workers that will affect relative wages (and/or unemployment).

The analysis of vertical intra-industry trade may be particularly relevant for the Italian case, given that the international specialization of the Italian economy is strongly oriented toward traditional goods. The impact of international trade on the labor market would be underestimated if only inter-industry trade were taken into account. Recent developments in empirical methodologies allow us to separate vertical IIT from horizontal IIT and then to consider product heterogeneity.

Table 10.3 reports Grubel–Lloyd indices of IIT, by distinguishing vertical and horizontal components. The methodology used (see Greenaway *et al.*, 1994, 1995) is based on a decomposition of the unadjusted Grubel–Lloyd index into vertical and horizontal IIT by using information derived from unit values of exports and imports.[3] It is assumed that for a high level of disaggregation of trade data, it is possible to use unit values as meaningful indicators of product quality. This implies that differences between the unit values of imports and exports of products in the same *i*th class can be used to distinguish between horizontal and vertical intra-industry trade and to decompose the latter into its positive and negative components.

The criterion used to discriminate between the two components of IIT is inclusion in the index of only the trade flows of those products whose unit value of exports relative to the unit value of imports was outside (or within) a certain range ($\pm 15\%$; $\pm 25\%$). In cases in which the absolute value of the difference was more (less) than 15 percent or 25 percent, the share of vertical (horizontal) IIT was obtained.

Values reported in Table 10.3 were obtained by using Italian trade data for the years 1990 and 1996 at four-digit CN levels for chapters from 24 to 99. We considered 1,040 commodities. The results show that most of IIT is vertical, especially in trade with developing Asian countries

TABLE 10.3. Level of total, vertical, and horizontal intra-industry trade in Italy, 1990 and 1996

	Grubel–Lloyd indices								
	Total	Horizontal 15%	Vertical 15%			Horizontal 25%	Vertical 25%		
			Total	Positive	Negative		Total	Positive	Negative
1990									
World	0.52	0.16	0.37	0.13	0.23	0.26	0.26	0.12	0.15
EU	0.56	0.15	0.40	0.09	0.31	0.28	0.28	0.08	0.20
Developing Asian countries	0.27	0.02	0.25	0.20	0.05	0.03	0.24	0.19	0.04
Transition countries	0.26	0.02	0.24	0.21	0.02	0.03	0.23	0.21	0.02
1996									
World	0.52	0.17	0.35	0.15	0.20	0.25	0.27	0.13	0.14
EU	0.55	0.15	0.40	0.10	0.30	0.28	0.27	0.09	0.18
Developing Asian countries	0.33	0.03	0.30	0.24	0.05	0.06	0.27	0.23	0.04
Transition countries	0.35	0.08	0.27	0.22	0.05	0.10	0.25	0.20	0.04

and with transition countries. Moreover, we can observe that most of vertical IIT by EU countries is negative, while Italy is a net exporter within each sector of relatively high-quality goods to the developing world. A comparison of 1990 and 1996 trade shows further that vertical IIT with developing Asian countries increased during the first half of the 1990s, as predicted by our hypothesis on the effects of globalization.

3. Product Quality and Sector-Specific Human Capital

The Basic Framework

In this section we develop a theoretical model of vertical product differentiation that is consistent with the empirical evidence shown above. We follow Rodriguez (1979), Falvey and Kierzkowski (1987), Flam and Helpman (1987), and Djajic and Kierzkowski (1989) in analyzing the interactions between product quality and trade within a perfectly competitive environment.[4]

Consider a small open economy that produces two commodities, a vertically differentiated good and a homogeneous good, by using three factors of production, unskilled labor, which is perfectly mobile between sectors, and two industry-specific types of human capital. The supply of the three factors is completely exogenous. The model we develop analyzes the role of an endogenous product quality within the specific-factors model.[5] The analysis is static and the context deterministic. Perfect competition is assumed to prevail in all markets.

The production function of the quality good, called X, is given by

$$XQ = \min[A(Q)L_X, H_X] \qquad A(1) = \bar{A}, \quad A'(Q) > 0 \qquad (10.1)$$

where X represents physical units of the good, Q is a quality index, XQ is the amount of 'quality units', L_X is the unskilled labor employed in sector X, H_X is the sector-specific human capital, and $A(Q)$ is the technical coefficient giving the marginal product of labor. We assume that the unskilled labor requirement per unit of quality good, that is, $A(Q)^{-1}$, decreases with quality.

Production function (10.1) assumes that there is no technical substitution between adjusted labor (i.e., expressed in efficiency units), $A(Q)L_X$, and human capital, but at the same time it implies that the human capital–'raw' labor ratio depends positively on quality.[6] The basic idea incorporated into eqn (10.1) is that higher quality can be obtained only through an increase in human capital intensity, according to the following technological relationship

$$\frac{H_X}{L_X} = A(Q) \tag{10.2}$$

The representative firm maximizes its profit by choosing the quantity of inputs employed and quality. Given the assumption of perfect competition in output and factor markets, the first-order conditions for profit maximization are[7]

$$\left[\frac{w}{A(Q)} + v_X\right]Q = p_X \tag{10.3a}$$

$$p_X \frac{A(Q)}{Q^2}\left[\frac{QA'(Q)}{A(Q)} - 1\right] = v_X A'(Q) \tag{10.3b}$$

where w is the wage rate of unskilled labor, v_X is the price of X-sector human capital and the p_X is the price of one physical unit of good X of a given quality.

Equation (10.3a) represents the zero-profit condition, stating that the average cost of a quality unit of good X is equal to price or, equivalently, that the average cost of a physical unit of the differentiated good is equal to the price adjusted for quality (p_X/Q). According to eqn (10.3a), a higher quality exerts two conflicting effects on the autarky price of X. On the one hand, the price is increased as the average cost of a quality unit rises with quality, but on the other hand it is diminished since quality lowers the unskilled labor cost expressed in efficiency units (w/A). We shall assume below that the former effect prevails, generating a positive link between quality and the output price for given input prices.

Equation (10.3b) is the optimal condition for quality deriving from profit maximization; it implies that quality must be such that the marginal revenue of quality per unskilled worker equals the marginal cost of quality per unskilled worker. The elasticity of the labor technical coefficient with respect to quality (i.e. $QA'(Q)/A(Q)$) must be greater than one (namely a positive effect of higher quality on total revenue occurs) to have a well-defined equilibrium. Substituting eqn (10.3b) into (10.3a) for v_X, we obtain another characterization of the optimal condition for quality

$$\frac{QA'(Q)}{A(Q)}\frac{w}{A(Q)} = \frac{p_X}{Q} \tag{10.3b'}$$

Equation (10.3b') asserts that the adjusted quality price must be a proportion of the wage expressed in efficiency units, where the factor of proportionality is greater than one from condition (10.3b).

The production function for the homogeneous good is

$$Y = G(L_Y, H_Y) \tag{10.4}$$

where Y represents physical units of the homogeneous good, L_Y is the unskilled labor employed in sector Y, and H_Y is the human capital specific to the industry. The function $G(\ ,\ )$ satisfies the usual neoclassical properties of regularity and is linearly homogeneous in the two inputs.

Letting Y be the numéraire ($P_Y = 1$), the optimal conditions for maximum profit are

$$G_{L_Y}(L_Y, H_Y) = w \tag{10.5a}$$
$$G_{H_Y}(L_Y, H_Y) = v_Y \tag{10.5b}$$

where v_Y is the price of Y-sector human capital.

Wage flexibility and perfect inter-sectoral mobility of labor assure full employment of unskilled workers:

$$L_X + L_Y = \bar{L} \tag{10.6}$$

where $\bar{L}$ is the fixed unskilled labor supply. Supplies of the two sets of specific human capital are completely inelastic with respect to variation in factor prices

$$H_X = \bar{H}_X \tag{10.7}$$
$$H_Y = \bar{H}_Y \tag{10.8}$$

Assuming that preferences of consumers depend on quality units of the differentiated good (i.e. XQ) and on the quantity of the homogeneous good, that tastes are homothetic and identical for all consumers, the supply side of the model, under the assumption of a small perfectly competitive open economy, determines the vector of factor prices, outputs, the sectoral distribution of the mobile factor, and quality.

Assuming, without any loss of generality, that A is an isoelastic function of quality—that is, $A(Q) = \bar{A}Q^\eta$, where $\eta > 1$ according to condition (10.3b)—the general equilibrium model, obtained by combining the optimality conditions of the firms operating in the two industries together with the equilibrium conditions on factor markets, is given by the following system:

$$\left[\frac{w}{\bar{A}Q^{\eta}} + v_X\right]Q = p_X \tag{10.9a}$$

$$\eta\frac{w}{\bar{A}Q^{\eta}} = \frac{p_X}{Q} \tag{10.9b}$$

$$\frac{\bar{H}_X}{L_X} = \bar{A}Q^{\eta} \tag{10.9c}$$

$$G_{L_Y}(L_Y, \bar{H}_Y) = w \tag{10.9d}$$

$$G_{H_Y}(L_Y, \bar{H}_Y) = v_Y \tag{10.9e}$$

$$L_X + L_Y = \bar{L} \tag{10.9f}$$

$$XQ = \bar{H}_X \tag{10.9g}$$

$$Y = G(L_Y, \bar{H}_Y) \tag{10.9h}$$

The system (10.9) determines the equilibrium values of the following endogenous variables: w, v_X, v_Y, Q, L_X, L_Y, X, and Y.

The sectoral allocation of employment plays a crucial role in the functioning of the model. An exogenous shock first has an impact on the allocation of labor and then feeds back to the other variables. The distribution of unskilled labor can be easily grasped by using the specific-factors diagram that combines labor demands (10.9c) and (10.9d) as well as the allocation constraint (10.9f).

Since the labor demand in the X sector depends on quality according to the production function (10.1), we can use eqn (10.9b) to eliminate Q from eqn (10.9c) and obtain the following relationship between w and L_X, that can be considered a sort of labor demand equation:

$$w = \frac{\bar{A}p_X}{\eta}\left(\frac{\bar{H}}{\bar{A}L_X}\right)^{\frac{\eta-1}{\eta}} \tag{10.10}$$

Function (10.10) is downward-sloping in the $L_X - w$ Cartesian space and is shifted upward by an exogenous increase in p_X. The distribution of labor is depicted in Figure 10.2, where the intersection of the two labor demand schedules simultaneously determines employment in both sectors and the wage rate measured in terms of the numéraire.

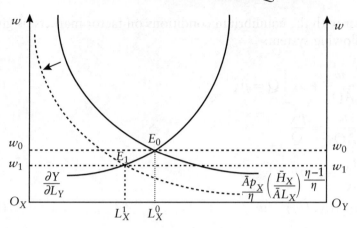

FIG. 10.2. Labor market effects

The General Equilibrium Effects of Globalization

The model developed in the previous section can be purposefully employed to investigate the implications of globalization. We assume that this phenomenon, stemming from increased world competition, can be represented by an exogenous shock that reduces the terms of trade, namely p_X.

Totally differentiating system (10.9), the basic model of the economy can be expressed in the following format:

$$\vartheta_{LX}\hat{w} + (1 - \vartheta_{LX}\eta)\hat{Q} + \vartheta_{HX}\hat{v}_X = \hat{p}_X,$$

$$\vartheta_{LX} + \vartheta_{HX} = 1, \quad \vartheta_{LX}\eta < 1 \tag{10.11a}$$

$$(\eta - 1)\hat{Q} - \hat{w} = -\hat{p}_X \tag{10.11b}$$

$$\eta\hat{Q} = -\hat{L}_X \tag{10.11c}$$

$$\hat{w} = -\frac{\vartheta_{HY}}{\sigma}\hat{L}_Y \tag{10.11d}$$

$$\lambda_{LX}\hat{L}_X + \lambda_{LY}\hat{L}_Y = 0 \qquad \lambda_{LX} + \lambda_{LY} = 1 \tag{10.11e}$$

$$\hat{v}_Y = \frac{\vartheta_{LY}}{\sigma}\hat{L}_Y \qquad \vartheta_{LY} + \vartheta_{HY} = 1 \tag{10.11f}$$

where $\hat{}$ denotes the relative change of a variable, σ is the elasticity of substitution between labor and human capital in the Y industry, ϑ_{ij} is the distributive share of factor i ($i = L, H$) in the value of output in industry j ($j = X, Y$), and λ_{Lj} is the fraction of the unskilled labor force employed in the *j*th sector ($j = X, Y$). The change in the quantity of the two goods, $\hat{X}$ and $\hat{Y}$, can be solved residually, using eqns (10.9*g*) and (10.9*h*), once the reduced forms for $\hat{Q}$ and $\hat{L}_Y$ are obtained. The imposed condition $\vartheta_{LX}\eta < 1$ implies a positive effect of quality on average cost.

Considering equations (10.11*c*) to (10.11*e*), we obtain the following relationship between quality and wage, both expressed in relative changes:

$$\hat{w} = -\frac{\eta\lambda_{LX}\vartheta_{HY}}{\lambda_{LY}\sigma}\hat{Q} \tag{10.12}$$

Equation (10.12), deriving from labor demands, can be considered as the log-linearized 'demand' for quality, in differential form, for any given price of unskilled labor. The relationship between Q and w (both expressed in logarithms) is negative, as represented by the *DD* curve in Figure 10.3.[8] An increase in the wage rate results in a lower demand for unskilled labor in the *Y* sector (from eqn (10.11*d*)), implying (given the adding-up constraint) an increase in the demand for labor in the quality good sector. The rise in L_X reduces the quality of the differentiated good, since it causes a reduction in the human-capital intensity for a given supply of the sector-specific input. The *DD* curve in Figure 10.3 is independent of p_X, since the terms of trade do not enter the labor demand equations and the allocation constraint.

Equation (10.11*b*) represents what can be called the 'quality equation'. It asserts a positive link between wage and quality for given terms of trade. This relationship is represented by the *QQ* curve in Figure 10.3.

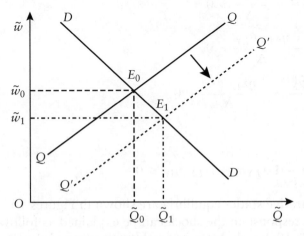

FIG. 10.3. Wage and quality

For a fixed p_X, a higher quality lowers the absolute value of the marginal cost of quality per unit of human capital more than the corresponding reduction of marginal revenue. Therefore, wages must increase to restore the marginal equilibrium condition for quality. A fall in p_X shifts the QQ curve downward to the right. Equations (10.11b) and (10.12) jointly determine the wage rate and the quality of the differentiated good.

The quantitative effects of an exogenous change in relative prices on the main endogenous variables are given by the following multipliers:

$$\frac{\hat{Q}}{\hat{p}_X} = -\frac{\lambda_{LY}\sigma}{\Delta} < 0$$

$$\frac{\hat{w}}{\hat{p}_X} = \frac{\eta\lambda_{LX}\vartheta_{HY}}{\Delta} > 0$$

$$\frac{\hat{w} - \hat{p}_X}{\hat{p}_X} = -\frac{(\eta - 1)\lambda_{LY}\sigma}{\Delta} < 0$$

$$\frac{\hat{L}_X}{\hat{p}_X} = \frac{\eta\lambda_{LY}\sigma}{\Delta} > 0$$

$$\frac{\hat{L}_Y}{\hat{p}_X} = -\frac{\eta\lambda_{LX}\sigma}{\Delta} < 0$$

$$\frac{\hat{v}_X}{\hat{p}_X} = \frac{\eta(\lambda_{LX}\vartheta_{HY} + \lambda_{LY}\sigma)}{\Delta} > 0$$

$$\frac{\hat{v}_X - \hat{p}_X}{\hat{p}_X} = \frac{\lambda_{LY}\sigma}{\Delta} > 0$$

$$\frac{\hat{v}_Y}{\hat{p}_X} = -\frac{\eta\lambda_{LX}\vartheta_{LY}}{\Delta} < 0$$

$$\frac{\hat{v}_Y - \hat{p}_X}{\hat{p}_X} = -\frac{\eta\lambda_{LX}\vartheta_{LY}}{\Delta} < 0$$

where

$$\Delta = (\eta - 1)\lambda_{LY}\sigma + \eta\lambda_{LX}\vartheta_{HY} > 0$$

The comparative statics equilibria are shown in Figures 10.2 and 10.3. The model response to the shock can be explained as follows. Considering Figure 10.2, a decrease in p_X shifts downward the labor demand in the X sector for a given labor demand in the Y industry, implying lower w. The reduction of the unskilled workers' wage in terms of the homogeneous good lowers the cost of labor for firms operating in the Y sector and therefore raises the amount of unskilled labor employed there. As a consequence, employment of workers in the quality-good sector is reduced, since the total labor supply is given. These effects on the labor market are described with the help of Figure 10.2.

The introduction of quality in a simple two sector-three factors model with no substitutability between inputs (i.e. Leontief production function for one sector) completely alters the effects of an exogenous change in the terms of trade. In the model with homogeneous goods, the relative price changes exert no effects on the sectoral composition of unskilled labor and henceforth on the wage. Since L_X is given by the technological condition and the assumption of a given supply of human capital in the X sector $(L_X = \bar{H}_X/A)$,[9] the change in p_X does not affect sectoral employment, the wage rate, and the price of human capital in the Y sector. The only consequence of this shock we observe is the change of the specific human-capital price, that moves in the same direction as p_X but by a larger amount (i.e., $\hat{v}_X/\hat{p}_X = 1/\vartheta_{HX} > 1$). When vertical differentiation is introduced into the model, employment of unskilled workers in the X sector depends (negatively) on quality. Quality in turn depends on the wage through the quality equation, so that an indirect relationship between unskilled labor and the real wage is introduced. Therefore through quality we restore the basic features of the neoclassical specific-factors model, even in the case of the Leontief production function, allowing for an endogenous change in sectoral employment.

Consider now the effects of globalization on quality. In Figure 10.3 the QQ curve is shifted downward for a given DD curve, which remains unchanged after the shock. The new equilibrium is characterized by a lower wage for the unskilled and higher quality. Increased competition from the rest of the world leads firms to raise the supply of quality at a fixed wage. A reduction of the wage rate is necessary, and this implies higher quality (since we are moving along the demand curve) to restore the equilibrium. Since the vertical shift of the QQ curve, corresponding to the relative change in p_X, is bigger than the equilibrium change of w, an increase in the real wage (i.e., the wage measured in terms of X) following the reduction of relative prices takes place.

The zero-profit condition (10.11a) implies that v_X diminishes as well and by a greater amount than w. The price of H_X also falls when expressed in terms of the quality good. The demand for human capital in the Y sector is raised by the exogenous shock, given the Edgeworth complementarity between unskilled labor and human capital in this sector. Consequently v_Y is raised. Henceforth, we observe that the price of skilled workers in terms of the homogeneous good is reduced in the differentiated sector and increased in the Y sector.

Finally, the physical quantity of the quality good falls, since $XQ = \bar{H}_X$ and Q is increased, while the amount of the homogeneous good rises due to the larger amount of unskilled labor employed.

4. Conclusions

This chapter has developed a simple general equilibrium model of international trade with vertical product differentiation and sector-specific human capital. The reduction of the unskilled-intensive good price stemming from increased competition generates a fall in the wage of unskilled workers and a reallocation of manual labor in favor of the homogeneous good, which crowds out employment in the differentiated good. This adjustment implies that the price of human capital in the homogeneous sector will increase, while that specifically employed in the differentiated sector will fall. This in turn will give the incentive to produce higher quality products generating a relative increase in demand for skilled workers in the industrialized countries.

If differences in qualities are associated with differences in skill content, so that higher quality products are associated with a higher content of skilled labor, then countries will specialize in different parts of the quality spectrum, depending on the relative convenience in terms of wages. Since the skill intensity of all production processes will be lower in skill-scarce than in skill-abundant countries, the factor endowment explanation of trade continues to hold and a country's trade will embody a net outflow of its abundant factor. Increased competition from low-skill abundant countries will lead an industrialized (skill-abundant) country to upgrade the quality of its product without this necessarily implying any inter-sectoral specialization. This phenomenon can be viewed as a sort of fragmentation of the product in different quality components.

The model describes a possible reaction to the increased world competition not considered in the traditional theory: a country can continue producing in the sector whose price is reduced by raising the quality of output.

The results provided by this model are particularly useful in explaining the recent evolution of the Italian trade structure, that, as we have shown, has been strongly oriented toward 'traditional' goods and has been characterized by an increasing share of vertical intra-industry trade with newly industrialized countries. According to our explanation, the upgrading in product quality within the 'traditional' industries was the result of the relative abundance of specific human capital in these sectors with respect to other countries.

Appendix 10.1. Grubel–Lloyd Indices

The total *intra-industry trade (IIT)* of a country is calculated as the share of its total trade, according to the following formula:

$$\text{IIT} = \frac{\sum_i (X_i + M_i) - \sum_i |X_i - M_i|}{\sum_i (X_i + M_i)} \tag{A.1}$$

where i denotes 4-digit-level product categories of CN classification manufacturing industry and X_i and M_i denote the value of exports and import respectively.

The numerator of index (A.1) can be evaluated by considering only those categories in which the ratio of the unit value of imports (UVM_i) to the unit value of exports (UVX_i) satisfies the condition:

$$1 - \alpha \leq \text{UVX}_i / \text{UVM}_i \leq 1 + \alpha$$

where $\alpha = 15\%, 25\%$.

Consequently index (A.1) can be expressed as the share of *horizontal intra-industry trade in total trade (HIIT)*:

$$\text{HIIT} = \frac{\sum_i \left(X_i^h + M_i^h \right) - \sum_i |X_i^h - M_i^h|}{\sum_i (X_i + M_i)} \tag{A.2}$$

The same procedure can be adopted to calculate the share of vertical intra-industry trade in total trade. In this case the numerator of index (A.1) can be computed by considering only those categories in which the unit value of imports (UVM_i) and the unit value of exports (UVX_i) satisfy the condition:

$$\text{UVX}_i / \text{UVM}_i > 1 - \alpha$$

or

$$\text{UVX}_i / \text{UVM}_i < 1 - \alpha$$

where α =15%, 25%. The result is:

$$\text{VIIT} = \frac{\sum_i (X_i^v + M_i^v) - \sum_i |X_i^v - M_i^v|}{\sum_i (X_i + M_i)} \tag{A.3}$$

The positive share of *vertical intra-industry trade* (VIIT$^+$) can be obtained by computing the numerator of index (A.3) and by considering only the categories in which UVX$_i$/UVM$_i$ > 1 − α, while the negative share of vertical intra-industry trade (VIIT$^-$) is obtained by using only the categories in which UVX$_i$/UVM$_i$ < 1 − α.

The above-stated assumptions imply that:

$$\text{VIIT} = \text{VIIT}^+ + \text{VIIT}^-$$

and

$$\text{IIT} = \text{HIIT} + \text{VIIT}$$

NOTES

We are grateful to Sven Arndt, Henryk Kierzkowski, and all the other participants of the Bürgenstock Conference for their useful comments and suggestions. We wish also to thank Barbara Annicchiarico and Barbara Piazzi for having prepared data on intra-industry trade.

1. For a survey of the labor-market effects of globalization see Freeman (1995), Slaughter and Swagel (1997), and OECD (1997).
2. See, for example, Krugman (1979, 1980), Ethier (1982), and Helpman and Krugman (1985).
3. See the Appendix for a description of these indexes.
4. Examples of models that consider vertical product differentiation in the more natural environment of imperfect competition are given, among others, by Grossman and Helpman (1991).
5. The classical references for the specific-factors model are Jones (1971) and Mussa (1974).
6. The Leontief production function, eqn (10.1), has been chosen for the sake of simplicity. A more general case would be given by the following technology: $XQ = B(Q, H_X/L_X)F(L_X, H_X)$, where $B_1 > 0$, $B_{11} > 0$, $B_2 > 0$, $B_{22} \le 0$, $B_{12} \le 0$, and $F(\ ,\ )$ satisfies the usual neoclassical properties of regularity and is linearly homogeneous in L_X and H_X. The qualitative results do not change if production function (10.1) is replaced with this more general technology.
7. The second-order condition for the maximum profit concerning quality, i.e. $2(A'(Q)/Q)[(QA'(Q)/A(Q)) - 1] > A''(Q)$, is assumed to be satisfied.

8. Note that in Figure 10.3 variables with ~ denote the natural logarithm of the corresponding plain variables.
9. Henceforth the labor demand for L_X would be vertical in Figure 10.2.

REFERENCES

Arndt, S. W. (1997). 'Globalization and the Open Economy', *North American Journal of Economics and Finance*, 8: 71–9.

Celi, G., and Segnana, M. L. (1998). Trade and Labor Markets: Vertical and Regional Differentiation in Italy, mimeo.

Djajic, S., and Kierzkowski, H. (1989). 'Goods, Services and Trade', *Economica*, 56: 83–95.

Ethier, W. J. (1982). 'National and International Returns to Scale in the Modern Theory of International Trade', *American Economic Review*, 72: 389–405.

Falvey, R. E., and Kierzkowski, H. (1987). 'Product Quality, Intra-industry Trade and (Im)perfect Competition', in H. Kierzkowski (ed.), *Protection and Competition in International Trade* (Oxford: Basil Blackwell), 143–61

Flam, H., and Helpman, E. (1987). 'Vertical Product Differentiation and North-South Trade', *American Economic Review*, 77: 810–22.

Freeman, R. B. (1995). 'Are Your Wages Set in Beijing?', *Journal of Economic Perspectives*, 9: 15–32.

Greenway, D., Hine, R., and Milner, C. (1994). 'Country-Specific Factors and Pattern of Horizontal and Vertical Intra-industry in the UK', *Weltwirtschaftliches Archiv*, 130: 77–100.

—— —— —— (1995). 'Vertical and Horizontal Intra-industry Trade: A Cross Industry Analysis for the United Kingdom', *Economic Journal*, 105: 1505–18.

Grossman, G. M. and Helpman, E. (1991). *Innovation and Growth in the Global Economy*, (Cambridge, Mass.: MIT Press).

Helpman, E., and Krugman, P. R. (1985). *Market Structure and Foreign Trade: Increasing Returns, Imperfect Competition, and the International Economy* (Cambridge, Mass.: MIT Press).

Jones, R. W. (1965). 'The Structure of Simple General Equilibrium Models', *Journal of Political Economy*, 73: 557–72.

—— (1971). 'A Tree-Factor Model in Theory, Trade and History', in J. Bhagwati, R. W. Jones, R. Mundell, and J. Vanek (eds.), *Trade, Balance of Payments and Growth* (Amsterdam: North-Holland).

—— and Engerman, S. (1996). 'Trade, Technology and Wages: A Tale of Two Countries', *American Economic Review, Papers and Proceedings*, 86: 35–40.

Krugman, P. (1979). 'Increasing Returns, Monopolistic Competition and International Trade', *Journal of International Economics*, 9: 469–79.

—— (1980). 'Scale Economies, Product Differentiation, and the Pattern of Trade', *American Economic Review*, 70: 950–9.

—— (2000). 'Technology, Trade and Factor Prices', *Journal of International Economics*, 50: 51–91.

Murphy, K. M., and Shleifer, A. (1997). 'Quality and Trade', *Journal of Development Economics*, 53: 1–15.

Mussa, M. (1974). 'Tariffs and the Distribution of Income: The Importance of Factor Specificity, Substitutability, and Intensity in the Short and Long Run', *Journal of Political Economy*, 82: 1191–203.

OECD (1997). *Employment Outlook*, Paris, July.

Quintieri, B. (ed.) (1995). *Patterns of Trade, Competition and Trade Policies* (Avebury: Aldershot).

Rodriguez, C. A. (1979). 'The Quality of Imports, the Differential Welfare Effects of Tariffs, Quotas, and Quality Controls as Prospective Devices', *Canadian Journal of Economics*, 12: 439–49.

Slaughter, M. J. and Swagel, P. (1997). 'The Effect of Globalization on Wages in the Advanced Economies', International Monetary Fund Working Paper, No. 43.

Wood, A. (1994). *North-South Trade, Employment and Inequality: Changing Fortunes in a Skill-Driven World* (Oxford: Clarendon Press).

11

[handwritten: selected countries]

International Subcontracting in the Textile and Clothing Industry

[handwritten: L67 F23 F14 L23 L24]

GIOVANNI GRAZIANI

1. The New Reality of the Textile and Clothing Industry and the Theory

Less and less of a Benetton shirt is assembled in Italy and more and more of it by independent external suppliers in South America, Asia, and Eastern Europe. Only the major strategic functions—design, cutting, quality control, and distribution—are still handled in-house in Treviso. Similarly, Levi's denim jeans are largely sewn in Asia and in Mexico, while Marks & Spencer sources its apparel items from a dozen developing countries. Some members of the business community have even suggested that 'made in Italy' or 'made in the USA' labels are obsolete and that one should rather stress the 'Italian style' or the 'American style'.

Outsourcing is a time-honored practice in the textile and clothing industry. What is relatively new is the increasing importance of offshore production and the extension of this production to the final (assembly) stage of the production cycle. In this sense, production is rapidly becoming truly international.

This widespread relocation of individual phases of the production process to the most cost-efficient regions abroad has fostered new theoretical breakthroughs: Dixit and Grossman (1982) model a theory of protection with multi-stage production, more recently seminal work by Jones and Kierzkowski (1990, 2000) explores the implications of fragmentation, and Arndt (1997) examines intra-product specialization.

The core idea of these theories is that fragmented technology divides the productive process into different production blocks connected by service links. In the limit, every production block and service link could be performed by a different firm in a different country (Jones and Kierzkowski, 1990). This more intensive use of service links at an international level is fostered by the fall in relative prices of many services, most notably in communications and transport, which brings with it a decline in coordination costs, and is supported by the progressive elimination of trade and investment barriers. In other words, we are witnessing a transition from purely domestic to international vertical integration, that is, a linkage between separate stages of production located in different countries.

Such cross-border segmentation of production allows for a finer degree of intra-product specialization according to comparative advantage. This promotes greater efficiency in resource allocation and, in the end, boosts trade flows, since the product of each production segment can enter separately into international trade.

Apart from the welfare implications, extensively explored in these models but not directly examined in the present chapter, the main prediction of these theoretical models appears to be that the location of each stage of the productive process will be determined by relative factor prices and productivities at an international level. As a consequence, labor-abundant and low-wage countries will retain labor-intensive fragments of production, while capital-rich and higher-wage countries will exhibit a comparative advantage in capital-intensive production segments. Countries and regions will then specialize in separate areas of the productive process and not necessarily in a whole industry or sector.

2. Textiles and Clothing

What is the relevance of these theoretical models for the textile and clothing sectors? In fact, this industry appears to provide a classic and in some sense archetypal case study of segmentation and relocation of production, first on a domestic scale and then on an international scale.

A fruitful approach is to consider the industry as composed not of two fundamental sectors—textiles and clothing—but as a value-added chain. This chain is composed of four main stages, each characterized by different factor intensities: (i) synthetic fibers production (very capital and technology intensive); (ii) textile manufacturing (relatively capital intensive in yarns and fabrics, less so for some finished textiles); (iii) clothing production (highly labor intensive); and (iv) distribution (capital and technology intensive) (among others, see Dicken, 1992). Roughly speaking, synthetic fibers are between three and four times more capital intensive than yarns and fabrics, which in turn are one and a half times less labor intensive than garments, finished textiles being somewhere in between.

Each link of the chain is composed of separate operations, which in turn exhibit different factor intensities even within the same link (Spinanger, 1992). So textile production requires spinning and weaving, where automation is very widespread, but also knitting and tufting, and each of these processes consists of many separate operations. Clothing manufacturing consists of upstream activities such as designing, pattern-making, grading, nesting, marking and cutting, some of which can be highly capital intensive and automated through the use of computer-aided design and manufacturing and computer-integrated manufacturing. There follows a midstream activity, sewing, which is not yet automated except in a minor way, and generally accounts for 80 percent of all labor employed, most of which is unskilled. Then comes product inspecting, pressing, dying, and washing, where some automation has been introduced; and finally packaging, inventory control, logistics, marketing and distributing, where capital- and scale-intensive techniques are becoming widespread and the labor required is relatively more skilled.

The industry produces a set of commodities that not only use a wide range of production techniques in terms of factor intensity, but also face widely varying elasticities of demand.

Companies may take part in only one link of the value chain. Within a single sector, one can find various typologies of firms: one might perform the entire cycle from tops to fabric, another transform tops into yarn only, with still another transforming the yarn into fabric. Some small firms may even specialize in one single operation within each segment.

The development of modern telecommunications and transport networks has allowed firms to divide production into separate stages, some of which, for example, sewing, can be located far away from the rest of the production chain without sacrificing quality and efficiency (Audet, 1996). Companies from the industrialized countries tend to retain only upmarket and niche production requiring special expertise or such production facilities as are needed to respond quickly to small runs and emergency orders. A firm can thus have its design, marketing, and distribution centers in Milan, New York, or Paris, while the garment assembly takes place in Hungary, Mexico, China, or Tunisia. At each stage, the firms involved can add value and extract profit. Retailing and trading firms have a much larger role in outcontracting the final product than in other industrial sectors. Large distributors tend to place big orders and to intervene in the choice of styles, quality, timing, and service standards (OETH, 1994). At the limit, one finds 'hollow' manufacturers, without factories.

3. Regional Polarization in Textiles and Clothing

Does fragmentation matter for the international pattern of production and trade? Let us look first at general world trends.

The textile and clothing industry is of major importance in the industrialized countries, in particular the *European Union (EU)* and the United States, in that it still accounts for a sizeable share of manufacturing employment and value-added. Consumption is still concentrated in the advanced countries.

At the same time, continuing a trend stretching over the last twenty-five years, production in both textiles and clothing has fallen almost continuously in the 1990s. The fall in output has induced a corresponding decline in employment, magnified by the restructuring undertaken in order to improve the industry's competitiveness. In the EU, almost 700,000 jobs (relatively more in clothing than in textiles) were lost in the last ten years, just under a third of all job losses in manufacturing as a whole. In the United States, employment declined by almost 40 percent in the last twenty-five years. Both production and employment declines were more pronounced in the textile and clothing industry than in manufacturing as a whole.

In contrast, Asian producers and exporters are growing fast. This is reflected in the trade data. In textiles, Western Europe accounted for 53 percent of world exports in 1990. In 1996, this share had dropped to 43 percent, almost on a par with the Asian share, which was only 35 percent six years earlier (WTO, 1997). By the end of the decade, Asia should emerge as the world's largest exporter of textiles. North America's share, although slightly increasing (from 5% to 6%), is only of minor importance. Hong Kong (the absolute leader, thanks mostly to re-exports), South Korea, China, and Taiwan figure among the top six world exporters of textiles, with India and Pakistan somewhat lower on the list among the top fifteen exporters (Table 11.1a). All of these countries increased their share of world exports over the last fifteen years. The other side of the coin is that, with the exception of the United States and Spain, all the industrialized countries saw a reduction of their share, including the two top performing nations, Germany and Italy.

Asia's advance is noticeable in textile imports, too. By 1996, Asia was importing almost one-third of world textiles, behind Western Europe, which still accounted for 38 percent of imports (down from 49% in 1990). Here too, North America's share is much less important, although increasing slightly (from 8% to 9%).

TABLE 11.1. Leading exporters of textiles and clothing (% share in world exports)

Country	1980	1990	1996	Annual % change 1990–6
(a) Textiles				
Hong Kong	3.1	7.4	9.4	9
of which re-exports	1.5	5.4	8.2	13
Germany	11.4	13.4	9.0	−1
Italy	7.6	9.0	8.8	6
South Korea	4.0	5.8	8.5	13
China	4.6	6.9	8.1	9
Taiwan	3.2	5.8	8.0	12
United States	6.8	4.8	5.3	8
France	6.2	5.8	4.9	3
Belgium–Luxembourg	6.5	6.1	4.9	2
Japan	9.3	5.6	4.6	3
United Kingdom	5.7	4.2	3.6	4
Pakistan	1.6	2.5	3.3	11
India	2.1	2.1	2.9	15
Netherlands	4.1	2.8	2.2	2
Spain	1.3	1.4	1.9	11
(b) Clothing				
China	4.0	8.9	15.3	17
Hong Kong	12.2	13.6	13.5	6
of which re-exports	0.8	5.4	8.0	13
Italy	11.3	10.9	9.8	5
United States	3.1	2.4	4.6	20
Germany	7.1	7.3	4.6	−1
Turkey	0.3	3.1	3.9	13
France	5.7	4.3	3.4	3
United Kingdom	4.6	2.8	3.2	9
South Korea	7.3	7.3	2.6	−10
Thailand	0.7	2.6	2.5	6
India	1.5	2.3	2.6	10
Indonesia	0.2	1.5	2.2	14
Portugal	1.6	3.2	2.2	0
Taiwan	6.0	3.7	2.0	−4
Netherlands	2.2	2.0	1.9	6

Source: GATT, *International Trade 90–91* (Geneva: GATT, 1991); WTO (1997).

The 1990s have also seen the establishment of the Asian region as the world leader in clothing exports. While its share was on a par with Western Europe's (43% each) at the beginning of the decade, by 1996 Western Europe's share decreased to 37 percent and North America's nearly doubled, albeit from a low level (almost 3% to more than 5%). Among individual countries, China established itself as the leading exporter (15% of world exports), followed by Hong Kong and Italy (Table 11.1*b*). Except for the United States, the more advanced countries have all lost position, as have Korea and Taiwan. Among the major emerging producers are China and Hong Kong, Turkey, Thailand, India, and Indonesia.

Finally, almost half of world clothing imports were still directed to Western Europe (down from 54%), 27 percent to North America (a slight increase), and 16 percent to Asia. The latter is on the increase on this front too.

A better understanding of the process may be obtained by examining the evolution of inter- and intra-regional flows of exports in the last two decades. Exports of clothes and textiles within Western Europe still represent the largest market, but are decreasing (Table 11.2). From 1990, a similar decline is observed in Asia in its exports of both textiles and clothing to North America and to Western Europe.

TABLE 11.2. Regional flows in exports of textiles and clothing

Country	1980	1990	1996
(*a*) Textiles			
Intra-Western Europe	40.0	39.0	30.0
Intra-Asia	12.5	20.6	27.6
Asia to Western Europe	5.2	5.8	5.3
Western Europe to Eastern			
Europe/former USSR	2.7	2.0	4.4
Asia to North America	2.9	3.6	3.5
Western Europe to Asia	1.6	3.0	3.1
Asia to Middle East	3.0	2.2	2.8
N. America to N. America	1.4	1.5	2.4
N. America to L. America	1.4	1.0	1.6
L. America to N. America	0.5	0.7	0.9
(*b*) Clothing			
Intra-Western Europe	37.1	32.7	28.3
Asia to N. America	15.0	19.5	15.8
Intra-Asia	5.1	8.8	12.3
Asia to Western Europe	14.6	14.2	11.0
L. America to N. America	1.6	3.1	5.1
E. Europe/former USSR to Western Europe	2.4	1.6	4.1
Africa to Western Europe	2.0	3.3	3.6*
N. America to L. America	1.4	1.2	3.0

Note: *EU only.
Source: GATT, *International Trade 90–91* (Geneva: GATT, 1991); WTO (1997).

One notable trend in the 1990s is the growing importance of export flows within the three main economic regions of the world. Most important of these are intra-Asia flows, both in textiles (28% of world exports in 1996, almost matching intra-Western exports) and in clothing (almost three times as large as in 1980). But one will note also the increase in Eastern Europe/former USSR–Western Europe and Africa–Western Europe export flows on one side, and of Latin America-North America flows on the other.

Four main features seem then to derive from this first level of empirical analysis. First, a growing number of competitors is gaining market share at the expense of traditional Western producers. Import penetration ratios have swiftly risen both in textiles and especially in clothing (in the EU 45%). Together with technological progress, growing import penetration is exerting downward pressure on Western domestic production and employment.

Secondly, the more advanced countries generally show a positive trade balance in textiles and a much larger and growing negative balance in clothing. The United States is a notable exception, in so far as it shows a deficit in textiles as well, which is however much smaller than the one in clothing. Italy is the only important producer among the industrialized countries to have a surplus in both sectors, as well as South Korea and Taiwan among the Asian *newly industrialized countries* (NICs).

Thirdly, in the clothing sector new countries from Asia, Latin America, Africa, and Eastern Europe are becoming exporters and displacing some of the first-tier NICs, which seem to concentrate on textiles. We would expect the evolution of revealed comparative advantages to show this new pattern.

Finally, there is a progressive reorientation of trade toward geographically proximate countries and regions in three definite clusters around the major players of the world economy.

4. The Central Role of Subcontracting

At first sight the trade data presented above would seem to call for a rather straightforward interpretation. Western textile and clothing producers are losing ground *vis-à-vis* new competitors from the developing world. At a certain development stage, countries abandon this type of labor-intensive production (in response to changes in their pattern of comparative advantage) for more high-tech undertakings. Meanwhile, rising import penetration seems to be responsible for the huge trade deficits in these goods (especially in clothing) and for part of the rising unemployment in the industry.

But the data do not reveal the structural changes taking place in the industry through subcontracting. *Subcontracting*, which can take a domestic and an international dimension, has been the most important type of redeployment in the textile and clothing industry, much more so than foreign direct investment (Graziani, 1998). The most powerful force behind firms' subcontracting has been the abatement of production costs (cost-saving subcontracting).

The most widespread form of subcontracting is a simple agreement to purchase the final product from a local producer (full package). At times, a firm buys locally or brings in the intermediate products necessary for production. In other cases, a firm will deliver semi-finished products to the subcontractor and buy back the finished product (assembly subcontracting). An extreme example of this type is the so-called '*impannatore*', a firm that retains only the design and marketing functions while contracting all other productive phases to outside firms ('*terziste*').

Domestic subcontracting is nothing new for the industry. One might recall the (in)famous 'putting out' system and the sweatshops of the early twentieth century. But its importance has continued unabated. In 1993, the clothing subcontracting sector employed 800,000 people in the EU, including 150,000 non-registered workers (Mercer, 1994). Similar numbers could be obtained for the United States.

What is relatively new in recent times is the explosion of subcontracting at an international level either in the full package form or in the assembly form; that is, the export of components and the reimport of the finished product. Even countries like Italy, which relied mostly on domestic subcontracting until the mid-1980s, have turned increasingly to its international form (Graziani, 1998).

No precise data exist on all the various forms of international subcontracting, with the exception of *outward processing traffic* (OPT) in the EU and the 9020/807 provisions in the United States, due to their special tariff regimes, plus some official Chinese statistics.

5. The OPT System in the EU

Outward processing traffic (OPT) takes place when some phases of the textile and clothing production chain—typically the sewing phase—are carried out by foreign subcontractors. Fabrics are shipped to the country of the subcontracting firm as temporary exports under an EU tariff-exemption regime. Prior to the *Europe Agreements (EAs)*, tariffs were levied only on the foreign value-added when the sewn product was reimported. Since then, tariffs have been abolished altogether, while reimports within normal *Multifiber Arrangement (MFA)* quotas continue to be subject to current tariffs.

Until 1982, OPT occurred within the MFA quotas for global textile and clothing imports. OPT reimports thus had to compete with other imports under MFA quotas. The 1982 regulation established an ad hoc regime, under which specific OPT quotas were reserved for EU producers of goods similar to those obtained with outward processing. On 1 January 1993, the European single market substituted a single community quota (for every combination of product/country of destination) for the existing national quotas.

The EU's official trade data allow us to distinguish 'direct' imports from OPT imports, plus the temporary exports for reimport. The latter are much more important in the textile sector than in clothing, which confirms that semi-finished textile products are shipped abroad in order to be processed for reimportation.

The European Union's OPT imports of MFA clothing products have dramatically increased in recent years. In 1988 their share of total imports was still only 8.1 percent (OETH, 1995), while in 1996 it was nearly 20 percent as a share of total imports of clothing (Table 11.3*b*). The share of the remaining imports ('direct' imports) has fallen accordingly. Germany is the leading OPT importer, with 63 percent of the total for the EU, followed by Italy (10%), France (9%), and Benelux, Denmark, and the United Kingdom following.

Geographically, two main regions have been targeted by EU firms: the Mediterranean countries, especially Tunisia and Morocco, and the Eastern European nations. Eastern Europe has been at the core of EU OPT trade for a long time, but its role greatly increased in the 1990s, partly due to the disintegration of Yugoslavia. Eastern Europe has come to rely almost completely on the EU for its textile and clothing trade. By 1995, more than 80% of EU clothing imports from and 60% of textile exports to Eastern Europe were represented by OPT (Table 11.3*c*). OPT looms very large in EU imports from Poland (78%), Hungary (72%), Slovakia (65%), the Czech Republic (58%), Romania (53%), and Bulgaria (45%) (Graziani, 1998).

In sum, the OPT system has been used extensively by EU firms with neighboring countries, due to the triple advantage of the favorable tariff regime, lower labor costs, and geographical proximity. Subcontracting

TABLE 11.3. EU imports of textiles and clothing

Country	1990		1995	
	Textiles	Clothing	Textiles	Clothing
(a) Total imports				
Eastern Europe	8.4	16.1	12.6	21.2
(incl. ex Yugoslavia)				
Mediterranean countries	12.3	23.2	13.2	25.1
Rest of the world	79.3	60.7	74.2	53.7
(b) OPT share as % of EU trade				
Imports	1990		1996	
Textiles	0.7		3.0	
Clothing	14.2		19.8	
Exports				
Textiles	13.8		21.6	
Clothing	4.0		9.3	
(c) OPT shares in EU trade with Eastern Europe, 1995				
	Imports		Exports	
Textiles	25.3		60.1	
Clothing	81.2		62.0	

Source: Taken or calculated from OETH (1997).

has drawn Eastern Europe into the larger process of globalization of production in the EU. Eastern Europe outpaced the Mediterranean countries in trade growth with the EU when the Interim Agreements eliminated tariffs on the value-added abroad. The Mediterranean countries are, however, still a relatively larger supplier to the EU (Table 11.3a). East European and Mediterranean countries have become extremely dependent on OPT for their textile and clothing exports to the EU.

While the elimination of EU tariffs on OPT imports from the *Central and Eastern European Countries (CEECs)* might explain the recent relative boom in this type of subcontracting, OPT as a tariff system may decline in importance after 1998, with the passing of non-tariff barriers on non-OPT imports. After 1998, OPT regulations no longer require the use of EU fabrics, so that EU firms can freely import clothing made from EU and East European fabric, while having to pay duty if fabrics from third countries are used.

6. The US 9802 Special Tariff Provision

In recent years, US textile and clothing trade with Mexico and the Caribbean countries has boomed thanks to tariff provisions similar to the European OPT system, which permit duty-free reimport of US-made components contained in articles assembled in those countries. Tariffs are levied only on the value added abroad.

Started in the early 1960s as a small concession to US producers, this arrangement was later formalized in the Custom's 806-807 program, a nomenclature which was changed to 9802 with the implementation of the Harmonized Tariff Schedule in 1988. This type of trade, especially in the case of Mexico, started growing at increasing rates only after the mid-1980s, when (i) sweeping changes occurred in Mexican policy, including unilateral trade liberalization and a move away from import-substitution trade policy; (ii) US producers, hit by rising labor costs and growing foreign competition, decided to widen their recourse to out-sourcing from Mexico; and (iii) Mexican producers started reorienting their operations from the domestic to the US market.

Table 11.4 shows the evolution of US clothing imports from Mexico and the Caribbean countries in the 1990s. It shows the importance of assembly trade in total clothing imports (over 80%). Between 70 and 80 percent of the value of these imports consists of US component exports (estimates by the US International Trade Commission and the *Association of Textile Manufacturers (ATMI)*). Mexico's share reached

TABLE 11.4. US clothing imports from Mexico and the Caribbean countries

	Annual growth rate (%)	As % of world imports	Share of 9802 trade (%)
Mexico			
1990		2.8	86.6
1991	28.1	3.1	87.7
1992	30.1	3.8	87.6
1993	19.8	4.2	88.7
1994	33.5	5.1	90.8
1995	52.2	7.2	88.6
1996	33.9	9.2	83.6
1997	38.3	10.8	82.2
Caribbean countries			
1990		7.8	74.3
1991	27.6	9.6	77.3
1992	30.0	10.5	77.5
1993	22.0	11.8	78.9
1994	13.0	12.3	80.1
1995	20.8	13.8	82.3
1996	10.9	14.6	82.5
1997	25.4	15.4	83.8

Source: Calculated from US International Trade Commission data.

a peak (91%) in 1994 and fell steadily thereafter (to 82% in 1997). This decline is due to the *North American Free Trade Agreement (NAFTA)*, which eliminated the tariff payment on value-added and allowed for the duty-free entry into the United States of articles assembled in Mexico from fabrics made in the United States, thus reducing the importance of cross-border production expressed through 9802 trade. NAFTA may also be encouraging full package subcontracting by allowing Mexican producers to use domestic fabrics for their exports to the United States (Bair and Gereffi, 1998).

Overall, US clothing imports from Mexico have almost quadrupled in the 1990s, establishing Mexico as the world's second largest supplier after China, with a share of 11 percent. At the beginning of the period, Caribbean exports to the United States were more than double the value of Mexican shipments. At the end of the period, the gap was reduced to only one and a half times. Until 1993, annual growth rates of exports from the two sources were almost identical. Starting in 1994, Mexican shipments grew much faster than Caribbean exports. Here again, the NAFTA duty-free clause seems to be the enhancing and discriminating factor in favor of Mexico, although both regions' producers continued gaining shares in US imports at the expense of major Asian exporters like China, Hong Kong, South Korea, and Taiwan. The share of assembly trade in total Caribbean clothing exports differs from Mexico's experience in that it continued to grow throughout the period. The Caribbean Basin, located outside NAFTA, may be locked into the role of an assembly export platform for the US market.

Both the EU and US cases reveal a new pattern of production that uses EU and US intermediate products in clothing exports destined mainly for the EU or US market. In both Europe and the United States special tariff regimes initially encouraged this type of trade, macroeconomic and trade policies allowed it to develop, while regional arrangements added the final touch by creating more favorable conditions for the partners, as in NAFTA, or by re-establishing parity conditions, as in the Association Agreements. In both cases, a relocation of clothing assembly to proximate countries benefits the textile industry of the relocating economy, which inevitably receives some orders for its intermediate products.

7. Textile and Clothing Redeployment in Asia

Asia has been the recipient of vast and successive waves of relocation of the world textile and clothing industry. The first occurred in the

1950s from Western industrialized countries to Japan. Imposition of *Voluntary export restraints (VERs)* and other restrictions by the United States gradually forced Japan to relinquish all but the higher value-added products and to shift production of the less sophisticated goods to Hong Kong in the 1960s and to South Korea and Taiwan in the 1970s.

The latter countries became large exporters in the 1970s and the 1980s as they developed both assembly and full package forms of subcontracting. Persisting quota restrictions, rising wage rates, labor shortages, and currency appreciations in the late 1980s pushed these countries, and Japan with them, to relocate segments of the industry to the new generation of exporters, namely China and various other Asian, Latin American, and African countries.

Quota restrictions have played a fundamental role in determining the strategic responses of the NICs and the development of their industries. Although every MFA round provoked its own responses, the typical strategy seems to have been one of switching production (either through affiliates, joint ventures, or independent producers) to low-cost countries which had quota advantages and then selling the products under their unfulfilled quotas (Moon *et al.* 1997). In this scheme, known as 'triangle manufacturing', the NICs' companies have come to play the role of coordinating intermediary agents, who receive orders from Western companies and execute them through the new emerging exporters' firms (Gereffi, 1996).

Interestingly, the links of these triangles are not chosen through a simple calculation of the labor cost advantage. Each NIC seems to have a preferred cluster of Asian countries to work with, strongly influenced by social (ethnic, language) and historical ties. Hong Kong and Taiwan show a preference for China, Macau, Mauritius, and South East Asia; South Korea for Bangladesh (but also the Dominican Republic); Singapore for Malaysia and Indonesia.

The case of China is most instructive and also one of the few where official statistics cover processing trade. The result of its policies has been a rather high share of subcontracting operations. At the end of the 1970s, the Chinese economy began to open to the world and welcome direct foreign investment on Chinese territory. In 1984, the State Council allowed the duty-free import of components and raw materials to be used in exports. Three years later a new strategy favored outward-oriented industries, especially in the coastal regions, with special tariff exemptions on imports, while tariffs on other imports were kept very high: 62 and 80 percent, respectively for textiles and clothing. In 1996 they were still 31 and 40 percent, respectively. According to China's customs statistics, roughly half of her total trade is due to processing operations. The textile and clothing industry accounts for one-third of total assembly exports and one-quarter of the imports destined for processing. In 1996 almost 60 percent of Chinese clothing exports were based on subcontracting and assembly operations (Chinese Customs). More than half of Hong Kong's, South Korea's, and Taiwan's exports of fabrics and clothing to China are intended for processing and re-export. Much of this processing is carried out in factories partially or wholly owned by Japanese, Hong Kong, Taiwanese, and South Korean firms. It is, moreover, the most dynamic part of China's trade, with growing surpluses, relative to the slow development of trade generally.

A sort of triangular pattern of subcontracting trade networks was thus established around China. Subcontracting and assembly imports are concentrated on Asian suppliers, most notably Japan, Taiwan, South Korea, and Hong Kong, which altogether represent roughly two-thirds of total subcontracting imports. Normal imports come, on the contrary, mostly from the EU, the United States, and Japan. These are also the countries which the major part of total Chinese clothing exports are destined for, together with Hong Kong which acts mostly as an intermediary base for goods to be shipped to the EU and the United States.

The more developed Asian countries have adopted a variety of approaches toward their processing operations in China. Japan reimports part of the output, South Korea and Taiwan re-export most of it directly from China, while Hong Kong's strategy tends to be more complex. After years of being the leading world exporter of clothing, Hong Kong is still second only to China (Table 11.1*b*), due mainly to the importance of re-exports, which in 1996 represented 88 percent of total Hong Kong clothing imports. Hong Kong has built a network of wholly or partly owned manufacturing, commercial, and financial companies in China. According to the Hong Kong Census and Statistics Department, 98 percent of clothing exports were of Chinese origin in 1993 and represented about 20 percent of China's total re-exports. A survey among Hong Kong industrialists estimated that roughly 65 percent of these clothing re-exports were produced by firms associated with Hong Kong investors. A similar function is performed by Hong Kong *vis-à-vis* Taiwan, where re-exports amount to 20 percent (Au and Yeung, 1995). Hong Kong is Taiwan's leading export market, serving mainly as a channel for shipping yarns, fabrics, and clothing to China for further processing (mostly in Taiwanese-owned factories) and re-export; it has also played the role of financial intermediary for Taiwanese investment in the Chinese textile and clothing industry.

8. Costs and Benefits of Assembly Subcontracting for the Developing Economies

Among the benefits of subcontracting is its ability to enhance the employment and industrial skills of the labor force and to generate various types of backward and forward linkages to other industries. These benefits derive from three main sets of factors. Firms (i) secure a guaranteed outlet and are able to market their products under the brand-name of their customers and through their distribution channels; (ii) cut storage costs of both inputs and output; and (iii) acquire quality advice, capital, technology, and managerial experience from the foreign partner. The learning process benefits from the principal's specifications and from direct training provided by the foreign partner.[1]

Among the drawbacks is the possibility that countries might get 'locked in' to their present structure of comparative advantage, with its stress on unskilled labor-intensive activities, while the exploitation of *potential* comparative advantage in higher-tech stages of production is delayed. Functions such as research and development, marketing, and financing might even disappear, since they are provided by the partners.[2] As more of the national production and exports come to depend on foreign firms' decisions and performance, economic uncertainty increases. A change in conditions, for instance, an economic downturn in the partner's country or a wage rise and/or a fall in productivity in the host economy, could cause the foreign partner to withdraw. Evidence that assembly subcontracting in the export-processing zones is the first to be cut in a recession and recent signs of reorientation of EU firms from Eastern Europe to lower-wage former USSR countries suggests as much.

Moreover, in the case of the OPT or the 9802 system, the requirement that subcontracting countries import fabrics of EU or US origin prevented the local textile industry from developing fully. This raises dependence on the foreign partner still further.

On balance, however, subcontracting offers firms the opportunity to expand their production and exports. Recent changes in the redeployment process itself offer subcontractors additional opportunities for upgrading and improving their performance. In the past, relocation and subcontracting were confined to the simplest tasks of the productive process. Today, clothing manufacturers are coming to realize that it is probably less convenient to relocate just the simplest tasks, since they are the ones that can most easily be automated and kept at home.

There has also been an improvement in the average quality of sub-contractors through the learning process. This is pushing entrepreneurs from more advanced countries to view international relocation as part of a global strategy where subcontractors are seen as pivotal in producing complex and high quality products. Furthermore, whereas relocation was traditionally limited to lower-middle market products, it now includes upmarket segments of production and is part of a move toward smaller, more specialized firms (Scheffer, 1994).[3]

9. Subcontracting and the Industrialized Economies

The impact on industrialized countries may be ambiguous and may differ in the short and in the longer term. In so far as subcontracting represents a substitution of domestic production and a derived demand for cheaper foreign labor, it tends to engender a contraction of domestic production and employment, and probably of exports, plus the possible erosion of the domestic supplier base. To the extent that offshore procurement of cheaper components makes firms more competitive in final-goods markets, employment and output would rise, as suggested by Arndt elsewhere in this volume (see Ch. 5). Offshore sourcing might result in the loss of externalities generated by domestic suppliers.

Particular production phases (i.e. assembly activities) and lower-skilled workers may be penalized, while other segments and higher-skilled workers are favored. By influencing relative factor prices, relocation tends to influence income distribution as well. Concentration on upmarket segments will require different skills and qualifications, causing changes in the employment structure.

It should be kept in mind, however, that alternative scenarios may also bring a reduction in employment, due to productivity gains, competition from other EU redeployers (higher quality segments), and competition from cheaper labor countries (lower quality productive segments). The latter will gain importance with the progressive abolition of MFA quotas and the consequent re-establishment of the developing countries' competitive advantage.

In the longer run, firms undertaking relocation could enhance their international competitiveness and thus expand their domestic production and exports, tending to offset the initial employment reduction. Meanwhile, subcontracting increases their flexibility, externalizes some of the production costs and risks, and often strengthens the position of domestic textile producers (Graziani, 1998).

10. Do International Trade Theories Explain Globalization in the Textile and Clothing Industry

The fact that international redeployment to the developing countries, in the form of subcontracting, licensing, and direct foreign investment, tends to involve the more labor-intensive aspects of garment production, rather than the more capital-intensive synthetic fibers and textile production, is certainly consistent with standard trade (and development) theory. According to the factor proportions theory, a country tends to export the goods which utilize larger quantities of its relatively abundant and cheap factor. Labor-intensive production appears to have moved to those countries where labor costs are comparatively lower: labor costs of some Asian countries, for example China, Vietnam, Indonesia, India, and Pakistan, are roughly 5 percent of the equivalent in the United States and even less of the equivalent in Italy or Germany (Table 11.5). The more countries climb the development ladder, the more they will move upmarket toward more capital-intensive and more value-added products (Anderson, 1994). These developments are also consistent with the product-cycle model and its more recent variant, the flying geese paradigm: mature, standardized products—and clothing is often classified as such—would be progressively lost by the more developed countries, which would concentrate on more sophisticated and skill-intensive goods.

However, production and trade developments within the industry differ markedly among branches and products. The textile and clothing industry is far from finished in the developed countries, some of which are still highly specialized either in both sectors, like Italy, or in one sector, like Germany and some of the NICs. Upgrading has been going on even within the production of individual goods.[4] Italian textile producers have improved product quality by enhancing the quality of the services that go with it: rigorous respect of delivery times, efficient technical assistance in the utilization of yarns, and the like. In the clothing sector, Italian producers have stressed the fashion content of their products.

Among 'newer' trade theories, the idea of *product differentiation* is useful. Very often the products of the clothing industry are classified as belonging to the mature phase when, according to the product-cycle thesis, goods are made by lower skilled workers, become standardized, are produced on a mass scale, and tend to compete on a price basis rather than on quality. But clothing production, and a large part of textiles, is marked by an increasing differentiation due to quality, design, and

TABLE 11.5. Labor costs in the textile and clothing industry (total costs per hour, USA = 100)

Country	Primary Textile Industry*		Country	Clothing Industry	
	1996	1990		1996	1990
Belgium	204	178	Japan	170	97
Japan	198	139	Germany	193	110
Netherlands	188	178	Netherlands	178	224
Germany	179	164	France	158	191
Italy	136	161	Italy	150	190
France	134	127	United States	100	100
United States	100	100	United Kingdom	98	122
United Kingdom	96	102	Portugal	41	35
Spain	75	77			
Portugal	39	27			
Taiwan	52	46	Taiwan	53	52
South Korea	46	32	South Korea	44	37
Hungary	26	12	Hungary	23	14
Poland	19	—	Poland	22	8
Czech Rep.	18	—	Czech Rep.	21	42
			Romania	12	26
Turkey	17	18	Turkey	15	20
Morocco	16	13	Morocco	14	14
Tunisia	15	—	Tunisia	10	22
Egypt	7	4	Egypt	6	5
Argentina	38	14	Argentina	36	16
Brazil	31	20	Brazil	20	15
Peru	16	12	Peru	14	13
China	5	4	India	4	5
India	5	7	Indonesia	3	2
Indonesia	4	2	Pakistan	3	4
Pakistan	4	4	China	3	4
			Vietnam	3	—

Note: *Includes spinning, weaving, dying, and finishing.
Source: Werner International.

presentation. Only one-third of clothing production is truly standard-ized (jeans, T-shirts), but even here one notes the growing importance of non-price factors (like fashion, design, advertising, and the like) which suggest product differentiation. The changeable nature of *fashion*—fashion goods tend to have only a few weeks' life—brings also to the fore *delivery time* as one of the crucial factors determining production locations. The need to be closer to consumers and to quickly respond to their requests affects the location pattern.

Conventional wisdom has it that the simpler parts of production are done in poorer countries and will drive the lowest value-added parts of the supply chain to where wages are lowest (*Economist*, 1998). But this may not always be true in the case of the textile and clothing industry. It will be more appropriate to decentralize production if (i) a product has a low fashion content (that is, the delays between the design and the final consumer market are not too short) and its design is not subject to frequent variation; (ii) it is standardized, that is, can be produced in large batches; and (iii) the share of assembly in total cost is significant. What matters is the fashion content and the labor intensity and not the simplicity of production. In fact it may be more convenient to subcontract the sewing of more complex goods, like men's jackets, because of the larger labor inputs required and the constancy of fashion, and less convenient to relocate low value-added operations, which require lower labor inputs and whose standardization may favor automation (i.e. the assembly of jeans).

Contrary to what happens in other industrial sectors, *internal economies of scale* are relevant only in certain limited portions of the chain. Firm size is on average much smaller in this industry, especially in clothing, which is characterized by low barriers to entry, a myriad of very small, often family-run enterprises, fierce competition, and a few large firms. Static scale economies are, however, relatively more important in fiber and textile production and in some downstream segments of the entire chain, namely distribution and other services. International relocation of production raises coordination costs, hence increasing firm size. Some new features of production, such as flexible production and the just-in-time system, may have an ambiguous impact on economies of scale. On the one hand, they may enhance the importance of scale economies because of the high capital outlays necessary for establishing a flexible organization, while on the other hand, they may reduce their role by giving birth to shorter production runs.

The relationship between globalization, segmentation, and agglomeration in the textile and clothing industry tends to be rather complex. On the one hand, trade liberalization leads to segmentation of the productive process in response to geographic differences in factor costs. On the other hand, it may also foster increased agglomeration due to both scale economies and geographic proximity, in some cases favored by specific trade policies. Mexico and China seem to be two cases in point, but with a major difference. While the clustering of textile and clothing operations near the US border and away from Mexico City was simply the consequence of trade liberalization culminating in NAFTA, the agglomeration of Chinese processing operations in the coastal zones was favored by a specific policy of the Chinese government.

The impact of *external economies* on industrial location, on the contrary, has been much more important. Traditional textile and clothing manufacturing in the older industrialized countries had the peculiar characteristic of clustering, a classic example of Alfred Weber's agglomeration economies. These economies go very far in explaining the Italian, US, and Japanese specialization in this industry and its location. International relocation appears, however, to suggest a weakening of external economies as a cause-and-effect determinant of trade patterns and to lend more importance to the labor cost-saving explanation.

At the high-fashion end of the spectrum, lean production, just-in-time deliveries, short runs, smaller orders, low inventories, and high quality are important. Fashion trends emerge and collections follow each other with much higher frequency than they used to. Thus, transport costs and, above all, geographical proximity and delivery time tend to be of paramount importance when deciding on FDI or subcontracting. In some cases, these factors may even offset the lower labor-cost advantage and keep the activity at home.

All in all then, one particular trade theory, be it standard or new, cannot by itself explain trade within this particular sector. Although the more labor-intensive assembly stage of clothing manufacturing seems to be consistent with factor proportions theory, product differentiation, external economies, distance, and delivery time also matter. Beyond that, new insights into the nature of production segmentation and of intra-product specialization push considerations of comparative advantage beyond the finished product. Within this new theoretical framework, particular features from both traditional (Ricardian relative productivities and Heckscher–Ohlin factor intensities and relative prices) and new trade theories (product differentiation, internal and external scale economies) may help explain the location of economic activity.

That redeployment of more labor-intensive goods will be directed toward labor-abundant countries tends to be true only in a general way. International relocation can relate to individual operations or whole links of the chain, but not necessarily to entire sectors. Moreover, within some of the links, technological progress can produce a reversal of comparative advantage, showing that relocation is not necessarily a one-way street. The example of the Hong Kong knitting manufacturers, who invested heavily in advanced machinery to bring the whole knitting process back home, is only one of the many examples of such reversal possibilities.

NOTES

1. This seems to be supported by the evidence from the experience of Czech firms working under subcontracting arrangements (Deardorff and Djankov, 1997).
2. See Graziani (1998) for details.
3. An important question is whether local firms can stand up to international competition when subcontracting comes to an end. A small survey of just over twenty firms in the Czech Republic and Hungary has shown that only one of them was able to turn a previous OPT relationship into autonomous production and sale under its own brand (Pellegrin, 1997).
4. Empirical analysis on the quality of Italian textile and clothing products shows that both export unit values and multilateral Fisher indices have been stable or rising in the last ten years and that they tend to be higher than import values, except in some clothing products subject to OPT (Faini and Hemler, 1991; Graziani, 1994*b*).

REFERENCES

Anderson, K. (1994). 'Fibers, Textiles and Clothing in Asia-Pacific's Economic Development', in D. K. Das (ed.), *Emerging Growth Pole: The Asia-Pacific Economy* (Englewood Cliffs, NJ: Prentice Hall).

Arndt, S. W. (1997). 'Globalization and the Open Economy', *North American Journal of Economics and Finance*, 8/1.

Au, K. F., and Yeung, K. W. (1995). 'The Competitiveness of the Hong Kong Clothing Industry', *Proceedings of the 3rd Asian Textile Conference*, Hong Kong.

Audet, D. (1996). 'Globalisation in the Clothing Industry', in *Globalisation of Industry* (Paris: OECD).

Bair, J., and Gereffi, G. (1998). 'US Companies Eye NAFTA's Prize', *Bobbin*, 39 (Mar.).

Corado, C. (1995). 'The Textiles and Clothing Trade with Central and Eastern Europe: Impact on Members of the EC', in R. Faini and R. Portes (eds.), *European Union Trade with Eastern Europe: Adjustment and Opportunities* (London: CEPR).

Deardorff, A., and Djankov, S. (1997). 'Knowledge Transfer under Subcontracting: Evidence from Czech Firms', World Bank Working Paper, 28 Oct.

Dicken, P. (1992). *Global Shift* (London: Paul Chapman).

Dixit, A. K., and Grossman, G. M. (1982). 'Trade and Protection with Multistage Production', *Review of Economic Studies*, 49.

Economist (1998). 'Manufacturing Survey', 20 June.

Faini, R., and Heimler, A. (1991). 'The Quality of Production of Textiles and Clothing and the Completion of the Internal Market', CEPR Discussion Paper No. 508, Jan.

Gereffi, G. (1996). 'Commodity Chains and Regional Divisions of Labor in East Asia', *Journal of Asian Business*, 12/1.

Graziani, G. (1994*a*). 'Trade Patterns and Comparative Advantages of Central Eastern Europe with EC Countries', in J. Gacs and G. Winckler (eds.), *International Trade and Restructuring in Eastern Europe* (Heidelberg: Physica-Verlag).

—— (1994*b*). 'Italy's Manufacturing Trade with Eastern Europe: Specialization Patterns and Possible Impact of Liberalization on Italian Industry', in *European Economy*, 6.

—— (1995). 'Threats and Opportunities for West European Industry Deriving from Trade Liberalization with Central and Eastern Europe', in R. Dobrinsky and M. Landesmann (eds.), *Transforming Economies and European Integration* (Aldershot: Edward Elgar).

—— (1998). 'Globalization of Production in the Textile and Clothing Industry: The Case of Italian FDI and Outward Processing Traffic with Eastern Europe', in J. Zysman and A. Schwartz (eds.), *Enlarging Europe: The Industrial Foundations of a New Political Reality* (Berkeley: International and Area Studies Publications).

Jones, R. W., and Kierzkowski, H. (1990). 'The Role of Services in Production and International Trade: A Theoretical Framework', in R. W. Jones and A. O. Krueger (eds.), *The Political Economy of International Trade* (Oxford: Basil Blackwell).

—— (2000). 'Globalization and the Consequences of International Fragmentation', forthcoming in R. Dornbusch, G. Calvo, and M. Obstfeld (eds.), *Money Factor Mobility and Trade: A Festschrift in Honor of Robert A. Mundell* (Cambridge, Mass.: MIT Press).

Mercer Management Consulting (1994). 'European Subcontracting in the Clothing Sector', report prepared for the Directorate General III of the European Commission, Brussels.

Moon, K. L., Leung, C. S., Cheng, M. T., and Yeung, K. W. (1997). 'Strategic Reponses by the Hong Kong Textile and Clothing Firms Toward the MFA', *Journal of Textile Institute*, 88, part 2/1.

Organisation Européenne du Textile et de l'Habillement (OETH) (1995, 1997). *The EU Textile and Clothing Industry* (Brussels: OETH), Apr.

Pellegrin, J. (1997). 'Linking Up with Western European Firms: On the Prospects of Outward Processing Traffic in Central Europe', in S. Baldone and F. Sdogati (eds.), *EU-CEECs Integration: Policies and Markets at Work* (Milan: Franco Angeli).

Scheffer, M. (1994). *The Changing Map of European Textiles: Production and Sourcing Strategies of Textile and Clothing Firms* (Brussels: OETH).

Spinanger, D. (1992). 'The Impact on Employment and Income of Structural and Technological Changes in the Clothing Industry', in G. van Liemt (ed.), *Industry on the Move* (Geneva: International Labour Organization).

World Trade Organization (WTO) (1997). *Annual Report 1997* (Geneva: World Trade Organization).

12

Joining the Global Economy: Experience and Prospects of the Transition Economies

HENRYK KIERZKOWSKI

1. Introduction

Nearly a decade ago, a group of countries in Central Europe embarked on the road towards a market economy. The transformation process was ignited by Poland, Hungary, and Czechoslovakia, but it spread rapidly south towards Bulgaria, Romania, Albania, and Yugoslavia. A huge wave of fundamental reforms has also swept across what was then known as the Soviet Union. Today, there are, all in all, twenty-six transition economies if the term is reserved for members of the European Bank for Reconstruction and Development. They represent a significant part of the world economy in terms of population, area, natural resources, and economic potential.

A relatively open trading system, introduced at an initial stage of the transition process, became a key policy objective, at least among the transition leaders. This need to open up the transition economies did not encounter any serious intellectual opposition in Eastern and Central Europe, which is not to say that governments are always willing or able to proceed with trade liberalization, nor that there are no pressure groups seeking individual favors.

The process of (re)joining the global economy has placed two tall orders before the transition economies: (i) a geographic realignment of their trade on the basis of economic profitability and (ii) an expansion of intra-industry trade. These are tall orders, indeed. But there is an even taller one. Economic transition in Eastern and Central Europe has been taking place against the constantly shifting external environment. Joining the world economy is like shooting at a moving target.

The world economy is undergoing a rapid process of globalization. Technical innovations, combined with falling trade barriers, increased ease of international capital movements, and ever-increasing freedom of establishment have made globalization possible and of interest to powerful countries and economic groups as it spreads across the world. Globalization implies that national economies are integrated not only through trade; they are becoming tightly integrated at the *production level*.

This chapter reviews the progress achieved by the transition economies in joining the global economy. Section 2 looks at the reorientation of their trade flows. Next, in Section 3, it is argued that to become a well-integrated member of the world economy means to engage in intra-industry trade. This type of trade offers a finer division of labor and additional benefits above and beyond those associated with the traditional inter-industry exchange. There is even a finer international specialization that can be achieved: fragmentation of production may lead to intra-product specialization. The question of globalization is taken up in Section 4. While trade reorientation has been largely completed, the potential for expansion of intra-industry trade has not been fully exploited yet. And participation of the transition economies in international production frameworks based on fragmentation of production is only beginning. However, given the existing factor-price differences between Western and Eastern Europe, transition economies could well fit into emerging international production networks, especially those centered on the *European Union (EU)*.

As stressed by the recent literature on geography and trade, spatial location and physical distance between economic agents and entities influence the intensity of their mutual trade relations. The contemporary history of Eastern and Central Europe shows how dramatically the economic geography of the region can change when political and economic barriers are removed. We have seen only the beginning of this process.

2. Trade Reorientation

Transition to market economy was never going to be an easy ride for Eastern and Central Europe. However, hardly anybody had anticipated that it was going to be that rough. A collapse in output observed in the region coincided with disintegration of the intra-regional trade regime.

How did the transition economies cope with the disruption of their commerce? The proper response to the trade shock was to forge new commercial links and expand in new markets rather than reinvigorate trade within the region. To be sure, it is only natural for neighbors to exchange goods and services and there is, no doubt, a large potential for intra-regional trade. However, past trade arrangements among the planned economies could not often be sustained in a competitive environment and developing a new intra-regional specialization would take time. In any case, a severe recession in Eastern and Central Europe was not the best time to expand one's exports there. Western markets offered a way out. It was not at all obvious at the time that Eastern and Central European producers would be able to seize upon this opportunity. Low quality of goods and the lack of marketing experience had been considered among the factors limiting an export expansion in Western markets. Geographic reorientation of imports could be more easily accomplished and will not be looked into in this chapter.

Table 12.1 tells how much exports of the transition economies changed between 1988 and 1996. The case of the three Central European leaders—the Czech Republic, Hungary, and Poland—is well known and documented. There was a very sharp curtailment of their exports to the ex-Comecon market; the relative share of that market was cut in half. Their export drive was directed toward the developed countries' markets and in particular toward the EU.

It is interesting to note, however, that other countries have undergone shifts just as dramatic in their export orientation as the Czech Republic, Hungary and Poland. In particular, Albania and Romania are now among the least dependent on the *Central and Eastern European Countries (CEEC)* market for their exports. Slovakia, on the other hand, is still locked into the traditional pattern for its exports to an unusual degree, as the only country outside the *former Soviet Union (FSU)* that directs more than 50 percent of its exports to the CEEC market.[1]

Inter-temporal comparisons are obviously not possible in the case of the FSU. Instead of a trade reorientation toward the developed markets, Table 12.1 only shows that present (i.e., 1996) trade links between the former Soviet Union republics and the developed countries remain rather weak in comparison with the Western-oriented countries of Central Europe. However, the Baltic States are an exception in this respect.

There is yet another difference in the patterns of trade of various groups of countries. In stressing the importance of the developed countries in helping transition economies in restructuring their trade flows, the role played by the European Union cannot be underestimated. It is that link that has proven crucial in forging new trade relations. Bulgaria, the Czech Republic, Hungary, Poland, and Romania have been remarkably successful in expanding their exports into the EU market. The Europe Agreements have no doubt played a very useful role in this

TABLE 12.1. Export orientation of transition economies

Transition economies	CEEC		EU		Developed	
	1988	1996	1988	1996	1988	1996
Albania	33.3	8.2	na	na	45.0	87.9
Bulgaria	35.6	23.6	19.3	40.0	22.7	44.2
Hungary	44.4	24.0	30.5	63.0	37.2	69.0
Poland	39.8	20.9	37.4	67.7	44.7	71.6
Romania	33.1	12.1	29.4	56.2	37.4	59.9
Czechoslovakia	54.5		30.1		33.6	
Czech Republic		30.0		58.6		62.8
Slovakia		51.2		41.4		44.2
Yugoslavia	29.7		43.0		51.5	
Croatia		35.0		51.0		54.2
Slovenia		27.3		64.7		69.3
Bosnia and Herzegovina		44.4		44.4		54.2
Macedonia, FYR		33.2		46.8		58.5
Serbia and Montenegro		10.7		81.4		84.3
Russian Federation		34.0		33.6		47.7
Estonia		40.5		52.6		56.9
Latvia		50.1		44.9		46.3
Lithuania		61.3		33.9		36.4
Belarus		83.1		9.7		11.3
Moldova		80.9		10.3		13.2
Ukraine		63.0		10.1		14.1
Georgia		68.9		15.5		17.9
Kazakhstan		60.0		18.4		24.2
Kyrghistan		80.1		4.0		8.0
Armenia		78.2		19.8		20.9
Azerbaijan		50.0		9.2		10.4
Tajikistan		47.3		34.7		46.9
Turkmenistan		8.2		6.0		55.0
Uzbekistan		53.9		22.2		30.8

Source: Direction of Trade Statistics, IMF 1995–7.

respect, but the export drive had begun even before the agreements were negotiated and implemented.[2]

A further step should be taken in identifying the crucial link in the process of trade realignment in transition economies in Eastern and Central Europe. The European Union now consists of fifteen members and it would be surprising if all of them expanded trade at the same pace with the new democracies in the East. This is certainly not the case nor should it be so except under very special circumstances.

TABLE 12.2. Three most important trading partners for selected countries (1996)

Reporting Country	Export markets	Share in total exports (%)	Import markets	Share in total imports (%)
Czech Republic	Germany	36	Germany	30
	Slovakia	14	Slovakia	10
	Austria	6	Russian Federation	7
Slovakia	Czech Republic	31	Czech Republic	25
	Germany	21	Russian Federation	18
	Austria	6	Germany	15
Hungary	Germany	29	Germany	24
	Austria	11	Russian Federation	12
	Italy	8	Austria	9
Poland	Germany	35	Germany	25
	Russian Federation	7	Italy	10
	Italy	6	Russian Federation	7
Romania	Germany	18	Germany	17
	Italy	17	Italy	15
	France	6	Russian Federation	13
Slovenia	Germany	31	Germany	22
	Italy	13	Italy	17
	Croatia	10	France	10
Estonia	Finland	18	Finland	29
	Russian Federation	16	Russian Federation	14
	Sweden	12	Germany	10
Latvia	Russian Federation	23	Russian Federation	20
	Germany	14	Germany	14
	United Kingdom	11	Finland	9
Lithuania	Russian Federation	24	Russian Federation	26
	Germany	13	Germany	16
	Belarus	10	Poland	5
Moldova	Russian Federation	48	Russian Federation	33
	Romania	14	Ukraine	27
	Ukraine	8	Romania	7
Kyrghistan	Russian Federation	27	Russian Federation	21
	Uzbekistan	23	Kazakhstan	17
	Kazakhstan	22	Uzbekistan	16

Source: UN COMTRADE database, 1997.

Table 12.2 identifies the three most important trade partners for a number of transition economies in 1996 and reports their percentage shares in total imports and exports. A number of interesting observations can be readily made: (i) the combined share of the three most important trade partners is usually close to or in excess of 50 percent of the value of exports and imports. Thus, trade concentration on a very small number of trading partners is very high for transition economies and quite likely higher than for other countries.[3] (ii) Germany plays an enormously important role in the trade of Central Europe and its role is also significant in the case of ex-Soviet Union republics. (iii) The other key trade player is the Russian Federation. One would expect that for a number of ex-republics but, surprisingly, this dependence is also strong for the Baltic States. (iv) A Western European country does not have to be large to be an important actor in East–West trade. Austria provides, no doubt with some help from geography, evidence that a small country can become a big partner. Table 12.2 also shows that a number of large European Union countries, notably the United Kingdom, are rather weakly represented in Eastern and Central Europe, as well as in the former Soviet Union.

The dominant commercial role played by Germany and the Russian Federation may change as the process of transition continues. Given the fact that reforms started later in the Soviet Union and perhaps were pursued less vigorously, the trade patterns of the new independent states have not yet fully settled. However, geography being such an influential factor, the presence of the European Union in, say, Asian transition economies may never become comparable to that observed in Central Europe. One may speculate that Japan, India, and a number of East Asian tigers are in a much stronger strategic position *vis-à-vis* ex-Soviet Union republics than the European Union.

How well are the transition economies integrated with the world economy? There is no single yardstick to measure the degree of openness achieved so far. In principle, integration can proceed on many fronts: commodity markets, labor and capital markets, and exchange rate arrangements. For this reason, a vast number of indicators would be required to capture the existing degree of integration with international markets.

Table 12.3 reports the values of three indicators: exports per capita, exports as a percentage of GDP, and foreign direct investment inflows per capita. The transition economies are compared with a number of developed countries, *newly industrializing countries* (*NICs*) and developing countries. It is clear that per capita exports are meager in the transition economies in comparison with other countries. Slovenia is by far the strongest exporter; in per capita terms it exports more than Portugal, Spain, the United States, Australia, and Japan! This is a remarkable achievement which puts Slovenia on a par with Italy. In addition to

TABLE 12.3. Indicators of participation in global economy

Transition economies	Exports per capita (US$)	Exports (% of GDP)	FDI per capita (US$)	Developed countries	Exports per capita (US$)	Exports (% of GDP)	FDI per capita (US$)
Albania	84.4	14.4	18.8	Australia	3,513.8	19.3	375.1
Armenia	213.2	36.8	0.7	Austria	9,545	37.3	129.5
Azerbaijan	211.8	38.5	4.9	Belgium	16,704.9	71.4	900.5
Belarus	1,376	60.3	1.4	Canada	6,320	33.4	252.3
Bosnia and Herzegovina	na	na	0	Denmark	10,082.2	34.7	645.2
Bulgaria	647.8	49.2	11.7	France	5,353.9	22.6	334.1
Croatia	1,363.4	45	17.6	Germany	5,936.5	22.7	25.5
Czech Republic	1,919.9	53.4	132.3	Greece	1,741.5	22.5	96.3
Estonia	897	74.5	128.3	Italy	4,520.2	25	60.1
Georgia	162.4	34.1	0	Japan	3,512.6	9.3	3.2
Hungary	1,217.8	30.1	260.5	Netherlands	11,682.3	51.6	449.5
Kazakhstan	520.4	35.5	12.3	Norway	11,368.4	38.4	303.2
Kyrghistan	240.1	31.1	1.8	Portugal	2,549.2	27.6	140.0
Latvia	1,157.7	54.1	57.6	Spain	2,829.8	21.8	219.3
Macedonia, FYR	366.2	40.8	0	Sweden	8,581.8	36.6	901.8
Moldova	310.1	32.7	6.9	Switzerland	13,597.5	36.1	327.3
Poland	647	25	62.7	United Kingdom	4,670.5	26.6	310.8
Romania	342.5	25.1	12.5	United States	2,739.4	10.8	193.1
				Newly Industrialized Countries			
Russian Federation	697.5	28.4	7.5	Korea, Rep.	2,723	30.8	21.7
Slovakia	1,703.2	63.2	36.5	Hong Kong	30,679.1	142.3	317.0
Slovenia	4,401.7	57.7	70	Malaysia	3,327.3	89	256.8
Tajikistan	339.8	84.3	1.4				
Turkmenistan	na	na	0	Developing Countries			
Ukraine	na	na	4	Brazil	293.6	8.4	19.6
Uzbekistan	475.8	48.8	3.1	Mexico	578.4	16.8	82.5
China	91.7	19.6	27.2	Philippines	326.2	33.8	21.4
Vietnam	75.3	32.8	10.9	Thailand	986.2	39	30.3

Notes: The data are yearly averages for the period 1993–5; na means not available.
Sources: 1. World Development Indicators 1997 on CD-Rom, World Bank, Washington; 2. *World Investment Report*, UNCTAD, New York and Geneva, 1996.

Slovenia, the Czech Republic, Slovakia, Croatia, Latvia, and Belarus make up the group of leading exporters. In general, the transition economies of Eastern and Central Europe export far more than China and Vietnam. Perhaps the most revealing indicator of openness is given by exports to GDP ratios.

The transition economies tend to be relatively open, some of them even remarkably so. A case could be made that an important part of relinking with the world market has already been accomplished. Indeed this conclusion is shared by Brenton and Gros (1997), who state

... that, in terms of the geographic structure of their trade, the more advanced countries in central and eastern Europe are indistinguishable from Western market economies. This reflects a substantial reorientation of trade away from former CMEA partners and towards the West, in particular, the EU. For other countries in the region this adjustment of trade is far from complete.

Becoming a part of the global economy also means that the financial markets of the transition economies should become increasingly integrated with international capital markets.[4] This is required in order to attract the foreign capital inflows that are so needed in the transition economies. Table 12.3 reveals that international capital still shies away from the transition economies.[5] Only Hungary attracts significant amounts of foreign direct investment per capita. Foreign investors still need more convincing before they move into the transition economies in a big way. This may suggest that integration through trade is easier to accomplish than integration through capital markets.[6] Of course, the recent financial crises in Asia make the leading transition economies in Central Europe quite attractive for internationally mobile capital.

3. Intra-industry Trade

Intra-industry trade deserves special attention in the assessment of reintegration of the transition economies with the world market. At the global level, numerous studies have documented the growing importance of this type of trade in international commerce. Would liberalization in the transition economies lead primarily to expansion of intra- or inter-industry trade? In fact, the question goes right to the problem of the place of these countries in the international division of labor.

Given the physical and economic proximity of the European Union to many transition countries, we propose to look at intra-industry trade in the European context. Table 12.4 reports the intensity of

TABLE 12.4. Total intra-industry trade with EU 12 (129 three-digit NACE sectors)

	1990	1991	1992	1993	1994
EU/CEEC					
Albania	23.4	23.3	23.8	25.1	21.1
Bulgaria	39.1	39.7	43.2	45.9	44.1
Hungary	50.5	51.5	53.9	50.5	50.9
Poland	42.8	41.3	44.3	44.3	43.7
Romania	32.1	38.9	34.7	34.4	36.1
Czechoslovakia	48.7	47.9	46.8	—	—
Czech Republic	—	—	—	51.0	54.1
Slovakia	—	—	—	43.8	47.5
Yugoslavia	51.7	55.4	57.1	—	—
Croatia	—	—	39.8	40.0	39.7
Slovenia	—	—	51.4	52.6	55.5
Bosnia Hercegovina	—	—	36.7	34.9	32.3
Macedonia, FYR	—	—	—	36.6	32.2
Serbia and Montenegro	—	—	—	25.8	24.2
Soviet Union	30.1	28.9	29.8	—	—
Russian Federation	—	—	26.1	25.9	22.8
Estonia	—	—	39.0	28.4	29.5
Latvia	—	—	37.6	31.4	27.2
Lithuania	—	—	30.0	27.5	29.0
Belarus	—	—	25.5	33.3	33.0
Moldova	—	—	36.3	30.9	27.2
Ukraine	—	—	28.8	27.3	28.8
Armenia	—	—	41.8	23.6	29.4
Azerbaijan	—	—	24.1	19.1	21.5
Georgia	—	—	22.1	20.6	25.0
Kazakhstan	—	—	17.4	14.1	18.0
Kyrghistan	—	—	20.9	27.7	19.6
Tajikistan	—	—	15.5	33.2	33.9
Turkmenistan	—	—	26.9	16.4	23.4
Uzbekistan	—	—	28.5	24.2	13.4
EU/EFTA					
Austria	62.4	63.1	62.0	63.2	64.0
Finland	43.5	46.9	48.9	50.6	48.4
Norway	36.8	37.6	39.2	39.3	36.7
Sweden	55.2	55.4	56.7	55.5	56.1
Greece	25.2	27.1	27.2	26.4	27.4
Portugal	41.6	41.2	41.0	43.2	42.3
Spain	64.2	60.9	61.1	62.3	62.4

TABLE 12.4. *Continued*

	1990	1991	1992	1993	1994
EU					
Argentina	35.5	31.3	25.7	24.5	21.8
Egypt	15.8	14.8	18.7	18.0	17.6
Malaysia	29.6	32.8	33.3	36.0	34.0
Mexico	33.1	34.6	29.9	33.1	30.7
Singapore	32.3	34.8	31.8	32.2	30.8
Thailand	31.6	34.8	34.9	31.5	35.5
Turkey	33.6	34.6	35.3	35.1	37.5
United States	56.6	58.0	58.3	57.4	57.1

Source: Eurostat Comext database, 1996.

intra-industry trade for 129 three-digit NACE sectors. The measure reported in Table 12.4 is the well-known Grubel–Lloyd index. In addition to the transition economies, a number of *European Free Trade Association (EFTA)* countries have also been selected for comparison (some of them have recently joined the European Union). We have also singled out Greece, Portugal, and Spain and treated them as if they were not EU members. These three countries have per capita incomes relatively close to what is observed in Central Europe and could provide a clue as to expected levels of intra-industry trade. Finally, a number of other countries are included in Table 12.4.

Obviously, there can be no general conclusions that hold for all the countries under consideration. However, it can be seen that at least a group of countries have achieved a remarkably high intensity of intra-industry trade with the European Union. These countries include: Hungary, the Czech Republic, Slovakia, Slovenia, and to a somewhat lesser degree Bulgaria and Poland. It is worth mentioning that Yugoslavia had managed to achieve a high level of intra-industry trade before the country disintegrated; at present only Slovenia and possibly Croatia engage intensively in this type of trade.

The leading countries mentioned above engage in intra-industry trade with the European Union at least to the same degree as Finland, Norway, Greece, and Portugal. They far outperform such countries as Malaysia, Mexico, Singapore, and Thailand; however, given the location of the latter group, this comparison may be quite unfair.

Our findings of a relatively high degree of intra-industry trade between Central Europe and the European Union confirm earlier studies carried out by Neven (1995), Drabek and Smith (1995), Hoekman and Djankov (1996), Aturupane, *et al.* (1997), Brenton and Gros (1997), and Carlin and Landesmann (1997), among others. Unfortunately, some of the findings reported in the above studies appear somewhat contradictory. More specifically, Landesmann (1997) established that, with the exception of Bulgaria, all of Central Europe experienced a burst in intra-industry trade after 1989. However, only the *Czech and Slovakia Federation Republic (CSFR)* and Bulgaria have managed to continue the trend in subsequent years. For other countries, the index of intra-industry trade stagnated or even declined slightly. Brenton and Gros (1997) have found that intra-industry trade between the EU and Czech and Slovak Republics has been growing continuously through the transition, although its greatest expansion occurred in 1989–92. A sustained growth of intra-industry trade has also been recorded in the case of Hungary. Brenton and Gros (1997) have also established that Bulgaria and Romania did manage to expand intra-industry trade with the EU after 1992.

Two other findings for Central Europe are worth reporting here. Drabek and Smith (1995) suggest the existence of causality between expansion of intra-industry trade and trade diversion from Eastern to Central Europe. In their somewhat pessimistic conclusion, the expansion of Central Europe–EU intra-industry trade represents 'mechanical growth not structural change'. Hoekman and Djankov (1996), on the other hand, identify increases in intra-industry trade not so much with trade reorientation as with foreign direct investment made by Western European firms in Central Europe.

Most of the existing studies on the intra-industry trade of the transition economies concentrate on Central Europe. Table 12.4 attempts to widen the discussion by including the ex-Soviet Union Republics in the analysis. It is quite clear that the difference between Central Europe and the FSU is striking in this respect. However, geographic location may be quite an obstacle to tighter trade relations with the EU for a majority of ex-Soviet Union Republics. The Baltic States are in a better position than other new independent states, but even in this case the intra-industry index is rather low.

It should also be added that much less progress with economic reforms has been accomplished so far in the former Soviet Union in comparison with Central Europe, so it is not altogether surprising that there is less cooperation and exchange with industries and markets in Western Europe. Future developments may well show that the former Soviet Union republics will tend to develop intra-industry trade not with the European Union but with Japan, China, Malaysia, Singapore, Thailand, or Indonesia.

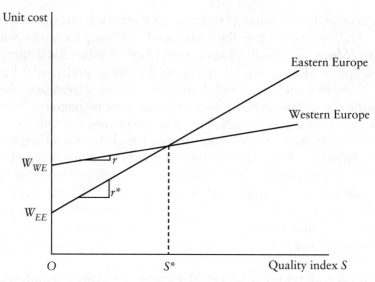

FIG. 12.1. Vertical product differentiation
Source: Falvey and Kierzkowski (1987).

Models of intra-industry trade require product differentiation.[7] In principle, there can be either horizontal or vertical product differentiation. When the first type of product differentiation is evoked, products differ because of one or more characteristics but they are basically the same in terms of quality, costs, and capital/labor techniques employed in their production. When it comes to vertical product differentiation, quality differences are brought to the fore in the analysis. Products are no longer the same from the point of view of unit production costs and factor intensities.

One may wish to know whether the intra-industry trade taking place between transition economies and the European Union reflects horizontal or vertical specialization. In the latter case, it could be predicted that lower quality goods would be exported to more advanced countries which, in turn, would export high quality goods to transition economies.

Figure 12.1 shows a particular industry producing various models of the same good differentiated by a quality index S. For the sake of simplicity assume that production of the lowest quality good requires only labor. Furthermore, assume that it takes one unit of labor to produce one unit of the lowest quality differentiated product. Thus, the vertical intercepts represent the wage rate in Eastern and Western Europe. Naturally, labor is assumed to be cheaper in Eastern Europe. Given the assumption that only labor is required to produce the lowest quality model and given that the labor requirement per unit of output is 1.0, the unit cost of production for the cheapest product is equal to the wage rate.

In order to produce the higher quality models only capital has to be added to the initial amount of labor; the higher the quality required, the more additional capital has to be employed per unit of production. This relationship between inputs, outputs, and quality may well be linear, à la Ricardo. If this were indeed the case, the unit cost function would be linear in terms of the quality index. The slopes of the two lines in Figure 12.1 represent the cost of capital in Eastern and Western Europe.[8] It makes sense to assume that capital is cheaper in Western Europe and hence the corresponding unit cost line is flatter.

Figure 12.1 shows that the unit cost of production for low quality models of the differentiated product is lower in Eastern Europe. This is so because lower quality models of the differentiated product require an intensive use of labor which is relatively cheap in Eastern Europe. It now becomes straightforward to show that Eastern Europe could outperform Western Europe in the production of lower quality models, all the way to S^*, and could therefore engage in exports of lower quality models. Western Europe, on the other hand, would remain a competitive exporter of higher quality models.

One could argue that vertical product differentiation may well be a revealing way of looking at intra-industry trade between reforming and Western countries. Figure 12.1 shows that wages have to remain relatively low for Eastern Europe to preserve its comparative advantage in lower quality models of the differentiated product. An increase in the wage rate of 10 percent would shift upwards the intercept of the cost line for Eastern Europe by 10 percent and result in a loss of comparative advantage of certain models. It can also readily be seen that as capital accumulation proceeds in Eastern Europe and capital gets cheaper there, the relevant cost line will become flatter. Eastern Europe would grow increasingly more competitive in higher and higher quality models of the differentiated good.

Two empirical questions pose themselves quite naturally: first, is it true that reforming economies of Eastern and Central Europe specialize in lower qualities of differentiated products? Secondly, is there any evidence to support the hope that transition countries can climb up the quality ladder?

The answer to the first question is rather clear cut. Landesmann (1997) comes to a well-documented conclusion that 'the development gaps even of the most advanced of the CEE economies in relation to the EU are very significant, showing up in patterns of intra-industry specialization and also in very considerable "quality gaps" in the products sold on EU markets'.[9] With regard to the second question, the evidence is rather mixed.

Carlin and Landesmann (1997) report that the Czech Republic, Hungary, Poland, and Slovenia narrow the quality gap *vis-à-vis* Western countries. However, the quality gap seems to widen for Bulgaria, Romania, and Russia. Carlin and Landesmann (1997) link the question of quality upgrading with industrial restructuring and foreign direct investment and arrive at a far-reaching conclusion:

In Poland—where growth has been most successful to date—reliance on small-scale *de novo* firms was reflected in the very limited catching-up in terms of export quality in the EU market. The recent influx of FDI, in conjunction with the privatization of a substantial chunk of large firms through mass privatization, may provide the appropriate complement in terms of scale of production to the *de novo* sector. By contrast, in Hungary, opportunities for nascent entrepreneurs have been closely associated with the substantial role of foreign capital in the privatization process. This has been reflected in the impressive upgrading of exports and the shift in structure towards more R&D-intensive goods.

This view of quality upgrading of exports by a number of Central European countries has been challenged by Brenton and Gros (1997) who claim to find 'no evidence that the changing geographic and commodity composition of the exports of transition economies has been associated with upgrading of product quality'. Drabek and Smith (1995) seem to be supporting the same conclusion based on the fact that unit values of Polish and Czech exports to the EU declined between 1988 and 1993.[10]

4. New Opportunities Associated with Fragmentation

Fragmentation of production and the emergence of new forms of international trade offer an opportunity for the transition economies to participate in a finer division of labor. Several preconditions need first to be satisfied for a reforming country to become a part of an international production network. The process of transformation should advance far enough so that interaction between firms operating in different countries is not hampered by rigidities of the old planning system.

One could imagine that even a state-owned enterprise could become a supplier of parts and subsystems for a Western firm. Indeed, a number of Western European firms had already begun to outsource production to Central Europe in the 1960s. Cheap labor offered sufficiently strong incentives to overlook the inconveniences, inflexibility, and risks inherent in dealing with planned economies. However, international production sharing with the involvement of Eastern European firms was condemned to remain a side-show.

As competitive firms in market economies shift from *just-in-case* production and inventory systems to *just-in-time* organization, the suppliers of parts, components, and subsystems are required to respond rapidly and with flexibility to changing market conditions. Large state enterprises operating under numerous constraints are not likely to play the role of a reliable partner. The need for rapid and elastic production response is further reinforced by the so-called *mass customization* of the market, being a logical extension of just-in-time organization of production. When the customer demands a product with individual specification and he or she is impatient, the organization of production must be remarkably well coordinated to respond to these new demands.

Economic reforms in Eastern and Central Europe open new perspectives for innovative and profit-motivated firms. Interestingly enough, a firm does not have to be large in order to join an international production network. The process of fragmentation offers small producers in Eastern and Central Europe a unique opportunity of transforming themselves from small-scale operations, set up to produce mainly non-trade goods for local markets, to international players. Fragmentation could thus contribute to the process of opening up Eastern and Central economies.

To what extent have the transition economies already joined the process of globalization based on fragmentation of production? The planned economies were practically excluded from the globalization strategy followed by transnational corporations in the 1970s and 1980s, which resulted in the rapid growth of intra-firm trade. But there is now some evidence that outsourcing is spreading into Central and Eastern Europe. Western European firms play a central role in this process.

Baldone *et al.* (1997) provide a systematic account of outward-processing trade originating in the European Union. According to their estimates, this type of trade grew from 3.86 billion ECU in 1988 to 11.04 billion ECU in 1994. The share of this trade captured by the

CEECs increased from 35.4 to 42.3 percent in the same period. In sum, the rapid expansion of outward processing trade

identifies a well-defined strategy of productive delocalization by EU firms. Delocalization of phases of the production process is mostly directed to countries with relatively low labour costs, yet endowed with industrial structures efficient enough to perform production activities of a quality acceptable to standards prevailing in EU firms supplying the intermediate products and marketing the final ones. This is the case of many CEECs. (Baldone *et al.*, 1997: 255)

Table 12.5 shows further details of the growth in EU–CEEC outward-processing trade. This type of trade was basically limited to the following areas ranked according to their relative importance: CEECs, the Pacific area, North America, the Mediterranean basin, and EFTA. The role of high-wage regions—EFTA and North America—has been systematically declining. However, the EU sectors involved in outward processing in EFTA and the United States are much more capital and technology intensive than those which look for subcontractors in Eastern Europe.

The textile and clothing industry is by far the most important case of EU–Eastern Europe fragmentation of production. The footwear industry appears to be the next likely candidate for intra-product specialization involving Western and Eastern European firms. The natural competitors of Eastern Europe in this respect are countries of the Mediterranean basin. Of course, international fragmentation of production may be undertaken within the European Union and countries such as Spain, Portugal, and Greece could well be attractive locations for labor-intensive stages of production. Germany is far ahead of other EU countries in promoting outsourcing in Eastern and Central Europe; it accounts for three-quarters of EU outward-processing trade with transition economies. Neither France nor the United Kingdom plays a significant role in this respect. However, Austrian firms find efficient subcontractors in their East European neighbours.

Geography counts for a lot in international fragmentation of production and this is so for a variety of reasons. Transportation costs associated with sending semi-products back and forth depend in an obvious way on the distance separating producers. However, other service links may be cheaper and coordination of various activities may be easier when producers are not separated by vast distances. After all, fragmentation takes place domestically before it spills over into international markets. Some transition economies are more natural candidates to join in the process of fragmentation initiated by EU firms because of their

TABLE 12.5. EU outward-processing trade (exports in million ECU)

Area of destination	1988	1989	1990	1991	1992	1993	1994
CEECs	1367.10	1701.70	2014.88	2508.89	3140.87	3879.53	4672.21
Mediterranean basin	338.43	589.08	689.22	814.26	910.06	954.51	1031.93
EFTA	429.59	588.94	683.47	857.93	842.11	972.29	835.12
Pacific area	792.31	1086.79	1235.30	1494.20	1673.99	2171.54	2544.70
Asia	49.46	58.26	102.11	96.64	134.44	135.87	154.38
North America	794.59	1142.60	1047.08	1537.88	1393.35	1289.80	1527.05
Central and Southern America	16.07	120.67	94.86	120.40	124.05	105.65	157.94
Sub-Saharan Africa	64.26	70.68	63.48	40.93	51.15	81.73	70.78
Oceania	10.09	2.15	2.28	9.13	13.36	23.33	24.44
Various extra EU	2.72	3.40	3.27	3.90	8.67	31.44	19.44
Extra EU	3864.61	5364.25	5935.95	7484.16	8292.06	9645.68	11038.00

Share (%)	1988	1989	1990	1991	1992	1993	1994
CEECs	35.37	31.72	33.94	33.52	37.88	40.22	42.33
Mediterranean basin	8.76	10.98	11.61	10.88	10.98	9.90	9.35
EFTA	11.12	10.98	11.51	11.46	10.16	10.08	7.57
Pacific area	20.50	20.26	20.81	19.96	20.19	22.51	23.05
Asia	1.28	1.09	1.72	1.29	1.62	1.41	1.40
North America	20.56	21.30	17.64	20.55	16.80	13.37	13.83
Central and Southern America	0.42	2.25	1.60	1.61	1.50	1.10	1.43
Sub-Saharan Africa	1.66	1.32	1.07	0.55	0.62	0.85	0.64
Oceania	0.26	0.04	0.04	0.12	0.16	0.24	0.22
Various extra EU	0.07	0.06	0.06	0.05	0.10	0.33	0.18
Extra EU	100.00	100.00	100.00	100.00	100.00	100.00	100.00

Source: S. Baldone, F. Sdogati, and A. Zucchetti; From Integration through Trade in Goods to Integration through Trade in Production Processes? Evidence From EU OPT Statistics.

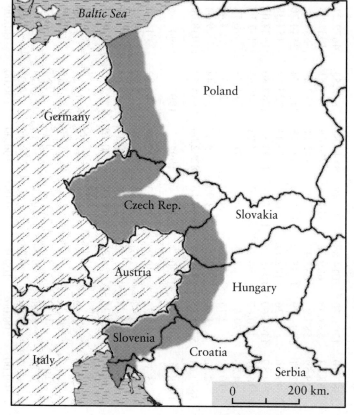

FIG. 12.2. Overlapping markets of the EU and transition economies

geographic location. In the map shown in Figure 12.2, the extent of market overlap between the European Union and Eastern Europe is captured by the shaded belt which is 100 km. wide. One could argue that within that belt information could spread rather easily, transportation costs are low, and coordination is easier. The experience of Mexico and China suggests that production associated with international fragmentation tends to be concentrated, at least initially, in border regions.

As our map shows, Slovenia is almost entirely situated within the border region. In the case of the Czech Republic, well over 50 percent of the country's territory is located within 100 km. of either German or Austrian borders. As far as Central Europe is concerned, there are also considerable zones of overlapping markets in Hungary, Slovakia, and Poland.

Can one expect that the western regions of the Czech Republic, Hungary, Slovakia, Poland, and Slovenia will become the maquiladoras of Europe? Geography gives those regions an advantage, but other factors are also important. Western European firms would compare wages and productivity in Central Europe and at home and also in other locations. The availability of certain services indispensable for fragmentation is another crucial consideration. And, of course, macroeconomic and political stability is a necessary condition that must be satisfied before Western European firms outsource production to transition economies.

There also exist regions of overlapping markets in the Baltic area and in Southern Europe. However, political and economic instability in Albania, Macedonia, and Bulgaria as well as the relatively limited economic potential of Greece constitute a serious obstacle to the emergence of Balkan maquiladoras. On the other hand, Baltic States may offer an attractive location for Swedish and Finnish firms.

Globalization has gone beyond the production outsourcing practiced initially by large multinationals. It is worth repeating that today, a firm does not have to be big to think international; in the limit, it can become international at the moment of birth. In fact, many do. Globalization has also expanded in scope in that in addition to manufactured goods it begins to include services as well, as witnessed by the offshore movement of banking, accounting, data entry, and software development.

The process of globalization presents new opportunities, and unfortunately new risks, for the transition economies as well as for developed and developing countries. As a finer international division of labor emerges, new production niches can be found and exploited. A country or a firm need not be a world producer of cars to benefit from the growth of the automobile industry; it is enough to be competitive in the production of a single part.

5. Conclusions

International trade has played a crucial role in the ongoing process of economic transformation of Eastern and Central Europe. By and large, the reforming countries did recognize the need to open up their economies and put them face to face with the competitive forces of the global economy. The remodeling of trade relations became all the more urgent because of the disintegration of the old commercial order.

The leaders of the transformation can be found primarily in Central Europe. They have already succeeded in reorienting their trade toward

Western markets, especially those in the European Union. Other countries, those who initiated the reforms later and pursued them with less vigor, have still to complete the task of trade reorientation. It is not clear, however, that they should copy the patterns established by Central Europe. Geography and distance still count for a lot in international trade. In a multi-polar world, some transition economies may end up being much more oriented toward the Far East than toward Western Europe.

A part of the trade-restructuring process involves an intensification of intra-industry trade flows. Again, we have seen that considerable progress has been made and some countries have already achieved high levels of intra-industry trade. However, progress in this area is less striking and the existing trends are not so impressive and clear-cut. Furthermore, there is no powerful evidence of product upgrading by the transition economies.

Further intensification of intra-industry trade and product upgrading will require a strong continuation of structural reforms and the transformation of the transition economies. These changes cannot come about very quickly. In the long run, sustained economic growth will make the transition economies look like present developed countries and therefore their patterns of trade will also converge and become similar. Interestingly enough, there is some evidence that foreign direct investment can help the process of industrial restructuring and also stimulate intra-industry trade and product upgrading.

The world economy is itself undergoing a transformation and therefore the transition economies face new challenges. Globalization offers opportunities to all involved but it also requires adjustment. It has the potential of increasing productivity all around. Fragmentation of production and the international reallocation that goes with it are not the zero-sum game alleged by some politicians.

An East or Central European country which was initially frozen out of producing a commodity may, with fragmentation, find that it can now compete successfully in a labor-intensive component. Thus, fragmentation and delinking of production should not be resisted in Eastern and Central Europe. Nor should it be resisted in the West. The resulting streamlining of production will not weaken Western European industries but, quite to the contrary, strengthen them. As a consequence, some benefits of growth will be transferred to reforming economies in Eastern Europe with consequent increases of real wages there. That may in itself reduce the desire of poorly paid workers to migrate. By spreading fragmentation of production into Eastern Europe, a new place in the international division of labor can be more harmoniously found for the economies that total about 300 million people and cannot be totally ignored in an increasingly interdependent world.

On the other hand, the government can influence the attractiveness of a country by running stable and responsible monetary policy, through its fiscal, environmental, and labor policies as well as through investments in infrastructure. A sound trade policy can also help a lot to make a country a winner in the contemporary world. Thus the role of the government has perhaps increased. The rewards for designing and implementing a good and mutually consistent set of domestic and external economic policies have become larger in the globalized economy. But so have the costs of failures.

NOTES

Parts of this chapter draw on my forthcoming article 'Challenges of Globalization: Foreign Trade Restructuring of Transition Economies', *Russian and Eastern European Finance and Trade*, special issue, 2000.

1. An obvious data problem makes it impossible to determine whether this dependence is diminishing or increasing over time.
2. For a more detailed discussion of the Europe Agreements and their impact on transition economies see Messerlin (1993), Baldwin (1994), Drabek and Smith (1995), Drabek (1997), and Kierzkowski (1996).
3. In some developing countries one finds a similarly strong concentration on a limited number of markets.
4. Again, one should be rather careful in suggesting how quickly and deeply this type of integration should proceed. The experience of Western European countries suggests, however, that total removal of capital market restrictions is a long and difficult process. The history of the European Payments Union could be a good guide to our expectations.
5. In interpreting this fact, one can argue that the transition countries have not yet opened up their economies to foreign capital. However, it can also be argued that it is foreign capital that is unwilling to enter in spite of the door having being opened.
6. We will not dwell on the integration of labor markets as East–West labor flows are practically non-existent at this stage. For economic and political reasons, movements of workers have become one of the least used channels of adjustment in the world economy. This stands in sharp contrast to nineteenth-century experience.
7. Actually, in the Brander model no product differentiation is required for intra-industry trade flows. In his one-commodity model, trade occurs because a domestic monopolist tries to invade a foreign market. The foreign monopolist responds by exporting the same good to the domestic market. See Brander (1981).

8. One can readily see this point by asking the following question: if the quality were to improve just a little bit, how much more expensive would the differentiated product become? Since only extra capital inputs are required for the quality up-grading, only capital costs will go up. The increase will depend on the going rental rate and this is captured in the slopes of the unit cost lines.
9. Quoted from Landesmann (1997: 137).
10. However, the unit values of Hungarian exports increased during the same period.

REFERENCES

Arndt, Sven (1997). 'Globalization and the Open Economy', *North-American Journal of Economics and Finance*, 8: 71–9.
—— (1998). 'Globalization and the Gains from Trade', in. K. J. Koch, and K. Jaeger (eds.), *Trade, Growth, and Economic Policy in Open Economies* (New York: Springer-Verlag).
Aturupane, Chonira, Djankov, Simeon, and Hoekman, Bernard (1997). 'Determinants of Intra-Industry Trade between East and West Europe', unpublished manuscript, (Washington: The World Bank).
Baldone, S., Sdogati, F., and Zucchetti, A. (1997). 'Emerging Patterns of Trade Specialization EU-CEECs', in Salvadore Baldone and Fabio Sdogati (eds.), *EU-CEECs Integration: Policies and Markets at Work* (Milan: Franco Angeli).
Baldwin, Richard (1994). *Towards an Integrated Europe* (London: Centre for Economic Policy Research).
Brander, J. (1981). 'Intra-industry Trade in Identical Commodities', *Journal of International Economics*, 11: 1–14.
Brenton, Paul, and Gros, Daniel (1997). 'Trade Reorientation and Recovery in Transition Economies', *Oxford Review of Economic Policy*, 13/2.
Campa, Jose, and Goldberg, Linda (1997). 'The Evolving External Orientation of Manufacturing Industries: Evidence from Four Countries', NBER Working Paper, Cambridge, Mass.
Carlin, Wendy, and Landesmann, Michael (1997). 'From Theory into Practice? Restructuring and Dynamism in Transition Economies', *Oxford Review of Economic Policy*, 13/2.
Collins, Susan and Rodrik, Dani (1991). *Eastern Europe and the Soviet Union in the World Economy*, Washington: Institute for International Economics.
Drabek, Zdenek (1985). 'Foreign Trade and Trade Policy', in M. C. Kaser and E. Radice, (eds.), *Economic History of Eastern Europe 1919–1979* (Oxford: Oxford University Press).
——(1997). 'Regional and Sub-Regional Integration in Central and Eastern Europe: An Overview', unpublished manuscript (Geneva: World Trade Organization).
—— and Smith, Alasdair (1995). Trade Performance and Trade Policy in Central and Eastern Europe, unpublished manuscript.

Falvey, Rodney, and Kierzkowski, Henryk (1987). 'Product Quality, Intra-Industry Trade and (Im)perfect Competition', in H. Kierzkowski (ed.), *Protection and Competition in International Trade: Essays in Honor of W. M. Corden* (Oxford: Basil Blackwell).

Feenstra, Robert (1998), 'Integration of Trade and Disintegration of Production in the Global Economy', *Journal of Economic Perspectives*, 12/4 (fall), 31–50.

Helleiner, Gerald (1981). *Intra-Firm Trade and the Developing Countries* (London: Macmillan Press).

Hoekman, Bernard, and Djankov, Simeon (1996). 'Intra-Industry Trade, Foreign Direct Investment, and the Reorientation of Eastern European Exports', unpublished manuscript (Washington: The World Bank).

Holly, Brian (1996). 'Restructuring the Production System', in P. W. Daniels, and W. F. Lever (eds.), *The Global Economy in Transition* (London: Longman).

Jones, Ronald, and Kierzkowski, Henryk (1990). 'The Role of Services in Production and International Trade: A Theoretical Framework', in Ronald Jones and Anne Krueger (eds.), *The Political Economy of International Trade* (Oxford: Basil Blackwell).

———(2000). 'Globalization and the Consequences of International Fragmentation', forthcoming in Rudiger Dornbusch, Guillermo Calvo, and Maurice Obstfeld (eds.), *Money, Factor Mobility and Trade: A Festschrift in Honor of Robert A. Mundell* (Cambridge, Mass.: MIT Press).

Kierzkowski, Henryk (1996). 'Central Europe Looks West', *The World Economy: Global Trade Policy 1996.*

Krugman, Paul (ed.), (1986). *Strategic Trade Policy and the New International Economics* (Cambridge, Mass.: MIT Press).

———(1996). *Pop Internationalism* (Cambridge, Mass.: MIT Press).

Landesman, Michael (1997). 'The Pattern of East-West European Integration: Catching up or Falling Behind?' in Rumen Dobrinsky and Michael Landesmann (eds.), *Transforming Economies and European Integration* (London: Edward Elgar).

Lawrence, Robert (1994). 'Trade, Multinationals and Labour', NBER Working Paper, Cambridge, Mass.

Messerlin, Patrick (1993). 'The EC and Central Europe: The Missed Rendez-vous of 1992', *Economics of Transition*, 1.

Neven, Damien (1995). 'Trade Liberalization with Eastern Nations: How Sensitive?', in R. Faini and R. Portes (eds.), *European Union Trade with Eastern Europe: Adjustment and Opportunities* (London: Center for Economic Policy Research).

Rodrik, Dani (1997). *Has Globalization Gone Too Far?* (Washington: Institute for International Economics).

INDEX